JERICHO

Hope you enjoy!
[illegible]

JERICHO

RACHEL MUMAW

NEW DEGREE PRESS

JERICHO

ISBN 978-1-63676-831-1 *Paperback*
978-1-63730-211-8 *Kindle Ebook*
978-1-63730-275-0 *Ebook*

CONTENTS

A NOTE FROM THE AUTHOR

When I started working on *Jericho*, I just wanted to write a story with a nonbinary lead about a family in a dieselpunk dystopian world. Then George Floyd was murdered. Then federal officers were deployed to Portland's streets. Then an insurgency swallowed the US capitol on January 6, 2021.

But let me start from the beginning.

Jericho began as a story about a family driving through the desert during the apocalypse. Initially, only three people in this family had names—Sergio, Ian, and Jen. This was because the story was told through a nameless character's perspective, and the most important thing to them was their chosen family, their community.

This one theme has remained the same from this original story concept—the importance of supporting and caring for the ones we love. I started writing this story during the COVID-19 pandemic, and with so many people out of work and getting sick, community is all the more important—even if we can't physically be in the same room.

At the time I was starting to develop this novel, one of my best friends began coming out as nonbinary. We realized pretty quickly that precious few novels had nonbinary characters, let alone nonbinary leads. So the narrator of that story became nonbinary and eventually got a name—Riley Jay.

It's always nice to see yourself represented in the media, and while I've had that in spades as a cisgender woman, my nonbinary friends haven't had the same luxury. Thus, it was important to me that Riley be nonbinary so my friends could see a representation of their gender identity in a genre we all love. Since Riley is nonbinary, they use they/them pronouns throughout the novel.

According to the Trevor Project, one in four LGBTQ+ people use pronouns other than she/her and he/him, so it's likely you will encounter someone like Riley Jay in your life who uses they/them pronouns.[1] If you haven't met someone who uses they/them pronouns yet, it can be a little confusing at first, especially since in the English language they/them is both a plural and a singular pronoun. I hope this novel gives you a chance to become more familiar with they/them singular pronouns.

Since the dystopian aspects in this novel arise due to the breakout of civil war, I didn't want to make this a sci-fi dystopian world with new gadgets and technology. Instead, I drew inspiration from the fall of the Roman Empire, where some of the greatest technological innovations from that time were lost, and the Western world was plunged into the Dark Ages.

War is often said to be one of the great drivers of innovation, but that's only for the countries that send their soldiers off to fight in *other* countries. When war comes to your land, it will tear it apart, leaving technology in the dust and people in the ground. I played around with this idea for a while, trying to develop a totalitarian regime that could've risen out of such a conflict. I was going to explore the consequences

1 "Research Brief: Pronouns Usage Among LGBTQ Youth," Blog & Events, The Trevor Project, updated July 29, 2020.

of turning a religion into a means of oppression, but all that changed when protests against police brutality exploded across the United States.

I started writing the first few chapters of this novel shortly before George Floyd was murdered, and within a few weeks it felt like the United States was sliding faster toward the dystopian world I was trying to create.[2] This was all the more true when federal officers were deployed to the streets of my home city of Portland, Oregon, without the request of the mayor or governor.[3] I watched in horror from Dallas as people were pulled into unmarked vans, choked by tear gas, and had their skulls shattered by "low-impact" rounds.[4] None of these tactics were new; they'd been used against protestors across the country for decades, especially Black and Brown protestors.[5] Federal officers had been deployed to Indian reservations violating their sovereignty, such as on the Standing Rock Indian Reservation when they protested the Dakota Access Pipeline.[6]

This time, the difference was that a state's sovereignty was being violated, and white bodies were on the line. We've been inching further and further into authoritarian territory for a while (Patriot Act, anyone?), but it's now louder and more in

---

2 Evan Hill et. al, "How George Floyd Was Killed in Police Custody," *New York Times,* May 31, 2020.

3 Marty Johnson and Lauren Vella, "Federal Agents Deployed to Portland Did Not Have Training in Riot Control: NYT," *The Hill,* July 18, 2020.

4 Jessica Lee, "Were Portland Protesters 'Kidnapped' by Federal Officers in Unmarked Vans?" *Snopes,* July 22, 2020.

5 Justin Hansford et. al, *Excessive Use of Force by the Police against Black Americans in the United States,* (Inter-American Commission on Human Rights, 2016).

6 Justin Worland, "What to Know about the Dakota Access Pipeline Protests," *Time,* October 28, 2016.

our faces than ever before.[7] And while some people have welcomed it, I've seen far more people be horrified by it. When the police tried to put down the protests across the country, the protests grew. When the federal officers came to Portland, a community of mothers, fathers, and veterans formed walls and used leaf blowers to protect the protestors.[8] Oppressive forces can never fully succeed in the face of resistance, when the people protest and work together toward change.

The dystopian genre is both a genre of privilege and a genre of desperate warning to resist oppression. In so many places around the globe, people are living through what most of us would classify as a dystopian nightmare—look at China and the Uighur Muslim people being tortured in state-run concentration camps.[9]

Only in the past few years did I start cracking open dystopian books and getting a more visceral fear of our reality becoming pretty close to that portrayed in the books. I bet you can relate at some level to the fear of an authoritarian regime too. For me this fear crystalized on January 6, 2021, when the United States stared down the barrel of a possible civil war caused by a man who wanted to hold on to power at all cost.[10] We came so close that day to seeing a massacre of legislators that would've changed our country forever—and, I believe, for the worse. We're not out of the woods yet either; as I'm writing this, very few people have been charged with crimes and those in Congress who supported this insurgency

---

7 "Surveillance under the Patriot Act," Multimedia, ACLU, updated 2021.

8 Laurel Wamsley, "In Portland, a 'Wall of Moms' and Leaf Blowers against Tear Gas," *NPR*, July 22, 2020.

9 Jen Kirby, "Concentration Camps and Forced Labor: China's Repression of the Uighurs, Explained," *Vox Media*, September 25, 2020.

10 Lauren Leatherby et. al, "How a Presidential Rally Turned into a Capitol Rampage," *New York Times*, January 12, 2021.

still have not faced consequences. I'm worried if they don't face consequences, someone will come along and try the exact same tactics to seize power, and we'll end up in a civil war just like the one in this book.

Dystopian fiction often serves as a warning against taking things too far, and that includes governmental control devolving into authoritarianism. In a similar fashion, the dieselpunk genre often delves into the horrors of authoritarianism and celebrates resistance to it. For this reason (and because it looks amazing), dieselpunk has always been one of my favorite "punk" aesthetics.

Most of the time, the authoritarian regime is the Nazi regime, such as in the *Wolfenstein* series or *The Man in the High Castle*, because dieselpunk technology and aesthetics come out of the 1930s and 40s, or alternative versions of those decades.

I chose instead to design my own regime and set it in the near future because authoritarian fascist regimes didn't die with the end of World War II. Heck, the Nazis didn't even die at the end of WWII. Look at any far-right protest, and you'll see plenty of flags that take inspiration from Nazi symbolism.[11] Fascism is still alive and well in the United States and other countries around the world, but so is resistance to it.

Calls for resistance and revolution can be scary because revolution is always inherently destructive, as the systems we know are broken down. But our current systems bring their own destruction—of lives, of families, and of communities. Just look at the system of policing that took the lives of George Floyd, Breonna Taylor, Tony Timpa, Jordan Edwards,

---

11 "Flags and Other Symbols Used by Far-Right Groups in Charlottesville," Hatewatch, Southern Poverty Law Center, updated August 12, 2017.

Tamir Rice, Michael Brown, and so, so many others.[12, 13, 14, 15, 16, 17] Look at the system of incarceration that imprisons one out of every five incarcerated people in the world.[18] Look at our healthcare system that forces people to choose between dying or being plunged into medical debt they cannot recover from.[19] Only by breaking down these systems can we hope to have a new way of doing things—one that is restorative instead of destructive.

The world you are about to enter sometimes feels just a breath away from our own, but it's a world we do not have to step into. People like my characters—Riley Jay, Sergio, Ian, and Jen—are everywhere. People fight every day for a better world than the one we have. People resist the slide into the world of Jericho. I hope reading this novel brings you some measure of hope.

---

12 Brad Parks, "George Floyd's Death Was 'Murder' and the Accused Officer 'Knew What He Was Doing,' Minneapolis Police Chief Says," *CNN,* June 24, 2020.

13 Eric Levenson, "A Timeline of Breonna Taylor's Case Since Police Broke Down Her Door and Shot Her," *CNN,* September 24, 2020.

14 Reis Thebault, "Police Laughed and Joked as He lost Consciousness in Handcuffs. Minutes Later, He Died," *The Washington Post,* July 31, 2019.

15 Kurtis Lee, "Officer Convicted in Killing of Fifteen-Year-Old Jordan Edwards—A Rare Outcome in Police Shootings," *Los Angeles Times,* August 28, 2018.

16 Safia Samee Ali, "Tamir Rice Shooting: Newly Released Interview Reveals Cop's Shifting Story," *NBC News,* April 26, 2017.

17 Raja Razek, "Missouri Police Officer Who Killed Michael Brown Faces No Charges," *CNN,* July 30, 2020.

18 Peter Wagner and Wanda Bertram, "'What Percent of the US Is Incarcerated?' (And Other Ways to Measure Mass Incarceration)," *Prison Policy Initiative,* January 16, 2020.

19 K. Robin Yabroff et. al, "Prevalence and Correlates of Medical Financial Hardship in the USA," *Journal of General Internal Medicine* 34 (2019): 1494-1502.

CHAPTER ONE

"Attention, citizens. The caravan leaves in ten minutes. Those who are not lined up in ten minutes will be subject to discipline."

"Riley, help me with this!" Ian pushed back stray black strands of hair hanging in his face. He was Korean-American, tall, thin, and all angles, but his quick smile was as soft as it was crooked.

Turning from the window where they'd been watching the Revolution loudspeaker trumpet the announcement, Riley Jay shouldered their medical backpack as they joined Ian. He nodded toward the other side of the cardboard box, and Riley crouched down to grab it.

"On three," Ian said. "One, two, three!"

Gritting their teeth, Riley hoisted the box up with Ian. They found that the box wasn't that heavy, just bulky.

Another long, low whistle pierced the air followed by a rolling *crash* that swayed the old office building. The bombs were hitting the outskirts of the city now. There'd been rumors that Command was getting closer, but it still felt like Philippi had become the front lines of this civil war overnight.

Riley steadied themself as the building stopped moving. "You want to go first, or you want me to go first?"

"I'll go first," Ian replied.

A low rumbling made Riley's heart leap into their throat. Was it their imagination, or were those bombs getting closer?

"Riley, go!" Ian said, his eyes wide.

"Then move!"

Ian sighed as the two of them backed out of the now-empty room. Riley reached to close the door before remembering there was no reason to. Trying to match their steps with Ian's, they followed him toward the stairs.

As the pair crossed the large, empty office floor, the door to another office room flew open. A middle-aged woman rushed out, cradling a young child in her arms. Two older kids peered out from behind the door.

"Hey! Hey, you're Riley, right? I need help!" The woman's blue eyes were so wide Riley could see the whites all around her irises.

"Help with what?" Riley asked.

"My daughter is sick. We've tried everything we could get our hands on, elderflower, chamomile tea, but she's burning up. I know you're a nurse. Please, help us!"

Everything in Riley seized up and they glanced around to make sure no one else had heard. "Why the hell would you accuse me of being a nurse?" they hissed. "You know that's illegal! You could get me killed!"

"Please, I'm desperate! Everyone's out on the streets lining up in the caravan. Now's the perfect time. I'll give you anything, especially if you have Tylenol."

Riley was about to say no, but then their eyes fell on the child. The little girl's hair was sweat-soaked, her cheeks bright red and almost glowing in the twilight. Every survival instinct they had screamed for them to run and not get involved. But they couldn't bring themself to turn away.

Looking over at Ian, Riley raised their eyebrows, asking either for permission to treat the girl and put them all at risk, or for a way out of it. Ian clenched his jaw and nodded.

"Help them. I'll manage."

"My son can help you," the mother said, turning around. "Matt! Help this man with the box!"

The oldest child hurried out of the room to stand by Riley's side. Matt couldn't have been more then twelve, with almost translucent skin and dull brown eyes. Riley wasn't sure he'd be able to lift a feather, much less help Ian carry the box.

"Attention, citizens. The caravan leaves in eight minutes. Those who are not lined up in eight minutes will be subject to discipline."

Riley shuffled over their end of the box to Matt, who struggled to get it balanced.

"Work fast," Ian said. "They'll be sweeping the buildings soon."

Riley nodded as Ian led the way to the stairs, slowing down so Matt could keep up. As soon as they were out of sight so they couldn't be charged as witnesses, Riley took off their backpack and knelt on the ground.

"Lay her down," they said, unzipping the backpack. "You're in luck, I've still got some kids' Tylenol. I can give you the rest if you promise to keep your mouth shut about where you got it."

"Of course. Thank you. I don't have much, but I can pay you back, thank you so much..."

Riley tuned out her gratitude as they pulled out their stethoscope and put the buds in their ears. The little girl didn't react when Riley put the cold stethoscope on her chest. Her heart rate felt more like a flutter than a beat, and her breathing was fast and shallow. If this was an infection, it was probably too far advanced for Riley to treat effectively. But they were already here, so they might as well try.

"Okay, first we need to wake her up," Riley said, unzipping one of their side pockets to grab a pen light.

"Freeze! Hands in the air!"

Riley knocked the pen light out of its pocket as they threw their hands in the air. The mother gasped. A door slammed shut, and Riley looked up to see the door to the mother's room had closed.

"Back away from the kid! Now!"

Riley kept their head down as they got up and moved two steps back. They already knew it was a Revolution soldier. They didn't need to see his ugly face to confirm it. The stethoscope bounced around Riley's neck, causing nausea to bubble up in their throat. They were dead. They were so, so fucking dead.

"Have you treated her yet?" the soldier asked.

Riley shook their head, glancing at the mother. Her gaunt face was white with terror, and she kept glancing from her daughter on the floor to the closed door behind her. Well, Riley was already thoroughly fucked, so might as well try to get everyone else out safely.

"I took the child from the mother in order to treat her," Riley said in a rush. "She had nothing to do with this. She got all treatments legally from Revolution healers. I couldn't stand to see the child suffer when those treatments failed."

"The treatments did not fail. She just did not have enough faith," the soldier replied. The mother squeaked, pressing her hands to her face.

Bull-fucking-shit. Riley had never known a mom who didn't have enough faith that their child would make it. Their blood boiled as they looked up at the soldier. His face was obscured in the shadows, but he was tall and gangly with a handgun pointed at the mother.

"Let the family go," Riley said, trying to ignore the thundering heartbeat in their ears. "She had nothing to do with this. She was trying to stop me."

The end of the soldier's handgun wavered, dipping down before swinging over to aim at Riley's face. Riley could feel their chest squeeze and their throat close up as they stared down the barrel of the gun.

"Get out," the soldier snapped at the mother. "Get your children and get in the caravan. Now!"

The mother babbled something that Riley couldn't make out and scooped up her daughter. Out of the corner of their eye, Riley could see the mother open the door.

"John! Get out here!"

Riley could hear small, rapid footsteps followed by a heavier set as the family ran for the stairs. They couldn't believe they'd done it. They'd actually talked the soldier into letting the family go. The squeezing in their chest started to ease, but beads of sweat were forming on their forehead.

"Attention, citizens. The caravan leaves in five minutes. Those who are not lined up in five minutes will be subject to discipline."

"Move away from the stairs. Take the backpack with you." The soldier flicked the end of the handgun to the right. Riley tried to swallow the lump in their throat as they scooped up their backpack to move away from the door and further into the room. Another blast went off nearby, and Riley stepped back. The soldier mirrored their movement with more grace, maneuvering so he was in between Riley and the exit.

"Name," the soldier demanded.

Riley tried to respond, but it felt like they were trying to talk through cotton balls. The office building rocked again as another blast went off nearby.

"Name!" The soldier switched the safety off, and Riley flinched.

"R-Riley Jay. Riley Jay Chasen."

"Riley Jay Chasen, you have been charged with providing illegal medical care in defiance of God and His Will and the laws of the Revolution. How do you plead?"

Why couldn't God's will ever include Tylenol with these people? "Just get this over with," they said. They knew Ian or Sergio would be barreling up the stairs in a minute to see what had happened to them. They wanted their body to be long gone before then.

The gun wavered. "I-I need an actual plea."

Apparently there was a lot of ceremony around shooting someone in the head. "Guilty, I guess."

"Throw the stethoscope toward me. And slide that backpack too. I'll need it for evidence."

Evidence. Why did Revolution insist on this mental torture? Pulling the stethoscope off of their neck, Riley went to throw it when they saw movement in the door that led to the stairs. The figure was fully obscured by the shadows, but by the way it crouched down, Riley knew it was Sergio.

Their heart leapt. They tried to keep their eyes off of Sergio so the soldier wouldn't become suspicious. Throwing the stethoscope at the soldier, they put their free hand back up and crouched down on the floor.

"Let me zip up this backpack so you don't lose any evidence," Riley said. Their mind raced. If they could get down and prepare to roll out of the way, Sergio could take out the soldier without having to worry about Riley getting shot.

"Hurry up!" the soldier said.

Riley went to zip up the side pocket when they remembered they'd knocked the pen light onto the floor. Glancing up, they saw the light lying at the soldier's feet.

Thank God. "Uh, sir, I-I dropped a piece of evidence by your foot."

The soldier glanced down, knocking the pen light a few inches away from him with his toe. Keeping his gun trained on Riley, he leaned down to pick it up, putting him in the perfect position for Sergio to pounce and get him in a chokehold.

Riley dove over their backpack and somersaulted, nearly smacking into the wall. With a loud *thump,* the soldier slumped onto the ground. Sergio snatched up the soldier's handgun and switched back on the safety.

"What the hell were you thinkin', Riley?" he asked in his soft Southern drawl. The dim light cast shadows on his tan skin and made his dark brown eyes look almost black. His curly black hair was sticking up straighter than normal.

He scooped up the penlight and tossed it to them. "Treatin' a patient right out in the middle of the floor?"

Riley threaded their arms through their backpack as they followed him to the stairs. "It was a child, Sergio. I didn't have time to think!"

"Honey, if they figure out why that soldier detained you, we're in a world of trouble."

He reached back to push them in front of him. Riley couldn't reply as they ran down the steps, needing all of their breath to move as fast as they could. Once they reached the first floor, Riley headed for the front door, but Sergio grabbed their shoulder.

"Lobby's filled with soldiers. This way!"

Spinning around, Riley followed Sergio out the emergency escape door. Riley winced as the alarm went off, but all thoughts of being caught flew out of their head when they rounded the corner and saw the line of beaten-up cars and trucks. Some were stuffed to the brim with belongings and people while others were close to empty. People scrambled to avoid the kicks and punches of the soldiers as they piled into cars, but few managed to escape the blows.

Skirting a floodlight, Riley sighed in relief as they saw the familiar white pickup truck their family owned. Ian was in the driver's seat while Jen was in the passenger's seat. The two were an odd pair—Ian a Korean-American in his early thirties, Jen a Black woman in her late seventies. But Riley didn't want anyone else in their corner; Jen treated them all like her own children, and Ian was the closest thing Riley ever had to a brother.

Sergio opened the back driver's side door and jumped inside. Riley followed him, slamming the door shut. Their anxiety eased as they heard the click of the car door lock. Looking up, they caught sight of their shaggy brown hair and pale face in the rearview mirror. Normally they were very fair, when they weren't pink from sunburn, but now they looked more like a ghost than a human.

"Attention, citizens. The caravan leaves in one minute. Those who are not lined up in one minute will be subject to discipline."

"What happened?" Jen asked, turning to look back at Riley and Sergio. "Ian said you'd stopped to treat a child, Riley, but then you didn't come outside with them!"

"Because they got caught," Sergio said before Riley could open their mouth.

Jen gasped, pressing her hand to her chest as her eyes went wide. Ian shook his head.

"I knew I should've waited for you," he said.

"You would've just gotten caught as well," Riley said. "Look, we're fine, Sergio knocked out the soldier. They can't tie anything to us."

They reached up to grab their stethoscope. Their fingers brushed through air instead of grabbing plastic tubes. Stomach lurching, they realized it was still on the soldier's body, but it was just a plain, cheap stethoscope. There was no way it could be tied to Riley.

"Is somethin' wrong?" Sergio asked, putting his arm around Riley's shoulders and pulling them in for a hug.

"No, we're good," Riley said. Closing their eyes and taking a few deep breaths, they tried to relax. They were okay. They were in the caravan. There was no way that the stethoscope could be tied to them.

Sergio kissed the top of their head. "You're all right, darlin'. I've got you. You're okay. The soldier didn't hurt you."

Riley opened their eyes and nodded, leaning their head to rest on Sergio's chest.

Flames shot up in the sky. A loud *boom* rolled over the truck, sharper than the thunder of the far-away blasts. Riley sat straight up, almost knocking their head against Sergio's chin. They squinted at the spot where the blast column had been, trying to see if anything around it had caught on fire.

"Why the hell are we not moving?" Jen said.

"Must still be sweeping the buildings," Sergio said, looking back at the office building that had been their home. "Shit, Riley! Get down!"

Riley dropped down onto the car floor, tucking their feet under them and pressing their back against the car door. "What is it?"

"He's already back up."

It took a minute for it to click. The soldier Sergio had put in a chokehold had already woken up. They'd been hoping he'd be knocked out for longer than that, long enough for their family to get out of Philippi.

"What do we do?" Ian asked, keeping his eyes on the blue SUV in front of him. Riley assumed he was attempting to look natural, but he looked as stiff as a tin soldier.

"Not much we can do," Jen replied, her voice even and steady. "Just stay down, Riley. Sergio, keep an eye on that soldier. We'll need to avoid him once we get to the next city."

"He starts givin' descriptions out and we'll need to avoid a lot more soldiers than just him," Sergio replied.

Jen tapped her fingers on the dashboard. "We're heading out the same way we came in. Anybody remember any side roads that led off the main road?"

Riley racked their brain, but they couldn't remember any. It'd been pitch dark when the four of them arrived in Philippi almost a year ago, and they'd still been recovering from heat exhaustion.

"There's one 'bout two miles out," Sergio replied. "It'll be on our left."

"Think there'll be enough dunes for us to get lost in?" Ian asked.

"Really hope so," Sergio replied.

"Look, this is insane," Riley said. "You'll all be in trouble if I'm found here. I'll hop out and hide amongst the people walking. Then we can meet back up at camp tonight."

Sergio shook his head, his thin lips pressed into a line. Riley heard the car doors lock again, and they looked up to see Ian glaring at them through the rearview mirror.

Jen stopped tapping on the dashboard. "Keep your ass on that floor until we say otherwise."

There was no way in hell this was going to work. Revolution had to have already stationed soldiers on that road to prevent people from running off. Riley was kicking themself. They should've just passed the mother by. They should've known it would be too dangerous to try and treat the little girl with the Revolution soldiers sweeping the buildings. Even as those thoughts crossed their mind, however, Riley knew there hadn't been another choice.

"We're moving," Ian said, shifting the truck into gear.

"Thank God," Jen breathed.

Riley scrunched themself up as tightly as they could as the pickup rumbled forward, trying to avoid the floodlights that swept in and out of the truck. They looked up at Sergio, who was staring straight ahead with his arm draped across the back seat. He'd switched the action off on the handgun he'd stolen, but he kept it hidden under his jacket on the seat.

"Where's the other gun?" Riley asked in a low voice.

"Glovebox," Sergio replied.

"Can I have it?"

He glanced out the window above Riley. "Too many soldiers around," he said. "Don't wanna raise their suspicions."

It made sense, but Riley felt vulnerable without it in their hand.

Nausea bubbled up in Riley's stomach as the truck swayed, so they looked out the window behind Sergio to try and quell it. They expected to see the stars, but all of the light pollution from the headlights and floodlights drowned them out.

The nausea was dulled by anger although Riley didn't know if it was only because they couldn't see the stars or because their life relied on how well they could hide on the floor of a car.

"Keep your eyes peeled, Ian," Sergio said. "Should be comin' up on the side road soon."

"You're going to have to give me warning to turn off. I don't want to hit anyone," Ian said.

"I'll try."

The caravan inched forward, slowly enough for the soldiers to walk alongside and make sure everyone stayed in line. Riley could tell when a soldier walked alongside the pickup truck, because Sergio would always hold his breath. Riley began to count how many times he did, taking satisfaction from knowing how many soldiers they'd managed to hide from.

After a small eternity Ian finally asked, "That the road you're talking about, Serg?"

Sergio leaned his head against the window. "Yeah, yeah that's it."

"All right. Keep an eye out for soldiers behind us. Okay? Don't really feel like hitting anyone."

Sergio nodded, glancing into the rearview mirror before looking behind him. "Soldier's heading this way. Jen, when we turn, we're going to need to duck."

"Got it," Jen replied.

Riley could feel their chest squeezing again as Ian came to a halt.

"When the caravan moves, wait to go so you can get some room for a fast start," Sergio said, turning back to look out the front windshield. "And kill the headlights soon as we're on that road."

"That's the idea," Ian replied.

Taking a deep breath in through their nose and out through their mouth, Riley resisted the urge to squeeze their eyes shut. They needed to stay alert in case they had to jump out of the car and run for it.

"It's okay, Ry," Sergio said, still looking straight forward. "We'll make it. It'll be all right."

Not enough emotion was in his voice to make Riley believe a word he was saying. He knew this was a long shot, but it was the only chance they had.

"Here we go," Ian said. "Where's the soldier now?"

Sergio glanced back. "Stopped at the car two behind us... Wait, no, he's turnin' this way."

Riley held their breath. It felt like every second was stretched into an age as they waited for Ian to stomp on the gas. The car in front of them had to be far enough ahead by now. They just wanted to get this over with, one way or another. The stress was killing them quicker than any bullet could.

"*Get down!*" Ian yelled.

Riley braced themself against the door as Ian hit the gas and turned the car. Their head smacked against the door as Sergio dropped onto the floor. The roar of the truck engine couldn't drown out the sharp patter of assault rifles. Riley shut their eyes.

"More people are trying to get away!" Ian said.

"Ignore it! Keep your eyes on the road!" Sergio replied.

All thoughts of being shot flew out of Riley's head, replaced by burning curiosity. Steadying themself, they crawled onto the backseat and pulled themself up to look out the back window.

Sergio grabbed the collar of their T-shirt. "What the hell are you doin'? Get down!"

Riley swatted his hand away, not able to take their eyes off of the sight in front of them. The caravan had collapsed, with cars and people scattering into the darkness. Soldiers were chasing them down on foot. Riley was sure some of the cars driving away were also undercover soldiers chasing down fleeing citizens. The gunshots got softer the farther away the family drove.

Sergio was still tugging on their shirt. Riley looked down at him. "I don't think the soldiers are shooting at us," they said. "Revolution's just trying to prevent as many people from getting away as possible."

"You think the soldiers would've blocked off this road, then," Sergio said.

"Maybe they didn't have the men to do it," Jen replied. She was crawling back up onto her seat, stretching out her knees and rolling her shoulders. Sergio gave in and also climbed back up, joining Riley in watching out the back window. After a minute he sighed and threw his arm around Riley's shoulders, kissing the top of their head.

Riley could feel their hands begin to shake as the adrenaline rushed out of them. The tightness in their chest eased, and they gulped in deep, sweet breaths. Tucking their head into the crook of Sergio's neck, they watched as the last headlights were swallowed by the dark, leaving the found family to the mercy of the cold desert night.

CHAPTER TWO

"You awake, Riley?"

Riley kept picking at the loose thread on the mattress. They didn't want to get up and face whatever survival crisis today would hold. Surviving was exhausting. They just wanted to sleep.

"Riley."

Well, by that tone, Jen already knew they were awake. "Yeah?"

"Come on. Sit up. We need to plan."

Riley didn't know if they had the energy to think, let alone plan. Rolling over to the edge of the mattress, they sat up, yawning and rubbing their eyes to get rid of the lack of sleep. "Wh-why did Ian go out a few minutes ago?"

"To check on Sergio," Jen said, nodding toward the door. It was one of those double-glass doors that had been common in storefronts. The glass was gone now, replaced by scrap wood fastened together with the few nails and screws the previous occupants could find. Most of the windows had been given the same treatment, except for one where the glass had one splintering crack in it. A white neon sign in the shape of a coffee cup with three gray steam curls coming out of it hung above the crack. The sign looked almost pristine, if not for the layer of dust that covered everything.

"Come help me get breakfast," Jen said.

Riley nodded, pushing themself up and stepping around an overturned table with two legs missing. Sergio and Ian had brought in some food, water, and the medical kit last night, but most of the supplies were still in the truck. It made it easier to get away if need be.

Jen untied the crate, and Riley pulled the lid off, setting it on a rickety chair.

"We need to eat these crackers before they go bad," Jen said, pulling out a small box. "So I'm thinking crackers and tuna. Hopefully we'll have time to search around these buildings. If any place is going to still have supplies, I think it's here."

She sighed, looking out the remaining glass window. "I miss the days when we could just go to the grocery store."

"You and me both," Riley replied.

The door creaked open, and Ian poked his head in. "Pack up. We need to move," he said.

"What? Why?" Riley asked.

"Sergio found two sets of footprints. He's worried there's more where that came from."

Jen grabbed two cans of tuna and the box of crackers, putting the food in the pockets of her skirt. Riley tied the lid back onto the crate, their calluses protecting them from the roughness of the rope. Ian helped Riley carry the crate of food out while Jen carried Riley's backpack of medical supplies and the two-quart water canteen. Sergio was already in the driver's seat, his eyes continually scanning the horizon. Jen put Riley's backpack on the floorboards of the passenger's seat and climbed into the back seat while Ian and Riley brought out the mattresses and bedding and threw them into the back.

"Make sure those aren't gonna fly out!" Jen yelled.

"They're not. They're fine!" Ian replied.

Riley moved one of the water containers to sit on top of the blankets before they and Ian closed the tailgate. "You want shotgun?" Ian asked.

"Yeah, thanks," Riley replied as the engine started up. Hurrying to the cab of the truck, Riley hopped into the passenger's seat while Ian climbed in beside Jen.

"You sure you got everythin'?" Sergio asked.

"Yeah, not like we brought a lot in," Riley replied.

Sergio nodded, shifting the truck into gear and pulling out onto the road. Most of the ten or so buildings around the coffee shop were in similar shape with boarded-up windows, chunks missing out of concrete walls, and a smattering of rubble connecting each store. A patio table was half-buried in the burnt golden sand, next to the legs of a wrought iron chair sticking straight up toward the blistering blue sky. Riley was surprised at how intact everything was, especially when less than a half-mile down the road, everything had been reduced to rubble.

"Where we heading?" Ian asked as everyone munched on the tuna and crackers. The truck was definitely going to stink the rest of the day.

"We need to look for a village," Sergio said. "Somewhere with plenty of people that'll provide us protection from bandits, but also ain't big enough for Command or Revolution to pay much attention to."

"Wouldn't a city provide us more protection? And more resources?" Jen asked.

"I haven't heard of a city that ain't under the control of either side," Sergio replied. "Even if there is one, it's probably gonna be the front lines soon. Either way, it's too dangerous for Riley to be in Revolution territory anymore, and I don't wanna risk Command bein' worse."

"Don't know how they could be," Ian replied. "Wait, is anyone former military? That might actually help us in Command."

"Not what I've heard. Command and Revolution treat former military the same," Sergio replied as Riley nodded their head in agreement.

Riley had seen what happened to former soldiers back in Philippi. The family's sixty-year-old neighbor had been held at gunpoint, weeping while being sworn into service. Then he'd been handed an assault rifle and forced into formation. They never saw him again after that.

Sergio took back his hand to swerve around a small crater in the middle of the road. He slowed down the truck to maneuver between two more craters and then pushed a little faster to get over a buckle. Riley braced themself against the dashboard as the truck bucked and jolted down the cracked road.

After a few miles the road finally started to smooth out. It was easy to figure out why because as the road calmed down, the amount of rubble began to decrease. Soon all that was left were sand dunes and a road only worn down by time. As the heat rose and the sun beat down, the lack of sleep from the night before caught up to Riley. Nothing was out here. They could shut their eyes for a few minutes…

"Baby, wake up."

Riley dragged themself out of their nap, stretching out the crick in their neck. The sun was dipping toward the horizon behind them, and when Riley looked into the rearview mirror, they saw that Ian and Jen were asleep. Ian had slumped over so his head was resting on Jen's shoulder.

"What?" Riley asked, looking over at Sergio.

"We're out of gas."

Riley glanced at the dashboard and sure enough, the needle was hovering over E.

"We've got more in the bed," Riley replied.

"Only good enough for another tank, I think."

Riley's heart sped up, and they could feel their chest tighten. "How far will that get us?"

He shrugged, pressing his lips into a thin line and refusing to meet Riley's eye. Everything went quiet as the engine sputtered off. Riley held their breath as Sergio navigated the truck to the side of the road, letting it glide to a halt on the shoulder.

"We need to find a house or business," he whispered.

"An empty house or business, right?" Riley said.

Sergio glanced back at Ian and Jen and slowly shook his head. "We can't get stranded out here."

"We could head back to the coffee shop. There had to be plenty of stuff back there we could scavenge."

"We didn't see anythin' comin' in, and I'm not riskin' gettin' stranded back there with the bandits," Sergio replied.

"What will Ian and Jen say? I don't want them to leave us."

"They won't. They'll understand."

"You have to remember how they talked about the looters and robbers in their home city."

"Situation's different. They'll know that."

"Wh-what are you guys talking about?" Ian asked.

Riley gulped down their protests and turned to see Ian yawning. He moved away from Jen, stretching out his arms in front of him.

"Tank's empty," Sergio replied. "Looks like we're stoppin' here for the night."

"You sure you've been driving, Serg?" Ian asked, poking his head between the front seats, looking out the windshield.

Riley snorted as Sergio glared at him. Ian gave him a shit-eating grin before turning to Riley.

"Want me to take the first watch since you haven't slept?" he asked.

"Excuse you, I slept," Riley replied.

"Really? Your eyes are completely bloodshot."

"So're yours."

"Yours are worse."

"I'm takin' first watch," Sergio said.

"The hell you are. You've been driving all day!" Riley replied. "And you took second watch last night!"

"Did Sergio just say he was taking first watch?" Jen asked.

"Good mornin', Jen. Sleep okay?" Sergio asked, looking back at her through the rearview mirror.

"Sergio Melendez, you need to *sleep* if you're going to be driving us on these dangerous roads!" Jen said, leaning over Riley's seat.

"We haven't seen another car since we turned onto this road. I could drive this in my sleep."

"Well, you don't have to. Have Riley or Ian take over next time!"

"Yeah, whose pickup truck *is* this?" Ian asked.

Sergio threw up his hands in surrender. "Fine. Ian can take first watch."

"Much obliged." Ian grinned, resting his arm on Sergio's shoulder.

"All right, Ian and I will fill up the tank and get a meal ready." Jen said. "You two take a look around and see if you can find a village or something. If the roads are this clear and the buildings still standing, it might've attracted more people than just us."

Everyone agreed and hopped out of the car. Sergio grabbed the two handguns from the glovebox, keeping one for himself and handing the other to Ian. Riley went to the back of the car to help Jen unload the truck bed.

"I've got it. You and Sergio get going," she said, rearranging Riley's mussed hair into some semblance of a style. "Keep your eyes open. All right?"

"All right. We'll be safe, Jen."

She tucked one last strand of hair behind Riley's ear before Ian joined them. "Sergio's about to leave without you."

"Like hell he is," Riley replied, rolling their eyes as they hurried to take Sergio's hand. But as the pair walked into the rubble, Riley turned to look back at the rest of their family. Jen was spreading an old quilt on the ground while Ian worked to rig up the tarp for some shade while laughing. Riley didn't want to watch their family starve, but they didn't want to risk Ian and Jen leaving either. So when Sergio tugged on their hand, they looked away from the truck and into the rubble. They just wished their heart would stop beating so fast.

"It'll be all right, sweetheart," Sergio whispered, pulling them close to kiss their cheek.

If Riley closed their eyes, ignored the heat, and blocked out the crunch of ash under their boots, they could pretend this was a normal date with Sergio, not a survival mission. But the second their shoulder brushed against an iron rebar that poked out of a concrete slab, they were yanked back into reality.

"Watch your step, honey," Sergio said, letting go of Riley's hand and putting his arm around their shoulders. Within a few minutes Riley felt their T-shirt stick to their shoulders, but they didn't want him to take his arm back.

Stopping in the shade of what looked like a storefront, the two surveyed the damage. Whatever this area had been—a shopping district, maybe?—it hadn't been completely reduced to ash. Some places only had one or two gray concrete slabs still standing, pockmarked with bullet holes and the paint blasted off by swirling sand. Twisted steel beams gleamed silver in the sun. Frames of storefront awnings stuck out in some places and were scattered across the ground in others. Riley broke away from Sergio and spun in a circle, trying to create a mental picture of what this place might have looked like. But it was impossible after the bombs and the guns had reduced it to chaos.

Sergio rested his hand on Riley's shoulder, holding them in place. After a second, he guided them deeper into the rubble. Sidestepping a large chunk of concrete and steel, Riley gasped as they spotted a smattering of bleached white bones behind it. Tibia, fibula, femur, patella…they were so small…

Sergio turned Riley away from the sight. "Stop tryin' to identify every bone you see. It'll just drive you mad."

Riley bit their lip and tried to swallow the lump that had formed in their throat. Sergio put his arm back around them, as the two stepped out onto the piecemeal asphalt that must have been a main street.

"No way we can tell who won," Sergio said. "Nothing's been rebuilt. Nothing's been left standing. Nobody cared."

Tears threatened Riley's eyes as they stared at the shattered buildings. The people who'd lived here had cared. But neither Command nor Revolution had cared about the people.

"One o'clock."

Looking to the other side of the road, Riley squinted at what Sergio was pointing at, unable to believe their eyes. The red brick building looked like it was still standing. So did the building across the street from it. "Should we take a closer look?" they asked.

"Kind of what we're here for."

As the two got closer, Sergio pushed Riley back and pulled out his handgun. Crouching down, Riley followed him behind a pile of rubble that blocked the street from view.

"Stay here," Sergio said, checking the ammo in the clip. "Anythin' happens, you haul ass back to the truck and you get Jen and Ian out of here."

Riley nodded as Sergio ducked to steal a kiss. Then he darted to the building, pressing his back against the wall. Glancing at the building across the road, he looked around the corner before disappearing behind it.

Riley took a deep breath, feeling their heart race as they sat against the concrete wall. Closing their eyes, they braced themself for the sound of gunshots, but all they heard was the wind. All they felt was the heat swirling around them. It was so heavy, so exhausting...

Footsteps crunched in the sand. Riley jumped to their feet. Trying to keep their breathing steady, they slid over to the end of the wall, peeking around the corner.

Ian.

Fucking. Shit. Fuckshit. How long had they been gone?

He was crouched behind a pile of concrete and melted plastic with his back turned to Riley. He seemed to be peeking at the building across the street. They debated on whether or not they wanted to get his attention or let him go, but they didn't want him to get spotted if there were people in the buildings up ahead.

Riley scooped up a stone and chucked it at Ian's feet. He whirled around and pointed the handgun at their head.

"Careful!" Riley hissed.

"RJ!"

"You didn't leave the gun with Jen?"

"She didn't want it, she—"

"Get over here!"

Glancing across the road, Ian scrambled to Riley's side, holstering his pistol.

"Where's Sergio?" he asked.

"Scouting ahead. Why didn't you give Jen the gun?"

"Didn't want it. She felt like something bad had happened to you, so she ordered me to find you guys. Besides, you've been gone for hours. Dinner's ready."

"What the hell's she going to do if she runs into bandits?"

"Feed them?"

Riley groaned, burying their face in their hands. "Sergio's going to be pissed at you."

"He can take it up with Jen. Come on, RJ. Let's go get Sergio and get back to the truck. I'm starving!"

He put Riley in a headlock, messing up their hair as he laughed. Riley frantically swatted at him, and he let go.

"RJ? What's wr—"

Riley clocked Sergio rounding the wall, and he froze as he saw Ian. "What the hell are you doing here?"

"Getting you for dinner."

Sergio glanced at Riley, his square jaw clenched. He'd found something. They had to stall, get Ian out of here. "We're still explorin'," Sergio replied. "We'll be back in a bit. Go tell Jen not to worry."

"She told me not to come back without you," Ian said. "Plus, if I come with you, we can cover more ground quicker."

"Or, if anythin' happens to us, Jen'll be left all alone," Sergio replied. "Do you want that?"

Ian gulped and shook his head. "But there's still safety in numbers. Right?"

"We can handle ourselves, Ian," Riley said, putting their hand on Ian's shoulder. "Jen's all alone right now, and I don't think any of us are comfortable with that. Go on back and tell her we'll be there in half an hour. All right? There's safety in numbers."

Ian sighed and nodded. "Stay safe," he said, giving Riley a quick hug and clapping Sergio on the back before taking off. Once he was out of sight, Riley turned back to Sergio.

"What'd you find?" they asked.

"Gas station about a mile up the road. Two adults, no kids, plenty of supplies. We've got to be near a city; I didn't see a car."

"Somebody else may be driving it right now. We'd better move fast in case they come back."

Sergio nodded, looking down at his handgun. "I've got ten shots with this."

"We do this right, you won't need them."

"Yeah, I'm thinkin' sneak in the back, knock them out, grab what we need, and go. Remember how to do a chokehold?"

"A chokehold?" Ian gasped. Riley spun around to see him pop up from behind a pile of rubble.

"What the hell are you still doin' here?" Sergio said, stepping in front of Riley.

"I knew you were up to something," Ian replied. "You're going to rob someone?"

"Ian, it's none of your business."

"The hell it isn't! Who's going to explain to Jen if you get..."

Riley bit their lip as they looked anywhere but Ian's eyes.

"We're not that desperate. Are we?" Ian asked.

Yes, but Riley didn't want to tell him that.

"You... you were doing this before we met. Weren't you? You're too confident."

Riley heard Sergio take a deep breath.

"Yeah. We were. That's how we survived so long without stayin' in a city. And if that's the only way I can keep my family alive, I'm gonna do it."

Glancing up to see Ian staring at Sergio with wide eyes, Riley stepped up beside Sergio and took his hand. "We promised we'd take care of you and Jen. Remember?" they said.

"Not like this!"

"Ian, we're running out of food, water, and gas," Riley said. "We don't know how far it is to a village. We could end up in the middle of nowhere with no options. We have at least one option here."

"But what about those people? What's going to happen to them?" Ian asked.

"We never take more than we need, we never take someone's last item, and we never hurt anyone unless it's in self-defense."

"You were literally planning on putting people in chokeholds."

Riley didn't have a reply to that. They didn't even consider it hurting someone anymore. There wasn't any pain. They just dropped unconscious for a bit, according to Sergio, but that was too much to explain right now with Ian as worked up as he was.

"I'm not watching you, Riley, and Jen starve to death in this desert," Sergio said through gritted teeth.

Ian locked eyes with him, and Riley could see the torment swirling there. It wasn't like Riley was happy with the options either. The first time they'd raided an occupied building, they'd hurled their guts afterward in guilt and shame. They still felt sick every time, but if the price for keeping the family alive was a stomachache, then they were happy to pay it.

"Fine then," Ian said, holding up his hands in surrender. "You're right. But we're doing this my way."

"Your way?" Sergio said.

"We're going to go up to the front door and ask nicely for help. Maybe even with a pretty please."

Sergio scoffed, shaking his head and grinning. Riley had to hold back a smile, too; Ian was so innocent.

"You think we haven't tried that before?" Sergio asked, chuckling. "They slam the door in your face if you're lucky. Put the end of a shotgun in it if you aren't."

"We do it my way, or I'm telling Jen."

Riley glanced over at Sergio, who had folded his arms and was biting the corner of his mouth as he stared at Ian. He looked at them out of the corner of his eye, and they nodded. Jen could not find out about this.

"Fine," he said. "We'll try your way first. But if it doesn't work, I take over. And give Riley your gun."

Riley held their hand out, but Ian just stared at them.

"Ian, give me the gun," Riley said. "I promise I won't shoot unless in self-defense."

He sighed, turning the gun around and handing it to Riley. "Thank you very much," Riley said, taking the clip out to check the rounds.

“Seven shots,” they said, putting the gun back together.

“Should be more than we need,” Sergio replied. “All right, follow me and stay down.”

“Hang on, I thought I was leading this!” Ian said.

Sergio raised his eyebrows. “Do you know where the gas station is?”

Ian shook his head, looking at his feet.

“That’s what I thought,” Sergio said. “Come on, let’s get this over with.”

Riley pushed Ian to follow right behind Sergio, making it easier to keep an eye on him. The stomachache that normally came after the raid had already arrived. Sergio led the way to the end of the building, pressing his back against the wall and peeking around the corner. As Ian crouched behind him, Riley could see his hands trembling.

“You don’t have to do this, Ian,” they whispered.

“Safety in numbers, right?” His voice was shaking too.

Sergio looked back at Riley and shook his head in frustration. “Ian, I don’t want you to—”

“We’re wasting time. Aren’t we? Come on. Let’s get to this gas station.”

“Fine,” Sergio said, sliding around the corner. Ian and Riley followed as they darted across the road to the fully intact building—a restaurant, going by how many overturned tables and broken chairs there were.

“Wait, why are we sneaking around?” Ian asked. “We’re just going to be walking up to the door anyway.”

“Because we don’t know if they’re the only people,” Sergio replied. “I’d rather make it hard for others to shoot us.”

Ian gulped. “Right. Forgot about that. Sorry.”

Riley put their hand on his back, trying to get him to calm down. If he froze up while they were trying to get away, it could be deadly for everyone.

"We've done this before," they said. "Just keep breathing and stay calm."

"I am calm!"

Uh-huh.

The group rounded the back of the building and sprinted to the next one. This building had a fair bit of bullet damage, but the sign with "CLARISSE'S CLOTHING BOUTIQUE" was still intact. Sergio scouted around the corner before beckoning Ian and Riley to follow him.

"We're going to cross over to that buildin'," he said, pointing at a boarded-up storefront. "Sneak around behind it, and then we'll be about thirty feet from the gas station. We'll walk on the road from there so we don't arouse the suspicions of the people in the gas station. I'll be in the lead until we get close, and then Ian can take over. Riley, figure out our quickest escape if things go bad. Understood?"

Riley and Ian both nodded, and Sergio led the way across the street. Tucking their gun in the back of their jeans, Riley moved to walk level with Sergio.

"I don't like this," Sergio whispered. "Ian's going to choke."

Riley gritted their teeth, trying to keep their voice steady. "I'll look after him."

"I need you helpin' me, not babysittin' him."

"I can hear you!" Ian hissed.

Riley and Sergio both shut up, neither one meeting Ian's eyes.

"I'm not going to choke," Ian said, ducking his head to force Sergio to look at him. "We're just going to go up to them, ask for help, and then leave. What're we running low on?"

"Water and gas," Sergio replied. "Food if they have extra."

Ian nodded as they walked up to the edge of the gas station. The gas pumps still stood, although their digital displays had gone dark and were covered in sand. The gas tanks underneath had to have been bled dry, and the cover above was caving in. As they skirted the cave-in, Riley saw that the convenience store was relatively untouched. It was still dingy, but it had obviously been scrubbed, and it had less bullet holes than the other buildings. The windows of the store were covered in thin plywood, blocking most of the light. What shone through the cracks flickered; Riley couldn't tell if it was candlelight or shadows from people moving around.

"All right, Ian, you're up," Sergio said.

Ian gulped, looking over at Riley. They shrugged, gesturing to the door. If this worked, Riley would be glad for it. If not, they could park Ian behind some rubble, go with their original plan, and hightail it out of there. Either way, it was time to move.

Rolling his shoulders back, Ian stepped up and knocked on the boarded-up door. Everything froze for a few seconds before the silence was broken by rapid footsteps. The door cracked open.

"Yes?" a gruff voice asked.

"Hello, sir," Ian said, putting on his crooked smile. "We're traveling through and our truck ran out of gas. We were hoping you had some water and gas to spare to get us on our way."

Sergio caught Riley's eye and nodded his head toward the boarded-up windows behind them. Nodding their understanding, Riley crept back to peek through the cracks. The only thing they could see were dozens of gallon-sized water bottles stacked on pallets.

"Sorry, no," the man replied, slamming the door shut.

"Liar," Riley hissed.

"I've got at least a dozen tanks worth of gas over here," Sergio muttered.

Ian joined Riley to peek at the water. "Why wouldn't they want to help us?" Ian asked.

"Because they're scared," Riley replied, feeling a little sorry for Ian. "They don't want to be without something when they really need it."

"I mean… do we have anything to trade?" Ian asked.

"Not that I can think of."

Sergio motioned toward the road, and Riley and Ian followed him out.

"Start walkin'," he said, heading back down the road. "We'll give it a bit and then sneak back and enter through the back door."

"They probably have it barricaded at this point," Riley said.

"Whoa, whoa, whoa," Ian said, running a few steps ahead of Riley and Sergio and throwing out his hands to stop them. "You're still going to rob them?"

Riley and Sergio stopped, turning to each other. Riley frowned in confusion, and Sergio raised his eyebrows.

"Yes?" Sergio said, turning back to Ian. "We still need gas and water."

Ian sputtered incoherently, and Riley put their hand on his shoulder to stop him. "You don't have to come with us," they said. "We'll find you a hiding spot, and you can look after the stuff until we're ready to take it back to the truck."

Ian continued to sputter until Sergio sighed and pointed at a partially collapsed building. "Get your ass in there and sit there until we come get you."

Ian shut his mouth, staring at Sergio with wide brown eyes. Sighing, he took a few steps away and then stopped and turned back to mess up Riley's hair.

"Don't do anything stupid, okay?" he said.

"Okay," Riley replied.

Ian turned toward the store again as Sergio caught his arm.

"You don't do anything stupid either," Sergio said.

"I won't."

Sergio slapped Ian on the back before he jogged off. Waiting until Ian had forced his way through the door and inside the store, Sergio turned to Riley and took a deep breath.

"We'll try the back door first, and if that doesn't work, we'll have to force our way in through the front," he said.

"I'm following you," Riley replied.

Sergio led the way as the two snuck back to the gas station. With each crunch of the sand and ash under their feet, Riley's throat got tighter and tighter.

Tiptoeing up to the back door, Sergio tried the doorknob and found it was unlocked. Pulling out their handgun, Riley pressed their back against the wall, ready to open the door. Sergio stood a few feet away, handgun raised. He nodded, and Riley turned the knob and eased the door open. Sergio scanned the doorway and ducked inside; Riley jammed the door open with a nearby crate before following.

Crouching next to Sergio behind a busted drink refrigerator, Riley could feel their heart pounding in their throat.

What if Ian had run back to Jen and told her everything that had happened? What if they had packed up and left? What if Ian was going to bust through the front door and try to stop them? What if...

A tap on the shoulder stopped Riley's thoughts in their tracks. Sergio pointed toward where a middle-aged woman was breaking down empty cardboard boxes. She seemed to struggle with tearing the flaps apart to get it flat, but she stomped on each box with great enthusiasm once she had. Her curly brown hair, sprinkled with gray, was wrapped up in a bun and held in place with what looked like rubber bands. The blue blouse she was wearing looked new, and Riley wondered where she'd managed to find it. Looking down at the flattened cardboard boxes near them, they saw words scribbled on them in sharpie. Riley managed to make out "canned goods," "clothes," and "hygiene items." Each box was signed with a "-K."

A man's voice was just audible from where he spoke across the store. "...think they can just come around and ask for shit? They probably don't even fucking need it. They just wanted to take advantage of us. How fucking entitled do you have to be to think that—"

Sergio pulled Riley close. "I'll take the woman hostage. You disarm the man if needed. I'll hold them, you grab what we can carry, and we're out. Good?"

"Good."

A quick kiss for luck, and Sergio was navigating the boxes and pallets as he crept toward the woman. Riley crawled further into the store, trying to figure out where the man was while also keeping out of the woman's line of sight. Hiding wasn't the hard part; trying to get around the mess of boxes, overturned snack carts, and empty wooden pallets was.

Sliding behind the counter, Riley glanced back at the woman before crouching to peek over the countertop. The man had opened the door and was looking up the road outside. He pushed back his dark gray hair and shielded his worn face from the setting sun. He was fairly short, maybe just an inch or two taller than Riley. They could probably take him if need be.

He dropped his hand and sighed, shaking his head. As he turned to let the door close behind him, Riley saw he had a shotgun tucked under his arm.

Shotgun. How in the goddamn hell had he gotten a shotgun? Sergio couldn't see it. At most he was expecting a pistol. He'd be thrown off, he'd freeze, the man would get a shot off, Sergio would be shot.

Riley scrambled back. They needed to warn Sergio. Turning around to crawl to the back, their foot hit a wire basket and kicked it out into the aisle.

Shit!

"Marine, was that you?"

Riley held their breath as boots thumped on the tile floor, closer, closer. They wanted to squeeze their eyes shut but they were glued open. Their lungs were on fire. Their heart was in their throat, strangling them. The man walked right past the counter. Riley's brain kicked into high gear. They jumped to their feet and jammed their gun into the middle of his spine.

"Drop it."

He did so, and Riley kicked the shotgun away. They could now hear scuffling from the back, and a minute later Sergio came out of the shadows. His hand was over the woman's mouth, his pistol to her temple.

"Tape 'em up," Sergio said, tossing a roll of duct tape at Riley and pointing his handgun at the man. Riley caught it one-handed and tucked their handgun into the back of their jeans before forcing the man's hands behind his back. They wrapped the tape seven times around his wrists, ensuring it was tight before doing the same to the woman. Sergio then sat the couple against the wall before taping their ankles together.

"I'm sorry about this," he said, checking to make sure the tape bonds were tight. "We're desperate. We're not goin' to take everythin'. We're just takin' enough to get to the nearest village."

"You motherfuckin' son of a bitch. What gives you the right? You'd better get the fuck out of here before I strangle the both of ya!"

"Yes sir, I understand," Sergio replied.

"You motherfucker—"

Sergio ignored him. Moving back, he took out his own handgun again and aimed it at the couple, keeping his finger off the trigger as he turned to Riley. "Move fast."

Riley ducked out of the back room. Passing by the counter again, they saw a mostly intact display of small Swiss army knives. Good, they could give it to the couple to free themselves right after they and Sergio left. Grabbing one, they pulled it out of the packaging while they assessed the supplies. Gallon-sized water bottles, five-gallon gas containers, and canned goods were scattered about along with several backpacks. Riley guessed that Sergio could carry two gas containers, one in each hand, while Riley could carry two gallons of water. The backpacks could probably hold another gallon of water each.

Shoving the Swiss Army knife into their pocket, Riley grabbed two of the backpacks and forced water bottles into them. In the gaps they put cans of food. Propping open the door with another water bottle, they set the gas containers, the last water bottle and one of the backpacks outside while putting the other on their back.

"RJ!"

Riley spun around and saw Ian sprinting up the street, pointing behind him at a beaten white sedan that was screaming toward him through the sand.

The car. The one that hadn't been next to the gas station. There was too much gas for them not to have a car. Of course there was another person.

"Ian, get back!" Riley yelled, pulling out their handgun, but Ian kept running toward them.

The car screeched to a halt, and a man jumped out, pointing his gun at Ian.

"Stay where you are!" the man yelled.

Ian froze, slowly raising his hands in the air. He stared at Riley, his eyes wide, repeatedly swallowing his fear. Riley clicked the safety off of their gun and aimed it at him.

"It's okay," they said, slowly stepping away from the shade of the gas station into the glow of the setting sun. "There's just a misunderstanding. Marina's helping my partner out, and we'll be on our way."

"The hell she is," the man growled. "Her name's not Marina!"

Shit. Fuck. What was her name?

"Drop your gun or he gets hurt!" the man yelled, pointing his gun at Ian.

"You hurt him, I drop you," Riley replied.

They heard the safety click off his gun as he raised it a little higher. "I said drop it!" he yelled.

He was too shaky. His stance was wrong. There was no way he'd ever fired that gun before. The bullet could go wild and kill Ian. Riley had to take the risk.

Letting out their breath, Riley squeezed the trigger. The muzzle of the man's gun flashed as his body collapsed into the sand, throwing up dust. Riley's stomach heaved at the blood pooling under the body as they racked the slide and tucked the gun back into their jeans.

"I'm sorry you had to—"

Ian collapsed to his knees and clutched his chest. Blood dripped through his fingers and pooled in the sand.

Riley couldn't breathe. They couldn't help the scream that somehow tore through their throat. They fell to their knees beside him and pressed their hand on top of his. The wound was high up, more on his shoulder than his chest.

"Oh my God, Ian. I'm so sorry. I'm so sorry. I thought… just keep your hand on it. That's it. Just keep up the pressure. We'll get you back—"

Ian groaned in pain, slumping against them and heaving for breath. Riley heard a strangled cry from behind them but didn't know who it was or what they had said. All they could comprehend was dark red blood running between their fingers and down their arm. Ian's blood. And it was their fault.

"Riley!"

Sergio's voice pierced through the fog, and Riley looked up to see him standing over them. He was aiming his handgun at the gas station, backpack on, gas container in the other hand.

"Get him up! We have to go!" Sergio hissed.

"Ian, come on. Stand up. We've gotta move. I can't carry you…"

Riley coaxed Ian to his feet. He stumbled forward as they tried to walk. Sergio stayed in between them and the gas station, walking backward. Keeping pressure on his wound, Riley glanced at the back of Ian's shoulder. No exit wound, which meant the bullet was still inside him. Fuck. That could bring on infection, or it may have bounced around and hit vital organs.

Riley's ears rang as a loud blast split the air. Sand sprayed up, scratching their face. They ducked away, pushing Ian, who cried out in pain.

"*Run!*" Sergio yelled.

Riley heard three quick shots. Ian broke away from them and began to run. Adrenaline pumped through Riley, and they ran too, making sure to stay behind Ian. Sergio fired off a few more shots before taking the lead. He kept looking back as he led them through the rubble, dodging piles of concrete bricks and jumping over steel beams. Ian tripped, but Riley caught him before he could fall. He slowed into a limping jog, breathing heavily.

"Come on, Ian. We're close. Just keep moving!" Riley said.

Whatever Ian tried to say came out as a whimper. Riley heard Sergio stop running ahead of them, and they looked up.

"Get him to the road and hide," Sergio said. "I'll pick you up."

Riley nodded, their chest squeezing in fear as he disappeared. Guiding Ian, they half-carried him the last fifty feet to the road. Finding a half-standing building, they helped Ian sit down before collapsing next to him.

"You're doing great," they whispered, leaning over to put pressure back on his shoulder. "We just gotta keep quiet and Sergio'll come get us."

Ian nodded before resting his head on Riley's shoulder. Panting, Riley laid their cheek on his spiky black hair, scanning the horizon for any sign of movement and straining for any sound of a car engine. They could only pray to whatever was above that it would be a pickup truck.

CHAPTER THREE

Riley didn't know how long it had been before they heard the growl of a car engine. They couldn't tell if it was coming from deeper in the rubble or from the road.

"All right, Ian, we need to move again. Let's get you up."

The bleeding started up again as Ian pushed himself to his feet and Riley hurried to press their hand to the wound. He was still panting, but it wasn't as desperate as it had been. He didn't complain once as Riley guided him to the side of the road.

"W-won't we get spotted? I-if someone drives by?" he asked.

"We just have to take that chance," Riley replied, sitting him back down against a building. "I'm more scared of the people from the gas station than someone on the road."

Ian nodded and leaned back against the wall. Riley stayed crouched on their feet, looking down the road for headlights. They didn't see any.

"I th-think it's coming from behind us," Ian said.

"Yeah," Riley replied. "Can you put pressure on this again?"

Ian slid his hand up and replaced Riley's hand with his own.

The bleeding seemed to have stopped again, but Riley wanted to make sure. They kicked themself for leaving the medical kit in the car. They knew better. At least they could've shoved some gauze into their pockets.

"RJ, it's getting closer," Ian said.

"I hear it," Riley replied, pulling out their gun and clicking off the safety. "Keep an eye on the road and tell me when you see the truck."

Riley didn't want to leave Ian, but they needed to know where the car was. The sun had gone down behind the horizon, making it difficult to see. Ducking around the rubble that hid Ian, they ran to the next pile of concrete and steel and peered into the darkness. The engine was getting louder. After a few seconds they saw the headlights flicker out from behind the rubble, bouncing over the sand.

Sergio needed to hurry the fuck up.

Backing away from the approaching car, Riley ducked back down next to Ian.

"Are they after us?" he asked.

Riley nodded, clicking the gun's safety back on while trying to ignore the anxiety that was threatening to burst out of their chest.

"How close are they?" Ian asked.

"Can't tell."

"You should get out of here."

"I'm not leaving you."

"I don't want you to die because of me!"

Riley couldn't reply. It was entirely their fault in the first place. They'd gotten Ian shot. He hadn't done anything wrong except try to warn them. "I'm not leaving you."

Two specks of light flicked on at the end of the road, and Riley's heart leapt. It had to be the pickup truck.

Come on, Sergio. Get over here.

"Should we try to get closer?" Ian asked.

Should they? If they started moving, they could get to the pickup truck faster, but they could also be easily spotted by the gas station people. Riley kept going back and forth before looking at where Ian was still clutching his shoulder. Every time they'd moved so far the bleeding had started up again. They couldn't tell how much blood he'd lost. He seemed okay, but that could change if he lost any more.

"We're staying put," they said.

"Yeah, this is where Sergio knows to find us," Ian replied.

Riley didn't know if Sergio would be able to recognize landmarks quickly enough in the twilight to find them. They'd have to wave him down once he got closer and risk getting spotted.

Ian shifted and groaned in pain. "Just stay still, Ian," Riley said as they covered his hand with theirs. That's when they realized how bloody their hand and forearm had gotten. It was almost completely dry. So was the blood on Ian's hand, arm, and shirt. Shit. It'd probably stuck his shirt to the wound and would be awful to peel off. Hopefully it wouldn't rip the wound further…

"Truck's almost here," Ian said.

"Ok, let's get you up," Riley said, tucking the handgun away. "Careful."

Riley kept Ian balanced as he got his legs under him and pushed himself up. Ian continued to lean on them as they watched the headlights of the pickup get bigger and bigger. They were going to make it.

Then a loud blast split the air.

Riley didn't realize they'd screamed until they felt Ian's hand fumble over their mouth. They stared at the pickup truck as it sped up. Dust sprayed up along the side of the truck bed. Another blast went off, and buckshot scattered in the truck's dust.

The truck came to a screeching halt beside Riley and Ian.

"Get in!" Jen said from the passenger's seat, pointing the handgun back down the road. Ducking, Riley hurried Ian the few feet to the truck and yanked open the door. A loud blast made them flinch as something whizzed by them.

"Get in! Get in! Get in!" Jen screamed.

Riley boosted Ian into the truck and he collapsed across the back seats. Jumping in after him, Riley slammed the door shut.

"Go!"

Sergio slammed his foot on the gas. Ian was nearly thrown to the floor, but Riley managed to catch him. He yelled in pain as his shoulder was slammed into the seat.

"Medical kit's on the floor by your head," Jen said, and Riley could see tears in her eyes. "What the hell happened?"

Nobody replied as Riley unzipped the kit and found the scissors. "I'm sorry, Ian. I'm going to have to cut your shirt off so I can assess the wound."

He nodded and Riley set to work, trying to ignore the continuing gunshots. It was difficult to keep from stabbing Ian with the bouncing of the car, but they managed to get the shirt cut down the center. Wincing, Riley peeled the shirt off of the bullet wound. Ian gritted his teeth and clutched the door of the car to keep from screaming.

"H-how bad is it?" he asked once his shirt was off.

"Not as bad as it could be."

It was Riley's practiced answer for when something was bad.

Sergio looked into the rearview mirror. "What do we need to do?"

"Get to the nearest city," Riley replied. "A village isn't going to have the medication I need to treat this."

Sergio nodded and pressed down harder on the gas. Jen had pulled the gun back inside the truck, switching the safety off. She was taking deep breaths, saying something in between them that Riley couldn't make out.

Riley turned back to Ian, hoping the bullet hadn't bounced around too much inside his shoulder. Without an X-ray, they couldn't be sure of the damage. They couldn't get the bullet out anyway. All they could do was clean and bandage the wound and then stitch it up once they got to the nearest city. They could only pray it wouldn't be Revolution controlled.

Another loud blast, and Riley instinctively ducked to protect Ian. Two quick shots followed with Jen returning fire.

"Here, for when that runs out!" they yelled, handing Jen their handgun before turning back to Ian. Digging through their medical kit they found the plastic bag with cloth soaked in vodka. Pulling a piece out and smoothing out the excess alcohol, they carefully began to dab at the dried blood on Ian's shoulder and chest. He sucked in air through his teeth as the car bounced and the cloth swept over the open wound.

"Sorry!" Riley gasped, jamming their leg under the driver's seat for stability. Moving as fast as possible, they cleaned off the blood from Ian's body and then pulled out a large gauze pad, some rolled gauze, and medical tape.

"You n-need me to sit up?" Ian asked.

"Not right now," Riley replied, trying to position the gauze while being jostled by the car.

"You gonna try and stitch him up?" Sergio asked.

"Not with the way you're driving!"

Jen's laugh startled Riley, and they also realized they hadn't heard a gunshot in some time. "Did the car stop following us?" they asked.

Sergio glanced in the mirror. "Nope, still back there, but they've stopped shooting."

"Why?"

"Dunno."

"Count our blessings and get Ian patched up," Jen scolded.

"Yes, ma'am," Riley replied, pressing down the gauze. After some adjustments they managed to get it taped down somewhat securely.

"Okay, now's the time for you to sit up so I can wrap this," they said.

Riley made sure Ian didn't put his weight on his injured arm as he struggled to sit up. They glanced out the back window to see the car only about ten feet behind them.

"They're so close!"

"Focus on Ian, Riley Jay," Jen said. "We'll watch the car."

Taking a deep breath, Riley turned back to Ian, who was now sitting up. Clambering up onto the seat next to him, Riley encouraged him to lean forward and began wrapping the gauze around his shoulder and chest. Ian was no longer wincing; he seemed to be succumbing to exhaustion. Riley prayed it wasn't because of blood loss, and just due to the adrenaline crash.

"They're backing off," Jen said.

Looking up, Riley frowned as the car behind them slowed to a halt before making a U-turn and driving away.

"What the hell?" Sergio muttered, looking in the rearview mirror.

"Oh, this might be why," Jen said, tapping him on the shoulder and pointing out the front window.

A massive barbed-wire fence had appeared in front of them after they'd gone over a small hill. A green metal gate blocked the road with a concrete tower on either side. Two soldiers manned each tower. Farther to their left, they could see an olive-green Jeep driving away from the road, through the sands that had been cleared of rubble.

Barbed wire. Olive green Jeep. Soldiers in green camo.

Relief swept over Riley, uncurling their shoulders and relaxing their chest. Ian slumped against Riley, most of the tension leaving him in a sigh. Jen buried her face in her hands, crying softly.

"We're okay," Sergio said. "We're okay."

They'd made it to Command territory.

The relief washed away as the family pulled up to the gate. Sure, this wasn't Revolution territory, but Command wasn't a walk in the park either. It was the remnants of the military and government Riley had grown up under, and they hadn't liked them before the Collapse that started this endless civil war. They were sure that opinion wasn't about to change.

Riley's stomach flipped as they saw one of the soldiers duck into the tower for a minute. Their guess was that they were radioing back to base that a strange car was approaching. Riley squinted to try and see in the shadows, but it was too far away. Hopefully they weren't getting orders to shoot first and ask questions afterward.

"Last chance to leave," Sergio said under his breath.

Riley looked down at Ian. "We don't have a choice."

The solider in the right guard tower motioned with his semiautomatic rifle for Sergio to pull the car forward. He did so, inch by inch, his knuckles white on the steering wheel. Jen slid the handguns back into the glovebox before folding her hands on her lap. Ian groaned in pain as the car went over a bump. Riley put their arm around his shoulders without putting weight on his injury. They racked their brain, trying to remember if they had any pain medicine in their kit. They hadn't seen any when they'd searched for the gauze, but it would be worth another look once they had passed the soldiers.

Jen was tapping her fingers on the car door, her lips pressed together as she flicked her eyes back and forth from one soldier to the other.

"Let me talk to them," she said.

"You sure you don't want me to?" Riley asked.

"No, I've got it. You just keep Ian comfortable."

Riley and Sergio nodded as the soldiers approached the car. The one on Sergio's side gestured for him to roll down the window. He complied, saying, "How're you doin', sir?"

"State your business here."

Riley could see Jen hesitate before she leaned forward. "We're seeking refuge, sir," she said. "Our city got caught in some crossfire and we had to flee."

"What city you from? Somewhere in Revolution territory?"

Sergio and Jen glanced at each other, and Riley tightened their grip on Ian. The other soldier strolled around the car, peering in the back at Riley and Ian. Riley waved in acknowledgment, and he nodded back.

If Jen revealed that they were from Revolution territory, then Command could accuse them of being spies and shoot them. If Command somehow knew, and Jen lied, they could be in serious trouble. But how could Command know they were from Revolution territory? It wasn't like they could hack into some database that would tell them. They could keep up the lie. Make up some sort of small-town name.

"Philippi," Jen said.

Damn it. They were done for.

The soldiers looked at each other before the soldier who'd been walking around the car hurried back inside his tower. The one who had been talking to Jen stepped a few feet back, shifting his gun to point it at the car.

"Why'd you tell him the truth?" Sergio hissed.

"The way they talked it sounded like there had been other people here from Revolution cities, especially those on the front lines," Jen said. Her voice was calmer than she had to be feeling. "They might be taking in refugees."

"Or they might be turnin' them away!"

Jen shook her head. "That's not what I'm getting from them."

To be fair, Jen's intuition had never steered them wrong. From running her black-market tailoring business back in Philippi to risking a negotiation with a Revolution pastor for elderflower because it might bring down Sergio's fever, Jen's gut feelings had kept them alive. But there was always a first time for everything. Riley hoped it wouldn't result in them getting dragged out of the truck and shot on the side of the road.

The soldier in the tower came jogging out to talk to the other soldier, and Riley tensed. The soldiers could just shoot up the truck. Sergio and Ian were right in the line of fire; there'd be nowhere for them to hide. Jen could make it out the door but not much farther. Riley had the best shot of getting away if they ducked fast enough, but where would they run? Back to the gas station?

Riley noticed that Sergio had shifted the car into reverse. He looked up into the rearview mirror, meeting Riley's eyes. Both of them took a deep breath as the first soldier approached the car.

"You're the first group here out of Philippi," he said. "But your story's been corroborated. You'll be escorted to City Hall to be registered and assigned to a district. Stay in your truck until you are directed to get out. Understood?"

"Understood," Sergio said. "Thank you, officer."

The soldier waved his arm above his head, and the gates creaked open. "Welcome to Jericho."

Sergio inched the truck through the gates. Four soldiers stood in the middle of the road. One of them beckoned Sergio forward for a few feet before turning to lead the way. The other three fell in around the truck, one on each side and one behind them. The road was lined with barbed wire, and any buildings that had once stood along it had been cleared out long ago. Now battered tanks, broken-down Jeeps, and dinged Humvees were grouped together by type. Memories of shiny, new tanks flooded Riley's mind, tearing up the street outside of the practice they'd worked for. It was getting harder and harder to breathe as they turned a corner and drove up to a tall, worn building of white marble and black windows that erupted into a ball of fire that threatened to engulf them all—

"Riley!"

Riley shook their head and realized the building was still in one piece, not burned to ash. They were confused for a minute until Sergio's hand on their knee brought them fully back into reality. It'd just been a flashback. They hadn't had one of those in a while.

"You're okay, baby," he said. "Just listen to my voice and keep breathing. You're okay."

Riley could feel their heart rate start to slow and their chest relax. They'd pulled up alongside the building and Riley could now read the dented metal sign that said "City Hall."

A soldier stood on either side of the door with four other soldiers spread out on the cracked gray sidewalk. All of them had their rifles in their hands, but none of them were pointed at the truck.

Ian was still passed out against them and Riley could feel themself beginning to panic. Clambering for his wrist, they took his pulse. It was fairly strong. His skin wasn't pale, and his breathing wasn't as rapid as Riley would expect from hypovolemic shock. He hadn't lost too much blood. He just had to be exhausted. At least, that's what they had to hope for.

"Get out of the truck!"

They all jumped. "Move," Jen said, and she and Sergio jumped out of the truck. Riley leaned over Ian to open the door, but Sergio got there first.

"Come on, Ian, wake up," he said, gently shaking Ian's non-injured shoulder. "We gotta get out."

Ian grunted, raising his head a few inches before it fell back against Riley's shoulder. They winced; their arm was starting to get sore.

"You can sleep later, buddy," Sergio said, ducking into the truck. Between him and Riley they managed to coax Ian out, careful of his injured shoulder. Even though Ian was steady enough on his feet after a minute, Sergio put Ian's arm around his shoulders, holding him up. Riley handed Sergio the gauze to put back on Ian's wound and then hopped out of the truck, threading their arms through the straps of the medical backpack.

"Hold it!"

Four assault rifles turned on Riley. They threw their hands up in the air, their heart racing as they felt their chest tighten. Jen stepped forward, but the soldier closest to her turned his gun on her.

"It's all right, Jen," Riley said. They hoped their voice was calmer than they felt. "Can we talk about this inside?"

"We need to check that backpack. Now."

God. The medical equipment. What if they confiscated it? Riley needed it to keep Ian alive.

Two of the soldiers stepped forward, one of them staying in front of Riley and the other one getting behind them. Riley was shoved forward as the soldier yanked the backpack from their shoulders. They wanted to run to the rest of their family but two soldiers were blocking their way. They heard the clatter of their medical equipment being thrown onto the pavement, but they didn't want to turn away from the soldiers pointing rifles at them. They could only stare at Sergio, Ian, and Jen, who were watching in horror. Jen glanced back and forth between Riley and the soldier dumping out the backpack, folding and unfolding her hands. Ian wasn't really focused on anything, but the soldiers kept catching his attention. Sergio's eyes never left Riley's. Every time they glanced away, he caught their eye again and took a deep breath, reminding them to breathe.

"You a doctor?" the soldier asked.

"What?" Riley asked, turning their head to look back at them. He had a black goatee that made him look like Dr. Faust.

"This is all medical equipment. You a doctor?"

"Learned some stuff from one on the road."

It was their standard answer ever since the Collapse. Neither side treated nurses well although no one knew exactly what happened to the ones Command managed to suss out.

"You patched him up?" Soldier Faust asked, nodding toward Ian.

"Yeah."

"Looks like you don't have any medication on you."

"Hard to come by in Revolution territory."

The soldier who looked like Faust dropped the now-empty backpack on the ground and waved at the other soldiers to stand down. "Pretty sure we've got some ibuprofen inside," he said. "Don't know what good it'll do."

"It'll be something," Riley said, holding their breath to see what the catch was.

Faust stepped over the medical supplies and up to the two soldiers who stood between Riley and their family. "Get those three inside and find somewhere for him to sit down."

The soldiers saluted and turned to Sergio, Ian, and Jen, holding their rifles sideways to push them away.

"What about Riley?" Jen asked.

Faust turned back to Riley. "Gather your equipment and then I'll take you in for processing. You'll be back with your friends soon."

Gulping, Riley tried to smile at the rest of their family as they were pushed back into the building. Sergio was eyeing one of the soldiers like he was assessing how best to take him down. He glanced back up at Riley, who shook their head. He could get hurt. Jen could get hurt. Ian could get even more hurt.

"Hurry up," Faust barked.

Riley scrambled to get everything back into the backpack and get it zipped. Shouldering the backpack, they were prodded by the two guards behind them to get moving. Faust was in the lead, and the guards on either side of the door saluted as they approached before pulling open the doors.

"After you," Faust said, stepping aside.

Riley's heart threatened to pound out of their chest as they walked into the building.

Riley was hit with the smell of bleach and sweat as soon as they stepped through the door. They expected to see the rest of their family once they got inside, but instead they were met by a dim room. A soldier was hunched over a large mahogany desk a few feet from the door with a floodlight sitting on his desk that illuminated the entire entrance. The two soldiers behind Riley grabbed their shoulders, forcing them to stop as soldier Faust approached the desk. His boots echoed off the cracked marble floors and the dingy gray walls.

The desk soldier closed the folder he was writing in and tossed it into a black plastic tray before looking up.

"This the last one, sir?" he asked.

"Yes," Faust replied, turning back to Riley. "Full name."

"Riley Jay Chasen. C-H-A-S-E-N."

Desk soldier wrote it out on the top of a file folder and then opened one of the drawers and pulled out a packet. "Standard procedure, sir. Holding cell twenty-five is open."

"Thank you, Private," Faust replied, taking the packet from him and turning back to Riley. He pulled a flashlight off of his belt and clicked it on. "Follow me."

One of the soldiers shoved Riley, and they stumbled forward. They resisted the urge to turn and glare, and instead they followed Faust past the front desk.

The echoes of footsteps died down as the group approached rows and rows of desks arranged to create a spacious middle aisle. The plain, metal tables had no cabinets underneath, but each had a metal folding chair tucked tightly in. All the furniture was immaculately clean but full of dents and holes and warped metal. The top of each desk was exactly the same with a black plastic tray on each top corner, a black cup with two pens on the bottom right corner, and... were those wired phones?

One of the soldiers stepped up from behind Riley and shoved open a metal door with his shoulder. It screeched as it swung open, and Riley winced as they were pushed inside.

The hallway was smaller than Riley expected it to be, lined with light wooden doors in various states of being on their hinges. The windows that still had glass in them were painted black, matching the black numbers on each door. Riley tried to listen for any signs of Sergio, Ian, or Jen, but they couldn't hear anything except for the muffled thump of the soldier's boots on the ragged carpet floor.

Riley tried not to gag as the smell of mildew and musk grew stronger. Faust stopped in front of a door marked "25," and Riley almost ran into him. He glared at them as he turned the key in the lock and pushed open the door. Riley hurried to the far side of the room.

Faust followed and locked the door. "Fill out this packet and then you'll have your photo taken for your ID," he said.

"Where's everyone else?" Riley asked.

"You'll meet up after you get your photo taken. Now, hand over your backpack. I will return it to you when you are done with the packet."

Riley had no choice. Faust handed them the packet and knocked on the door. One of the soldiers on the outside opened it and exchanged places with Faust. The lock clicked as the door closed. The soldier left in the room set a lantern down and switched it on. The dim light threw shadows onto the walls, but a glint in the corner next to the door caught Riley's attention. It was an old-school security camera that had to be hooked up to some sort of CCTV system. They doubted anyone was on the other end of it, though, especially since the soldier was standing in front of the door. Thank goodness he at least had his rifle across his shoulder.

On the other side of the room stood a desk that was almost identical to the desks outside, except there wasn't a phone. Pulling out the metal folding chair, Riley sat down while keeping an eye on the soldier. He hadn't moved since taking up his position by the door.

Taking a deep breath, Riley took one of the pens out of the cup and turned their attention the packet. Name, X for gender marker, date of birth, city of birth... Were they allowed to put down the original city name? Riley didn't even know what the new name would be, and they didn't really feel like asking the soldier if he knew.

Deciding to skip it for now, Riley continued on to the physical description questions. Height, weight (how the heck were they supposed to know that?) eye color, hair color, boxes for fingerprints, and that was all the biological information.

Flipping the page, Riley sighed when they saw "FAMILY" in large letters at the top of the page. Now to decide which family to put down—their biological one or the one they'd had for the last year. Deciding to go with the latter, Riley scribbled everyone down—Sergio Rosémond Melendez, Ian Cho, and Jennifer Joanne Smith. Riley stared at the spaces that were marked "Relationship." They scribbled "Partner" into the one next to Sergio, but Ian and Jen were trickier. They finally settled on "brother" for Ian and "mother" for Jen, which were close enough.

Riley's head shot up at the sound of a safety being switched off. The soldier was aiming his gun at them. Jumping to their feet they flinched when the metal chair clanged against the ground. They put their hands in the air.

"H-hey, what's going on?" Riley asked, trying to ignore the tightness in their chest. "What'd I do?"

The soldier didn't reply.

"Look, whatever I did, I'm sorry. Just put the gun down. I'm not armed. I can't hurt you."

Soldier still didn't reply.

"Please?"

After a pause, he took a step forward, and Riley stepped back, pressing their back against the cold concrete wall. He took another step forward. Riley assessed the room; the door was locked so escape wasn't an option, but if they could clear the desk and get in a good kick to his stomach, maybe they could get the rifle out of his hands.

Another step forward.

Was the desk thick enough to stop bullets? Maybe they could kick it up and use it as a shield long enough to get behind him and knock him out. Chokehold could work, or they could sweep his feet out from under him.

Another step forward.

Fuck it, throw the chair and hope it stunned him. Riley glanced down at it. They'd have to kick it up in their hands. They wouldn't have time to duck, but would they be able to throw it before...

Click.

The soldier switched back on the safety and stepped back. Slinging his rifle back to his shoulder, he took up his position by the door.

Riley's heart raced as they tried to catch their breath. Fumbling for the chair, they somehow managed to get it righted and plopped down into it. Struggling to take deep breaths, they pressed their fingers to their pulse. After a minute they could feel their heart rate begin to go down, so they tried to relax and turned back to the packet. They didn't fully comprehend what they were writing down. They just wanted out of the room. Scribbling their signature on the last page, they threw their pen into the cup and jumped to their feet.

"I'm finished."

The soldier nodded, giving no indication of what he'd done earlier, and knocked on the door. It opened after a few seconds and the soldier stepped outside, the door closing behind him. Riley didn't know what to do. They settled for just standing by the desk, feeling awkward.

After a few minutes Faust came back in and held the door open for them. "I will take your packet now."

Riley handed it over and slipped out into the hallway. A new soldier was waiting outside, yawning. Faust took the lantern out of the room before closing and locking it. He took the lead down the hallway, holding the lantern out in front of him. Riley tried to follow but their feet felt heavier than lead. The new soldier shoved them from behind, and Riley tripped forward, finally able to walk down the hallway.

CHAPTER FOUR

"Don't smile."

Riley couldn't have mustered a smile if their life had depended on it. Their eyes burned, their stomach ached with hunger, and every part of their body felt like it was weighed down by molasses.

The lightbulb flashed and Riley jumped. It took them a second to realize it hadn't been a muzzle flash from a gun. Stumbling out from in front of the camera while trying to blink away the large black spot that had appeared in their vision, they nearly tripped over a backpack that had been placed on the ground. The medical kit.

"Ian Cho's bandages needed to be re-taped, and Jennifer Smith was able to do it with your supplies," the soldier explained.

Had their taping really been that bad? Granted they'd been in a speeding pickup truck getting shot at, but they felt like they had better skills. They'd have to inventory their bag later and see what was taken. Riley shouldered the backpack and followed the soldier to the ID card desk.

"Here you go," the soldier behind the desk said, passing over a thin card. It reminded Riley of their pre-Collapse driver's license, except it was a plain white card with black writing and their ID photo in black-and-white in the top left corner. Across the bottom of the card was written, "TIER ONE, FOXTROT."

But hey, the photo was just as hideous as their pre-Collapse ID photo. Some things never changed.

"Keep it on you at all times," the soldier behind the desk said. "You'll need to show it whenever you cross through district checkpoints and at morning reveille."

"Morning reveille?"

"You will gather in the square at seven a.m. sharp tomorrow morning for reveille. When you leave here today, you will head directly to the grocery store to pick up your rations. These are meant to supplement your earnings from work. Once you have obtained your monthly rations, you will be able to move into any available housing in Foxtrot district. Do you understand?"

"Yes, thank you," Riley said, sliding the card into their pocket. Their escort soldier led them away from the photo counter and back out into the hallway. A low siren rang out, and Riley froze.

"Just the warning that the lights are turning back on," the soldier said.

Sure enough the lights flickered back to life. Electricity must be rationed here. The electrical grid must've been damaged in the fighting, so they turned it off at night so the grid wouldn't be overloaded. Given that the City Hall also got turned off at night, Riley was sure Command was still in the process of trying to fix it instead of keeping all of the juice for themselves.

The soldier led the way to the back door, pushing it open for Riley. "The rest of your family will be joining you soon. Welcome to Jericho."

He shoved Riley out the door and slammed it shut. Stunned, Riley turned around and was relieved to see Jen leaning against the pickup truck. Behind the truck, two soldiers were guarding a gate that looked like it blocked the road that led into the rest of the city. But Riley was mainly focused on Jen, who had visibly relaxed with a relieved grin on her face. Somehow, Riley managed to find the energy to run up to her.

"Jen, you're okay! Where're Sergio and Ian?" they asked.

"What took you so long, Riley Jay?" Jen asked. Riley could tell she was trying to act cool, but they could see the tremors at the corners of her mouth when they got close. They wanted to ask if she and Ian had been held at gunpoint too, but they didn't want the soldiers to overhear, and they didn't want Jen to worry further if the two of them hadn't.

"Ian's sleeping in the back of the truck, thank goodness, but I haven't seen Sergio yet," Jen said. "One of the soldiers gave us ibuprofen. It looked all right to me and Ian was in so much pain—"

Riley snatched the bottle from her hand and opened it. The few pills left looked like ibuprofen, and the number on each pill was correct as far as they could remember.

"It didn't take away the pain but at least took the edge off so he could fall asleep," Jen said. "Because he was injured, the soldiers told me I could stay with him."

"Thank goodness for that," Riley sighed, looking back up at the truck. "When was the last time you checked on him?"

"A few minutes before you came out," Jen said as Riley put the cap on the bottle and slid it into the side pocket of their backpack. "Just relax, Riley. It's been a long night."

She held out her arms. Riley accepted the hug, resting their chin on her shoulder. Jen began to hum as she rubbed their back. Tears began to threaten Riley's eyes—from exhaustion, sadness, or anger, they couldn't tell. They wanted to let go and actually cry for once, but they couldn't seem to relax enough for the lump in their throat to slip.

"It's all right, Riley Jay," Jen whispered.

After a minute Riley pulled back. "Can I see your ID card, out of curiosity?"

Jen nodded, pulling the card out of her dress pocket. Riley took it and held it up in the dim morning light to get a better look at it. It was almost identical to Riley's, except for different biographical information of course, and across the bottom of the card was printed, "TIER THREE, FOXTROT."

"Ian's says Tier Two," Jen said.

"Mine's Tier One."

"I can't for the life of me figure out what it means."

Riley was going to reply when they heard the doors to City Hall screech open. Turning around, they saw Sergio taking something from a soldier—the keys to the truck, Riley guessed. He gave the soldier a stiff nod before jogging toward Riley and Jen. The soldier slammed the door shut. Sergio broke into a sprint and then pulled Riley into a hug, resting his chin on top of their head. Riley hugged him back, his rapid heartbeat and shaky breathing filling their ears.

"You all right, Sergio?" Jen asked.

Riley felt Sergio nod as he squeezed them tighter. After another minute Sergio let them go, giving them a peck on the lips before turning to give Jen a quick hug and a kiss on the cheek.

"I'm guessin' Ian's in the truck?"

Jen nodded. "Then let's get goin'," Sergio said. "We've gotta go get those rations and find a place to live."

Ian jolted awake as Riley opened the back door of the truck. "It's okay," Riley said, squeezing themself in between the front and back seats. "How're you feeling?"

Ian grunted, pushing himself up on his uninjured arm. Riley helped him sit all the way up and then hopped up on to the open seat next to him. They leaned across Ian to check his bandages, and sure enough it had been re-taped. Guess they'd done a bad job after all.

They could feel a hand on their head, and they looked up to see Ian's tired grin as he mussed their hair. "Well you seem to be doing a lot better," Riley said.

"Doesn't hurt as bad," Ian said. "Still aches, though."

"Well that's an improvement."

The door behind Ian opened and Sergio stuck his head in. "Hey, man," he said, a small smile on his face. "How you feelin'?"

"I'm okay," Ian replied. Sergio hesitated and then pulled Ian into a hug. Riley lurched forward to keep him from hurting Ian, but he'd made sure not to touch Ian's shoulder. Ian returned the hug, his voice muffled against Sergio's shoulder. Whatever he said seemed to comfort Sergio, who patted Ian's back before letting him go.

"Ry, I could use your eyes lookin' for somewhere to stay," Sergio said.

"You okay without me?" Riley asked Ian. He nodded as Jen opened the other backseat door.

"Here, Ian, I got you another shirt," Jen said. Riley switched places with her and, once Jen got settled, closed the door. Sergio started the truck as Riley hopped into the passenger's seat.

“Accordin’ to our IDs we’ve been assigned to Foxtrot district,” Sergio said. “Let’s hope they have housin’.”

“Hopefully we’ll get a senior executive suite this time instead of a junior one,” Riley said.

Sergio snorted, and Riley’s heart leapt to see a genuine smile on his face, as tired as it was. He turned the truck toward the gate as the soldiers pushed it open. As soon as the soldiers were out of the way, Sergio drove through.

Jericho was in a lot better shape than the area around the gas station. Plenty of buildings had been beaten up with plywood sheets layered on sides of buildings, windows missing, and empty doorframes. And, of course, all of the road signs were gone to prevent the other side from being able to navigate with them. But there weren’t any piles of rubble, and the streets were clear enough for Sergio to drive on without having to swerve. Most of the buildings still seemed sturdy, whether they’d been reinforced or seemingly untouched by war.

The missing glass in a storefront window had been replaced by black-painted plywood. A white “HU228” was painted on the center panel; as they drove by the next building Riley could see that “HU226” was sprayed on the door.

But the building after that didn’t have a number on it, and the empty windows hadn’t been boarded up. It was leaning slightly to the left with large chunks missing from the outside walls. A blue tarp hung over the doorframe. It was completely dark inside, but when Riley squinted, they saw movement inside—way too big to be a cat or mouse. *Please, God, please let us be able to find housing.*

As they approached an intersection, Riley looked out the window to see a brown sign with “Block 200” written in white letters. A woman standing under the sign was laughing at something her partner said as they waited for a squadron of soldiers to march by in the street.

"I... I didn't expect Jericho to be like this," Jen said, watching with wide eyes as a mother carried her baby down the sidewalk, bouncing the infant on her hip.

"This had to have been a major city," Sergio said.

"Where are the skyscrapers, then?" Riley asked.

Sergio shrugged. "Blown up?"

Obvious answer was they'd been the place where a lot of people had tried to hole up for safety. Those who were smart enough to get underground or get out instead were the ones who'd survived.

Overall, the concrete buildings were less pockmarked with bullet holes then they'd been outside of the city. Riley figured that most of the fighting would've occurred in the city, but it looked like both sides had been trying to keep the infrastructure of the city intact. Not well, though, if the Command kept having to turn off the electricity at night.

Riley rolled down the windows as the heat started to get unbearable. The truck filled with the rancid smell of diesel fuel. They looked up to see two Jeeps sputtering along in front of them, coughing up black exhaust smoke. Ian coughed before groaning in pain.

"Sorry!" Riley said, rolling the windows back up. The exhaust was becoming thicker as they trundled on behind the Jeeps. They were pulling up to what Riley assumed was a checkpoint—a red-and-white gate bar attached to a small concrete box with a soldier standing in front of the doorless opening. Behind him, Riley could see another soldier standing in front of a similar opening on the other side of the box. The soldier closest to them walked inside the box and the gate raised to let the Jeeps through. But as soon as their pickup truck pulled up, the gate was lowered back down.

The soldier meandered up to the truck. "IDs."

Riley scrambled in their pocket for theirs before reaching back to take Ian's and Jen's. Ian was sitting up as straight as he could, but Riley could tell from the look in his eyes he was starting to slip. All they could do was pray he'd hold on for just a bit longer.

Sergio handed over all of their IDs. "Just the four of us, sir."

"What's your destination?"

"Foxtrot district to obtain rations and housin'," Sergio said.

"Well this is Foxtrot," the soldier said as she went through their IDs. "Keep straight on this road and you'll run right into the square with the grocery and everything."

She was about to hand back their IDs to Sergio when she glanced into the backseat. Yanking the cards back, she leaned through the driver's side window to look back at Ian and Jen. "You all right?"

"What? Y-yeah," Ian stuttered, trying to smile. Riley winced at how pained it looked.

The soldier turned back to Sergio. "Make sure you get him registered at District Hall when you get your rations. Only way he's going to get medical help."

Riley had hoped they would be able to re-stock, that Command would be more open with their medical supplies. False hope, they guessed.

Sergio thanked the soldier as he took back the IDs and handed them to Riley. Riley passed Jen's and Ian's back to them as Ian was settling back against Jen's shoulder again and closing his eyes.

"We're almost there," Riley said.

"You don't know that," Ian replied. "'Sides, we have to go get food first."

Riley and Jen looked at each other and shrugged; he was right. The gate raised, and Sergio pulled the pickup truck through. He lowered the windows again since the Jeeps were gone, but the air still tasted of diesel fuel.

Significantly fewer people were on the streets in Foxtrot, except for a squadron of soldiers that marched down the sidewalk toward them. Riley could feel the hairs raise on the back of their neck as the squadron marched passed the truck. The soldiers looked like they were facing forward, but Riley could swear they were actually looking through the windshield.

The District Square came up faster than Riley expected, and it was a lot smaller than they thought it would be. Unlike the sidewalks, nobody was just strolling through here. The only person Riley could see on foot was a hunched-over man with a cane, hobbling as fast as he could away from the largest building in the square. The large black letters across the top of the box said "DISTRICT HALL" although the only difference between it and the other concrete boxes was that it had two large, wooden doors and a second story.

Two Humvees were sitting in the middle of the square, facing opposite directions. The one facing toward them had two soldiers in it, whose eyes had locked on to the family's pickup truck. Riley looked down at the console until the pickup truck rolled to a halt.

"Jen, you still have Ian?" Sergio asked as he shut off the engine.

Riley looked up into the rearview mirror to see Jen nod.

"Then let's go, Ry," Sergio said, opening the door.

The grocery store was right next to the District Hall, identifiable by the "GROCERY" sign in similar black letters to District Hall. Like the other two buildings it was just a concrete box with a wooden door that had two small, rectangle windows on either side of it. A soldier walked up on the other side of the building as Riley and Sergio approached, stopping in his tracks and narrowing his eyes. Riley clenched their teeth as they looked down at their feet.

Sergio held the door for Riley, and they stepped into the cool air of the store. Naked lightbulbs hanging from the ceiling only provided dim illumination, causing the store shelves to throw shadows onto the cracked tile floor. The shelves almost reminded Riley of a grocery store before the Collapse with tin cans and boxes of food on the shelves. But now almost all the tin cans were dented, the boxes were battered, and some of the shelves were slanted and threatening to collapse. Everything was covered with a thin layer of dust.

"Hey!" a voice called from the back. Riley could feel Sergio step right up behind them. A young East Asian woman, a little shorter than Riley, was standing behind a counter that stretched almost the entire length of the back wall. She was putting her long black hair up into a high ponytail, grinning as she looked up after tying it off.

"Don't think I've seen you around before. I'm Katherine, but I go by Kit, and I run this grocery store. What're your names?"

"Riley Jay, and this is my partner Sergio," Riley replied. "We just arrived here and were told to come here to get rations."

"Nice to meet you both," Kit said, throwing a jaunty two-fingered salute to Sergio before turning back to Riley. "Let me break this down for you, then. Every month you'll get rations depending on your tier level—oh, yeah, can I see your IDs?"

Riley could feel Sergio shift back on his feet. "We've got two more people in the truck," he said. "You need to see them in person?"

"No, just their cards, thanks."

Sergio squeezed Riley's shoulder, and they turned their head to watch him head out.

"So, the rations cover food, bottled water, and some hygiene items like toothpaste on a monthly basis, other hygiene items like shampoo and soap every three months, and clothing on a semiannual basis although it's not much fashion-wise, I'm afraid," Kit said. "Gas is tightly controlled. You'll be given some if Command thinks you need it."

Riley turned back to look at her, and she grinned wider than Riley'd seen anyone smile in a while. They could tell it was forced, though, because it didn't quite reach her eyes.

"Is there anything else you're going to need?" Kit asked.

"Huh?"

"Anything else, like toilet paper, cleaning supplies—"

"Yeah, actually," Riley said, shifting to look around the shelves just in case they'd missed the medication section when they walked in. "Do you happen to have any ibuprofen or Tylenol? And antibiotics?"

"I've got some ibuprofen," Kit said, pulling a clipboard off the wall. "I'll need payment within a week, though, since you're new. After that you'll have to pay up front. And you'll have to register at District Hall to get medical care."

"It's not for me. And I don't need a doctor. I just need the medication," Riley said.

Kit looked up from where they'd been scanning the list. "You a doctor then or something?"

"It's just not that bad. We don't need a doctor. Just the medicine."

Riley saw the corners of Kit's mouth turn up, and a hollow pit formed in their stomach. They were in trouble.

The door swung open, and Riley could hear Sergio's footsteps as he strode up the aisle.

"IDs," he said, panting a little as he handed them over the counter to Kit.

"Thanks, man," she said, shuffling through them and holding them up to the dim light. "So, two Ones, a Two, and a Three. You should be okay. Wouldn't recommend heading to the doctor, though, not when you've already got someone on Tier Three."

"What do you mean?" Riley asked, but Kit seemed to not hear them. Instead, she was humming to herself as she headed into the back room, closing the door behind her.

"What the hell was that about?" Sergio asked.

"I don't know, but she's suspicious. Told her I didn't need a doctor, just medication, and she just smiled."

"That don't mean anythin', Ry."

Riley knew that, but they also knew something was up. The back door swung open, nearly fell shut, and then swung back open again with a bang as Kit sidled her way back into the main room with beige burlap bags hanging off her arms.

"And here we go—a month's worth of rations," she said, banging the bags on the counter. "Your group's ration card is in here too. Every time you come in, you bring it and the bags back, and I give you more stuff and mark off your card. Easy peasy."

Riley stared at the bags. Five of them were the size of plastic shopping bags, and one was about half as big.

Nothing was poking out the top, nothing bulged out the sides, but at least they were filled enough to stand on their own. Barely.

"Is this it?" Sergio asked.

Kit raised her eyebrows. "Yup. Two Tier One rations..."

She tapped four of the larger bags.

"...one Tier Two ration..."

She tapped the fifth large bag.

"...and one Tier Three ration."

Her hand landed on the final, smaller bag.

"And let me just get that ibuprofen for you," she said, ducking down behind the counter. "I can give you a small bottle without it seeming suspicious, but hopefully the Reverend'll have more for you."

"The Reverend?" Riley repeated as Kit popped back up. She reached out to hand over the bottle. Riley took it. Kit's smile flattened into a thin line as she grabbed Riley's wrist and pulled them in closer.

"Hey!" Sergio yelled, lurching forward to grab Riley, but Kit glared at him, shaking her head and digging her fingernails into Riley's wrist. Riley yelped, and Sergio froze.

Kit pressed a piece of paper into Riley's hand with the bottle of pills. "You'd better keep your mouth shut with what I'm about to tell you. You register anyone in your family for medical treatment with Command, maybe you get it, maybe you don't. Only thing that's for sure is they'll knock you down a tier, unless you're already at Tier Three. Then, they'll probably take you in and you'll never be seen again."

Riley's blood ran cold as their chest tightened. "Why are you telling us this?"

"Don't wanna see anyone starve. Don't wanna see anyone disappear. Now, your best bet for medical help is going to be Reverend Rafael Jameson. He lives in Echo district. He's converted a warehouse into a chapel of sorts, holds services on Sundays, offers spiritual comfort to the community, all that. These directions'll get you there. He's also got some sort of connections that lets him get his hands on medicine and medical supplies that're normally off limits. If you tell him I sent you, he'll be willing to help you out. You can't tell anyone, and make sure the Command isn't on your tail when you go visit. Just say you're going to visit a friend. Capiche?"

Riley nodded and Kit let go of their wrist, a smile coming back to her face. It still didn't reach her eyes. Sergio pulled Riley back behind him and took the ration bags, passing two of them along with the half-bag back to Riley.

"See you in a month," Kit said with a grin on her face. "And good luck with your patient."

Riley's thanks stuck in their throat at the word "patient." Sergio grabbed their arm and hustled them down the aisle as Kit watched the two of them go. As soon as Riley and Sergio reached the front of the store, she ran into the back room, the door slamming shut behind her.

"What the..."

"Don't talk," Sergio said as he shoved open the door and pushed Riley outside. "Don't talk, don't say anythin' about this to Jen and Ian just yet. We'll talk it over once we've found somewhere to live."

The two of them hurried back to their truck, keeping their eyes down and away from the soldiers. Ian opened his eyes for a few seconds when Sergio opened the back door, but he closed them just as quickly. Jen didn't say anything as Sergio and Riley arranged the groceries on the empty back seat. She just shook her head and held Ian a little tighter. Sergio hopped into the driver's seat and started the truck as Riley climbed into the passenger's seat, rubbing the nail marks on their wrist.

"Keep your eyes open. Preferably for a house that's somewhat stable," Sergio said, pulling out onto the road.

Riley tried to focus, but the battered buildings blurred into one long streak of gray. Kit's smile had burned itself onto their eyes, and they kept replaying Kit running into the back room and slamming the door behind her. Something was up. No way had she told Riley everything. She wanted Riley to go to the Reverend, for some reason, and Riley didn't really want to figure out why. Besides, Riley'd just wanted the antibiotics as a preventative measure, just to make sure Ian's wound didn't become infected. They didn't really need them. It would just be nice to have. Maybe if they kept repeating that, they'd actually believe it.

"This looks promising," Sergio said.

Ignoring the worry bubbling in their stomach, Riley turned away from their window and looked up to see a large blue sign with "HOTEL" written in white letters. The pole holding the sign up had a kink in the middle of it, making the board bend over like it was trying to intimidate whoever passed by. Taped to the bottom of the pole was a cardboard sign with "VACANCY" scribbled on it in black letters. They drove up to the dingy white, four-story building, which had one of its front double doors replaced with rough-hewn planks. Some of the windows were illuminated, highlighting silhouettes of people moving about their daily lives. Riley could see one silhouette bent over, sweeping a broom across the floor, while two others in a different room seemed to be playing with a baby.

"It's not an office building," they said.

"It's not an office buildin'," Sergio repeated as he found a parking spot toward the end of the lot. "I'll go in and see if they have a vacancy. I'll be back in a minute."

Ian deteriorated as they waited for Sergio to return. He went from sleeping somewhat peacefully to breathing heavily with sweat pouring down his face.

"He was just fine when we got here!" Jen said as she laid Ian out on the seats and hopped out so Riley could take her place.

"He's got no more adrenaline and the ibuprofen must be wearing off," Riley said, crouching on the floor of the truck. "Get a water bottle out of the bed."

Every breath Ian took was a groan of pain, and he didn't even acknowledge when Riley pressed the back of their hand to his sweat-soaked forehead. He didn't feel feverish. He was just hot from the sun like they all were. What Riley wouldn't give for a sterile, cool environment.

"Ian? I'm going to give you more medicine, but I need you to sit up."

Ian's next groan seemed to acknowledge what they'd said, but Riley wasn't entirely sure. Either way, he was going to sit up. With Jen's help, Riley managed to push him to a sitting position without him screaming in pain. They managed to get a few of the pills down his throat, leaving only four in the bottle. One more dose in about four hours, then they'd have to crack into the new bottle.

The door on the other side of the truck opened and Sergio stuck his head in. "Hotel's got room… what the hell happened?"

“Ibuprofen ran out and he’s on an adrenaline crash,” Riley replied.

“Landlord said there’s a bed in one of the rooms already,” Sergio said, tossing the truck keys to Riley. “I’ll get him up there, you pull the car around back to the metal double doors.”

“You sure you don’t need my help?” Riley asked.

Sergio shook his head. “Get the truck around and grab as much medical stuff as you can. I’ll stay with Ian.”

“Okay,” Riley said, wiping the sweat on their hands off on their jeans. “Ian, we need to get you upstairs. Can you walk?”

Ian nodded once and managed to get out of the truck with Riley and Sergio’s help. But as soon as he was on his feet, he collapsed against Sergio.

“Ian, buddy, this is gonna be a lot quicker if you let me carry you,” Sergio said.

Ian nodded again, so Sergio scooped him up and cradled him in his arms, bridal-style.

“Fourth floor, rooms 406 and 408. Move fast,” Sergio said as he headed for the front doors.

Jen had already hopped into the passenger’s seat and buckled in. Riley didn’t bother with their seatbelt as they drove the truck around the building, and for once Jen didn’t badger them about it.

“I’ll stay with the truck,” she said as Riley pulled out their medical kit. Nodding, they headed to the back of the truck and grabbed more water bottles and their suture kit before heading for the doors. Sprinting up the stairs, they felt sweat dripping down their back as they forced the door open.

406…406…406!

Sergio had left the door unlocked, and when Riley pushed it open, they found a dingy room with off-white walls and a light wood baseboard. A king-sized mattress sat on a rickety frame in the middle of the room with a battered brown love-seat across from it facing the bed. A roughed-up wooden desk was shoved into the corner of the room with a metal folding chair tucked under it. Closing the door, they realized a small kitchenette was also along the wall next to the door, but that was it for furniture. The stained carpeted floor creaked under their feet as they hurried to Ian's side.

"I'm going to stitch him up," Riley said as Sergio stood up and stepped back so they could take his place next to the bed. "Jen's staying by the car."

"Fortunately we don't have that much to bring up," Sergio said. "But I'm gonna need your help with the mattress at least."

"Save it for last. I should be done by then."

"Good luck, baby," Sergio said, kissing their cheek before heading out. Pulling out their "surgical tray"—a collection plate they'd found in an abandoned church—Riley sterilized it and their equipment as best they could with the vodka. Setting their needle driver, forceps, alcohol pad, and scissors in the plate, they dug around in the suture kit, trying to find if they still had a needle and thread in its sterile pack.

They did. Thank God. One thing going right.

They opened the pack and set it in the plate, still in its wrapper. Turning to Ian, they pulled the tape off the bandages and threw it in a ball on the floor. After pulling out the small bottle of soap and grabbing one of the water bottles, they headed over to the small sink to scrub up. They'd run out of gloves before meeting Ian and Jen and hadn't seen any since. They just did their best with soap, bottled water, and vodka, hoping it was enough. It had been so far.

"How's it goin', honey?" Sergio asked as he opened the door, lugging in the water they'd managed to steal. Riley's chest squeezed when they saw it, and they felt their stomach begin to bubble with guilt. If only they'd sent Ian back to the truck before raiding the gas station, none of this mess would've happened.

"Haven't started yet. Will in a second. Anybody hanging around?"

Sergio shook his head. "Truck's hidden from the road and nobody's come down the alley from what Jen's said." He kissed their cheek before heading back out.

Taking a deep breath to calm their boiling stomach, Riley pumped soap into the water bottle and swished it around. They walked back to Ian's side and checked his breathing. It had slowed down a bit, but it was still labored. As far as they could tell he was asleep. Hopefully his exhaustion would keep him knocked out since Riley had never managed to find topical anesthetic. Grabbing the scissors, Riley got up on the bed and straddled Ian to get the best angle. Cutting off the wrapped bandage and hoping a long enough piece could be salvaged, Riley pushed the scraps away. Picking up the forceps and steeling themself, they slowly peeled back the gauze.

The slow-moving round had left a large hole in Ian's shoulder, which gaped up at them. It seemed to laugh, demanding to know what Riley was going to do about it since Riley had put the wound there in the first place.

Well, stitch it up. That was what they were going to do.

Come on, Riley Jay. Running stitch, quick and clean as possible. You've done this dozens of times before. Just one more time. Just one more time.

Swallowing back the bile that rose in their throat, Riley leaned over and grabbed the soapy water and a clean cloth. Ian didn't react as Riley started cleaning around the wound. In a panic they pressed their fingers to Ian's throat, trying to find his pulse. It was there, rapid and weak, but it was there.

Sighing, Riley finished cleaning up as best they could, trying to keep the soap out of the wound. Hopefully Ian would stay unconscious for this. Once they were satisfied, they set aside the soap and cloth and grabbed their needle driver, which they used to pull the needle out of its pack. Taking a deep breath, Riley braced themself and began to suture.

They could feel Ian tense under the first poke, but he didn't seem to wake up. Pushing the needle through on the other side, a soft groan escaped his lips. He wasn't going to stay fully unconscious for this. Damn it.

"Riley?"

Riley looked up and noticed that Sergio had snuck most of the stuff in while they were distracted. "All that's left is the mattress. You ready to go?"

"I-I just started. Had to clean the wound first."

Sergio sighed. "You can do it, Riley Jay. I know you can. I'm gonna get Jen."

"Yeah, do that."

He turned and left, leaving Riley to face their fears again. They could do this. It was just another patient. Just another patient they could mend. Just another patient they'd gotten shot when they'd promised to always protect them...

No, no, no. Focus.

Riley's hands were shaking. Taking a deep breath, they forced them to relax, only moving when they were ordered to move. The first few stitches were jagged and clunky, but they began to flow easier with every push and pull of the needle.

Move down the forceps, stitch under, pull up, stitch over, repeat. Riley found the flow of the needle, working with the tensing and relaxing of the skin while forgetting everything but making sure each stitch was perfect.

They were tying off the last stitch in the double square knot when the door opened again. Riley didn't look up as they cut the thread and quickly returned the needle to its packaging. They looked up as they were getting off the bed to see Sergio and Jen maneuvering the mattress into the hotel room.

"Woah!"

"We've got it, Riley. You focus on Ian," Sergio said.

Riley still considered running over to help, but a groan from the bed made them turn back to Ian. His eyes were still closed, but his hand was fumbling toward his shoulder.

"Nuh-uh, hands down," Riley said, pulling his hand away. "I'm not letting you get those stitches infected."

After pulling a fresh patch of gauze out of their kit, Riley taped it down, thankful that Ian had at least not fully woken up while they were stitching him up. But at the same time, it was worrying how exhausted he was…

"How is he?" Jen asked as she walked in from the adjacent room, panting.

"Well I got him stitched up, but he's not as responsive as he should be," Riley replied.

"We haven't slept in over a day, a lot's been going on, and he just got shot," Jen said, leaning forward to put her hands on her knees. "He needs to sleep. *You* need to sleep. I'll keep an eye on him and wake you if something goes wrong."

Riley opened their mouth to protest, but a large yawn came out instead.

"What were you going to say?"

"Nothing."

"That's what I thought." Jen smiled as she pulled Riley into a hug. "Sergio's getting the mattress set up for the both of you. Get some rest. You've had a long day, and you did a good job with Ian."

Whatever dam had been inside Riley broke, and all the guilt and fear from the past few hours came flooding out. They could barely hear Jen shushing them through their sobs, but they could feel her rubbing their back. The tenderness made Riley cry harder. They didn't deserve this. Everything was entirely their fault. If Jen knew what had happened, Riley was sure they'd be getting slapped instead of hugged.

After a minute they could hear the low rumble of Sergio's voice. Their throat stung as Sergio's warm hand stroked their hair, and they pulled away from Jen to lean against Sergio's chest.

"I'll tell you later, Jen," Riley could make out Sergio saying as he wrapped his arms around them and pulled them a step back from Jen. "Let me get Riley to sleep. They need it."

"Yes they do," Jen replied. Through watery eyes, Riley could see her reach out and push a strand of hair out of Riley's face. "We'll be able to talk once you're both rested."

CHAPTER FIVE

"Riley! Sergio!"

Riley peeled their eyes open, wincing at the dim morning light as they felt Sergio sit up beside them. They assumed he asked Jen what was up, but their ears weren't fully functioning yet. They envied Sergio's ability to wake up at a second's notice.

"Ian's bad," Jen said, sounding like she was speaking through water. "I gave him more ibuprofen, two more. I know it's early but he's bad."

"It's fine. Takes about thirty minutes for the medication to kick in," Riley said, finally pushing themself up and rubbing the sleep out of their eyes. Their tongue was thick in their mouth, and the dry air wasn't helping any. "When'd you give it to him?"

"Just now, but that's when I noticed red streaks coming out from under his bandage."

Riley's feet were on the floor and sprinting into the other room before their brain caught up. Ian was propped up in the bed, tucked in under a quilt Jen had pieced together, and he offered up a weak smile.

"Hey, RJ," he said, his voice still creaky and faint.

"Hey," Riley replied, hopping on the bed next to him and looking at his shoulder. Jen was right; little red streaks were beginning to peek out from under his bandage. Ian was shivering as well, and Riley could feel the feverish warmth radiating off of him.

"Shit," Riley said under their breath, getting back off the bed and heading for the sink.

"Wh-what's wrong?" Ian asked. "I-is it infected?"

"Afraid so," Riley replied, scrubbing up at the sink with half of a bottle of water.

"Do you need help?" Jen asked as she and Sergio walked back into the room.

"Get the medical kit open so I can get some new gauze and tape, and grab the ibuprofen out of one of the ration bags. I think it's in the smaller one," Riley said. "I'm going to clean out the wound again and re-bandage. We've got to find some antibiotics."

Swishing soap into the rest of the water bottle and grabbing a clean cloth, Riley pushed Sergio out of the way as they hurried back to Ian's side. Sitting on the side of the bed, Riley set their materials down on the rickety side table and gritted their teeth as they peeled back the gauze bandage.

Angry red streaks reached out from each stitch. Light green pus oozed out, sticking to the gauze as Riley pulled it back.

Damn it!

"H-how bad is that?" Ian asked as he took the two ibuprofen Jen offered him.

"I've seen worse," Riley replied. The infection had just set in, but infections could be unpredictable. The sooner they could treat it, the better.

"Sergio, can I talk to you?" Jen asked. Riley felt Sergio kiss the top of their head before heading into the other room with her.

"Th-think he's going to tell the truth?" Ian asked.

"Doubt it," Riley replied.

"It's not your f-fault. You know th-that."

"Kinda is."

"The man would've sh-shot anyway."

Riley looked up at Ian, raising their eyebrows. Ian's eyes seemed slightly unfocused, probably due to exhaustion, but he seemed resolute in his interpretation of events. Well, he could believe whatever he wanted to believe. Maybe it was better that way.

"D-do I really need antibiotics?" Ian asked.

"Yeah," Riley replied, feeling their anxiety rising in their throat.

"H-how are you going to find some?" Ian asked.

Riley thought about the piece of paper Kit had pressed into their hand. It was still in the pocket of their jeans, untouched. They were pretty sure it was directions to the converted chapel. They just didn't know if they wanted to follow those directions, especially if those directions led to a pastor. They weren't in the mood to trust any supposed men of God after living in Revolution territory. Unfortunately, that pastor was the only connection they had to the medication they desperately needed. But Ian didn't need to know that right now.

"Like I always have," Riley replied. "Ask around, find someone who knows someone. There's always people with connections."

A groaning creak made Riley turn around to see Sergio walking in from the other room. Yanking the door shut behind him, he headed over to Riley's side. "Jen's horrified at the state of our room, so she's cleanin' it up. How're you feelin', Ian?"

"Just p-peachy," Ian replied, forcing a weak smile. Sergio's returning smile seemed normal, but Riley knew him well enough to see a lot of worry behind it. He looked over at Riley, who could only shake their head.

"Hey S-Serg," Ian said, lowering his voice to a hoarse whisper, "wh-what did you tell Jen?"

Sergio glanced at the other room and lowered his voice as well. "Told her the truth. We got ambushed by a man with a gun and you got shot."

Ian nodded, "Good."

Yet again, Riley was reminded that they didn't deserve Ian. Sergio grabbed Ian's hand in gratitude, and Ian squeezed it tightly. He then reached up his other hand to run it through Riley's hair.

A booming, mechanical horn split the air, and Riley clapped their hands over their ears. "What the hell?"

"Gotta be reveille!" Sergio yelled.

The horn cut out, replaced by a mechanical voice that was lower and more resonant than the high screeching voice in Revolution. "Attention, Tier One citizens. Report for reveille in five minutes. Only Tier One citizens are to report today. Attention, Tier One citizens."

Riley's shoulders dropped in relief. Ian wouldn't have to get out of bed and be forced to stand for who knows how long. Thank God.

"Riley, we need to go," Sergio said.

"Where?"

"According to the soldiers yesterday, we're supposed to stand in front of our building with nothing in our hands and nothing in our pockets. If we get chosen for work, they'll give us all we need for the day."

Shit. Command probably didn't have the manpower to frisk everyone in a timely manner, so it was easier to say not to bring anything. But that meant Riley couldn't take their backpack. "How long is it going to take?" they asked.

Sergio shrugged, and Riley could feel the panic rise in their chest. The infection didn't look too bad, not yet, but they knew that could change in an instant. They needed to go get the antibiotics now before it got worse.

"What do you think happens if we don't show up?" Riley asked.

Sergio glanced at Ian but then shook his head as he looked back at Riley. "I don't know if you could go anywhere with everyone else standin' in front of buildings. You'd get spotted quick."

Damn it, he was right. "Okay. Give me a minute and I'll be ready to go. I'll tell Jen we're out too,"

"I heard the robot voice," Jen said as she came through the door right in front of Riley. She was carrying Riley's jeans from yesterday and a plain gray T-shirt. "I'm not that deaf yet."

"Just Sergio and I have to go, it sounds like," Riley said, ducking around the doorframe into their room to change.

"You two be careful and stick together. Don't want you running afoul of these soldiers. I don't want to learn how trigger-happy they are."

"We'll be safe," Riley said as they chucked their pajamas onto the bed and headed back into the other room.

"Well, I can't ask for that much," Jen replied. "I'll have your packs ready for you when you get back so you can grab them and go get the medication."

Riley didn't know whether to smile or frown at her comment as they kissed Jen on the cheek. Heading over to the door where Sergio was already standing, Riley waved to Ian, who offered a weak wave in return. Sergio also kissed Jen on the cheek and waved to Ian as Riley slid on their shoes.

"I'll keep Ry out of trouble," Sergio said as Jen kissed him on the cheek as well.

"The hell you will. I'm relying on them to keep *you* out of trouble!"

The weak chuckle from Ian made Riley's heart both leap and sink at the same time. They had to go to Echo district and get those antibiotics the second they could. They didn't have another choice.

"Come on. Let's go," Sergio said, putting his hand on their shoulder. "Don't think we should be late."

Riley sprinted down the stairs after Sergio, trying not to run into other people. Everyone was scrambling down the stairwell as fast as they could, skipping steps and sometimes jumping over railings to get ahead. Hair was still mussed from sleep, jackets had been haphazardly yanked on, and one man nearly tripped when Riley accidentally stepped on his untied shoelace. They tried to apologize, but the man shoved past them, his shoelaces still flopping against the concrete. His eyes had been somewhere between sleepy and fully alert, giving him a wild-eyed stare that was more than a little unsettling.

When Riley reached the ground floor, they headed for the door to the lobby before Sergio grabbed their hand and tugged on it. Confused, they followed him to the back door. A few other people were running outside, trying to avoid the crowd in the lobby.

"You're new around here," a tall, thin man with bright blue eyes, dark brown hair, and pale, suntanned skin commented as they hopped out the door. He was holding the hand of a shorter woman with almond-shaped brown eyes and ebony hair, thrown up into a braid. She wiggled her fingers at Riley, a small smile on her face. Riley couldn't help but smile back, but something about the woman made them uneasy. Maybe it was the fact that she seemed to be nice for the sake of being nice and not to get anything out of it.

"When'd you get in?" the man asked.

"Last night," Sergio replied.

"Well, welcome to Jericho, I guess. I'm Carter, she's Nozomi. Come with us. We'll show you the ropes."

He swept his arm toward the street, and the small group hurried down the side of the hotel. Whatever had been the building on the other side was now just a pile of rough concrete slabs stacked high, threatening to topple over.

"Put your toes on the edge of the sidewalk and try to keep a few inches between you and the people next to you," Carter said.

Riley and Sergio did as he said, squeezing into the line that had formed and jostling for those few inches of space. Unfortunately, with how many people were trying to get into line, they were pressed shoulder to shoulder. Sergio was on Riley's left with Carter on his other side. On Riley's right was a tall, burly man with bright red hair and blue eyes set deep into his pink face. Across the street was another line, a motley group of young and middle-aged people. Some were staring straight ahead, eyes wide, while others whispered to each other, stealing glances up and down the road.

"What're your names?" Carter asked, barely audible over the crowd's murmur.

"I'm Sergio. They're Riley."

"You both Tier One?"

"Yes, sir," Sergio replied.

"Good. They do random card checks and they'll detain people who aren't the tier they asked for. You don't want that."

Frantic voices bubbled up to the left of the group, and Riley leaned forward to see what was going on. A figure was lying curled up in the street, with another figure bent over it. Riley stepped into the street to go help, but Nozomi grabbed their arm and pulled them back up onto the sidewalk between her and Carter.

"Whoever's next to him will get him back on his feet," Nozomi said, staring straight ahead. "There's not much we can do."

Pre-Collapse, Riley would've said they were a nurse, pushed aside Nozomi, and rushed to the patient's side. Now, memories of being held at gunpoint cemented their feet into the sidewalk. They couldn't even watch. They just stared at the line of people on the other side of the sidewalk. Some of them were staring back at Riley, their mouths pressed into thin lines and their eyes screaming in terror. Others were stealing glances at the collapsed person, but refusing to watch for long.

Two troop transports rumbled into view, massive pick-up-truck-looking vehicles with open roofs and benches lining each side of the truck bed. Both of them already held a smattering of people who were either exhausted, relieved, or a mix of both. The trucks screeched to a halt, too loudly for how slow they were going, and the four soldiers in the back of each truck jumped out. They paired up, with one soldier in each pair holding a clipboard while the other held an assault rifle.

A scream split the air, and Riley turned to see the collapsed man being yanked off the ground by a soldier. A woman grabbed the back of the man's shirt. Another soldier swooped in and grabbed her, pushing her back into line. She kept screaming, banging her fists on the soldier's chest. Riley tensed, bracing themself for what was going to happen. Sure enough, the soldier pulled a black taser off of his belt and thrust it into the woman's stomach. She went rigid, collapsing forward. Only the rumbling of the truck and the footsteps of the soldiers could be heard as the soldier dragged the woman to the nearest truck and threw her in the back.

"IDs, all four of you."

Riley turned to see one of the pairs of soldiers standing in front of Carter. The soldier with the clipboard was skinny and pale, her face hidden by the shadow of her olive-green bucket helmet. Behind her, the soldier holding his assault rifle was burly with dark tanned skin, his face similarly obscured. Riley couldn't help but think of buddy cop shows, where the fresh-faced rookie and the grizzled veteran were mismatched together to take on the world. It almost made them laugh, either from nerves or from how dumb their brain was being.

Nozomi elbowed them as she pulled out her ID, and Riley did the same. Skinny with the clipboard took all the little plastic cards and laid them out on her clipboard. She looked each of them up and down before making a few marks on the chart. Riley held their breath.

Please don't pick me! Please don't pick me. Please don't pick me!

"All right, you and you in the truck," she said, pointing at Nozomi and Sergio before handing back all four of the IDs. Riley breathed a small sigh of relief. They could go get the antibiotics! That didn't help the tightening in their chest or the nausea in their stomach as Sergio stepped off the sidewalk and followed Nozomi to the nearby truck to the right. He glanced back at Riley, giving them a little wave before patting the air, palm downward. It was his signal for them to stay calm, that everything would be all right.

"He'll be back at dark, perfectly fine with a little bit of cash," Carter said. "I promise."

Even with both of those reassurances, Riley couldn't help but bite their lip as they saw Sergio help Nozomi into the truck before climbing in after her. The soldiers hopped in after the two of them and closed the tailgate to the truck.

"*Move out!*" the burly soldier yelled, and the truck engine roared as it trundled forward. Nozomi blew a kiss to Carter with a small wave while Sergio forced a smile and waved again to Riley. They tried to smile back, but they were sure it came off as more of a grimace than a grin. All of the transports rolled out of sight, heading west toward the outskirts of Jericho.

"Dismissed, dismissed," the robot voice intoned. A collective sigh went up as people began to scatter back into their homes or headed off down the street.

"Getting picked up on the first day is rare," Carter said. "Normally it takes a day or two for people to show up on the population spreadsheets."

Riley shrugged as they turned back toward the hotel. They expected Carter to let them go, but he stayed right next to them. At least he walked as fast as he talked.

"Granted, Command's been trying to get a new ammo factory up and running on the outskirts of Golf district," he said. "I worked there for a few days last week. If Sergio and Nozomi aren't there, they'll be in one of the established factories or plants."

"What're those?" Riley asked as they followed him back down the side of the hotel.

"One's packaging food. That's the smallest, so they're probably not there. One deals with processing metal into a variety of things, and the last one makes uniforms for the soldiers. They're still trying to get Jericho up and running. Most of the stuff here still needs to be shipped in from deeper in Command territory. Makes some things harder to get, but we're not too bad off. At least we aren't on the front lines anymore."

Riley was tempted to ask what that was like, but they didn't really want to have an hour-long conversation. They needed to get Jen and Ian up to speed and then head for Echo district.

"Do you know how hard it is to cross between districts on foot?" Riley asked as Carter opened the back door.

Carter's eyes widened and he frowned slightly, probably startled by the sudden change of subject. "Uh, it's not that bad. You'll just have to look out for trucks coming up when you get in the middle of the road to cross. No different procedure than being in a car. They might search bags. They might not. No real rhyme or reason."

"Thanks," Riley replied, stepping inside the building.

"Where you thinking of heading?"

Riley debated on whether or not to tell him the truth, and they settled on a shrug. "Just in case we have to cross a checkpoint. You seem to know a lot about Jericho, and we just got here last night."

Carter shrugged back, "We've been here for about six months. You'll catch on fast. Don't worry. It's pretty simple, until it's not."

Riley snorted, shaking their head. "Good to meet you, Carter. Better go figure out what I'm going to go do with my day."

"Yeah, good idea. And hey, we're room 315 if you need anything."

"Thanks," Riley replied, heading up the stairs. They were pretty sure Carter expected for them to give their room number in return, but they weren't willing to give up that information. Not until they knew for sure he was trustworthy.

Pulling out the crumpled-up paper Kit had given them yesterday, they studied the rough sketch of a map of Foxtrot and Echo districts with arrows and an X over one of the buildings in Echo. They turned it over and looked at the "TO REV" scrawled in spidery black ink.

Riley only had so much trust to give in a day.

Jen was more relieved than Riley was about Sergio being picked for work. "We could use the cash," she said. "I've inventoried everything; our toothbrushes are about to give out, we need more shampoo than they gave us to last us three months, and Ian definitely needs new shoelaces for his boots."

"I don't know how much Sergio's gonna make in a day," Riley said. "And we don't know how much things cost around here. We still have to pay for the ibuprofen."

"Don't worry. I'm making a priority list," Jen said, nodding to the little black backpack at Riley's feet. "That's still good to go, at least."

Riley nodded as they scooped up their pack, which had food, two bottles of water, a change of clothes, a blanket, and a smaller version of their medical kit that was packed into a hidden compartment. All of the members of the family had one of these survival kits. It was something they'd all started carrying in Philippi after Sergio hadn't been able to make it home before dark one time. He'd spent a miserable night hiding in a dumpster before being able to get home the next morning.

"Might need to replace the food in it if we can," Riley said. "It'll do for today. I don't think I'll get caught in Echo if I leave now."

Jen looked like she was about to disagree, but she nodded and kissed Riley on the cheek again. "Be safe, and be back before dark."

"I will, I promise."

Riley looked over at Ian, tempted to say goodbye, but they didn't want to wake him up. So they just kissed Jen on the cheek and headed out the door.

It was a surprisingly short walk to the Echo-Foxtrot checkpoint, which wasn't in high demand. Only one man stood on the sidewalk next to the checkpoint booth, and the soldier was examining his ID through a window. If the soldier was in the booth, hopefully that meant he wasn't interested in searching backpacks.

Riley stood a few feet back, pulling out their ID before looking into Echo district. It was much busier than Foxtrot with people actually milling about and lounging on stoops in front of what Riley assumed to be their homes. Children were actually playing in the street, laughing and screaming as they kicked around a scuffed-up soccer ball.

The man was let through the gate, and Riley stepped up to the window. They were shocked to see that it still had clean, completely intact glass.

"ID."

Riley handed it over and the soldier held it up to compare the photo to their face. "What's your business in Echo district?"

"Visiting a friend," Riley said, praying Kit's instructions weren't about to get them into trouble.

But the soldier nodded and handed back their ID. "Curfew's at sundown. I'd recommend you be back home before then."

Riley nodded, breathing a sigh of relief as the soldier raised the gate for them. Hurrying through, they headed for the other side of the street so they wouldn't get in the way of the kids' soccer game.

Echo district was full of townhouses and duplexes instead of apartment buildings and converted storefronts. There weren't any stores, converted or otherwise. This had to have been where the rich people had lived before the Collapse. But now, looking at the state of the houses compared to the buildings in Alpha and Foxtrot, Riley could tell that this was just as cared for as Foxtrot was, if not less so. The windows weren't officially boarded up; instead sheets hung to block the windows or were boarded up with scraps of wood. Instead of the housing unit numbers being neatly painted onto the doors or window boards, they were haphazardly spray painted on the sides of the building, wherever there was room, just like the apartment unit number on the hotel.

At the next crossroads Riley turned right, heading toward what the paper Kit had given them said was the outskirts of Echo district. The houses had disappeared, replaced by dilapidated warehouses and trailers that had probably served as office buildings for the warehouses. Just as many people were here, though, with children running in and out of homes and people sitting on the steps to the trailers. Riley could feel eyes on their back as they looked for the black wooden cross on the wall of a warehouse.

The air felt thick with suspicion. One woman jumped and threw her hands up in front of her face when Riley stepped up onto the sidewalk in front of her trailer. A small boy missed a kick, his foot soaring over the scuffed-up and faded basketball as he watched Riley pass by the game of kickball he was playing with his little friends. His eyes were too narrow and too wary for his age. They should've been wider with the innocence of pure trust.

They finally spotted the cross on the next street over. Ducking between two other warehouses they stopped in the street and stared at the Meeting Space. It was similar to every other warehouse in this area, except that it was almost completely made of wood and a large black cross was nailed next to the door.

There was no way the Reverend could be part of the Revolution. It would be so dumb to hide being a Revolution agent by pretending to be a pastor. That being said, Riley seriously doubted he was actually a pastor. He had to have some sort of medical background if he was medicating people on the down low and nobody had reported him to Command. Granted it seemed like Command cared less about this district than Foxtrot or Alpha.

"Attention, citizens. Echo district is under lockdown. Please return to your homes and remain there until instructed otherwise. I repeat, Echo district is under lockdown."

All of the motion that was happening in the street flowed back into the warehouses and trailers. Riley froze as shouts and footsteps swirled around them. A young man jumped off of the steps to grab an older woman by the arm, coaxing her and her conversation partner into his trailer. Two teenage boys kicked down their stall made up of rotting boards and snatched up the stall sign that said "Tools for Rent" before ducking into an alleyway. An older woman corralled a gaggle of elementary-aged children into a trailer, the children's high-pitched voices a cacophony of whining about having to give up their game of tag.

"You idiot, get inside!" a woman snapped at Riley. That unstuck their feet and they bolted across the street for the Meeting House door. They raised their fist to knock on it, but the door opened before they could.

"Get in."

Riley was shoved inside. Turning around, they saw the man step out into the road, arms crossed, watching everyone scurry into their homes. He was Black, tall, and had a twist-out hairstyle that Riley was surprised he had the materials to do. Jen had complained before how she didn't have the hair styling stuff to do twist-outs anymore.

He had to be the Reverend Rafael Jameson.

The street was almost cleared, except for another man who was walking down the road. He also had black skin, but his curly hair was cropped short. He jammed his hands into the pockets of his jeans as he strolled down the street, whistling. Riley didn't recognize the tune, but it was cheerful and jarring when compared to the scramble from a few minutes earlier. But there was something else to the cheeriness, some tension. A warning.

The man was also looking up and down the street, which by this point was empty. Nodding to the Reverend, the man headed to a trailer across the street. His whistling trailed off as he walked up the ramp, and everything fell silent as he closed the door behind him.

The Reverend began backing toward the still-open door. Riley stepped back as he got back inside, closed the door, and slid the lock shut.

"Good to meet you, Riley Jay."

Riley's heart raced and their chest squeezed. They wanted to bolt out the door, but the Reverend was blocking it with his arms crossed.

"Kit let me know you were coming," he said. "Something about needing antibiotics and more ibuprofen?"

"Something like that."

"Let's talk in my office."

The Reverend gestured toward a battered wooden door. Riley kept their eye on him as they stepped toward the office. He didn't move until they were halfway to the office, just passing the final column of metal folding chairs that faced an altar made of a plastic folding table, a cross of scrap wood, and a small stack of Bibles. Even then he made sure to stay behind them until they were fully inside his office. Then he closed the door and sat in the metal folding chair on the other side of his dinged, rickety wooden desk. A filing cabinet sat behind him under a grimy window that had a jagged hole in the lower left pane.

"So, Riley Jay, how can I help you?" The Reverend folded his hands and rested them on the desk.

"Kit told me you were the person to go to for help if I didn't want to register someone for medical treatment," Riley said. "Something about having medicine that's otherwise hard to get your hands on."

"Antibiotics and prescription-strength ibuprofen would definitely fit into that category. What kind of antibiotics?"

"Something that can stop an early infection in a gunshot wound."

"Ah, so something broad spectrum."

Oh, he definitely had some medical background.

"I have some cipro, I think," the Reverend said, pulling a clipboard out of his desk and flipping through the pages of what Riley assumed was an inventory list.

"You sure you don't have anything better?"

"Like what?" he asked, looking up and raising his eyebrows in expectation.

Shit. The question had been out of their mouth before they could stop it.

The Reverend rolled his eyes, "Look, Riley Jay—"

"It's just Riley, honestly."

"—stop bullshitting me," the Reverend continued. "You walked into Kit's grocery asking specifically for ibuprofen and antibiotics, saying you don't need a doctor even though it's a *gunshot wound,* and then you come here playing dumb like you don't know what medication you need. I assumed you've already stitched up the wound as well since your patient hasn't bled to death and there's no way pressure alone's going to stop the bleeding of that wound. You're hiding something."

"I'm not!"

"Like I said, bullshit."

Riley crossed their arms and bit their lip. They glanced at the closed door that led to the main area of the Meeting Space.

"What about you, then?" they asked. "I've never heard of a pastor who had more antibiotics than he had Bibles."

"Bibles don't cure diseases," the Reverend replied, setting his clipboard down before leaning back and crossing his arms. "Can't tend to my flock's spiritual needs without tending to their physical ones."

"Can't tend to your flock's spiritual needs without enough Bibles, either."

"People can share."

"Not when you've got one Bible for each row of what, ten? Fifteen? *You're* hiding something."

The threat didn't have the visible impact Riley hoped for. The Reverend stared back at them, smiling a bit, as if they were just having a friendly conversation. But behind his dark brown eyes Riley could see the storm clouds forming. They swallowed down the fear that had risen in their throat and looked away. They didn't want to know what would happen when the lightning struck.

"Where'd you learn that there's better antibiotics than cipro?" the Reverend asked. His voice was soft and cajoling, inviting Riley to confide in him. But when Riley looked back up at him, the storm clouds hadn't gone anywhere.

"Picked some stuff up on the road," Riley replied.

The Reverend laughed, high and clear, a mocking melody that did nothing to cut the tension. "You wanna know how many times I've heard that phrase? All of them now work for me, and they're damn good at their jobs."

"Work for you doing what?" Riley asked.

The Reverend tensed, but his face smoothed over into a less-than-natural smile. "Helping me get the medications, of course."

"Stop bullshitting me," Riley said, leaning forward and planting their hands on his desk. "You're providing medical care to people so they don't have to register with Command. Pretty sure that's illegal by the way Kit was acting. What's to prevent me from reporting you?"

"Nothing, I guess," the Reverend said, shrugging. "But, for one thing, you don't have any proof besides your word about this conversation. And for another—"

He pulled open the top drawer of his desk, took out a small, clear, yellow-orange bottle, and set it on the desk.

"—you wouldn't get this."

Riley's heart sped up, and they nearly choked. Thrusting their hand forward, they tried to grab the bottle, but the Reverend snatched it back off the desk and put it in his drawer.

"I can't be giving anything out for free, Riley Jay," he said. "For one thing, I need to know your specialty. Tell me that, and I can give you the ibuprofen, and cover the cost for the ibuprofen Kit already gave you."

Fair enough. Riley glanced out the window and leaned toward the Reverend, lowering their voice. "Nurse practitioner, pediatric specialist."

The Reverend leaned back, his eyes wide. A slow grin spread across his face.

"Good," he said, opening another desk drawer and setting a white bottle on the table. Riley snatched it up, holding it up to the light to see "Ibuprofen, 800mg" on it. Hallelujah.

"What about the antibiotics?" Riley asked, stashing the ibuprofen in their pocket.

"I'll need more from you if you want those," the Reverend replied.

"So let's talk trade," Riley replied, sitting back up. "We've got gas, water, bedding—"

"No, no, no, no, I'm not talking about that," the Reverend said. "Here's my deal. You work for me, and I'll pay you in antibiotics."

"What? Work for you as a drug runner?"

"Of course not, not with your skill set. I need you to help me with patients. Command doesn't want weaklings in their cities, people who're a drain on resources without contributing anything back." He spat the words out, glaring back at the window as if he could stare down the entirety of Command. "That's why they cut rations as you get older, if you get hurt, if you get sick. No use wasting stuff on people who aren't potential soldiers or who can't work regularly in the factories. Well to hell with that, I aim to keep everyone alive."

"Doubt the Command's happy with that idea," Riley said.

"What Command doesn't know won't kill them. Or us."

Riley's chest squeezed as if a hand had reached into their body and was holding them in a vise-like grip. "You're asking a lot from me, Reverend."

"I'm not asking you to do any more than I'm willing to do. I've been doing this for almost a year now and I haven't been caught."

"You don't have a family. I do. You're asking me to put them at risk."

"Their lives were at risk the second those soldiers took over the capitol and massacred all those legislators," the Reverend replied with the same venom as when he'd talked about Command.

"Yeah, but I didn't have control over that. I've got control over this. The answer is no, I can't risk anyone getting hurt."

"What about your patient? Who are they, your brother, sister, lover? You can't be treating a stranger, not the way you're acting right now."

Riley stared at him, white hot guilt bubbling up in their gut. The last time they'd tried to help a stranger, they'd gotten the end of a gun for their troubles. So sue them if they didn't want to repeat that experience. Survival came first. That's how they'd stayed alive this long. But the guilt of not helping people, especially when their skills were in such high demand, just would not go away.

"Whoever they are, they've already been hurt," the Reverend continued. "And you'll be taking a pretty big chance with their life if you don't get them medication."

"You're the one keeping it from me, *doctor.*"

The Reverend sat back, stunned, staring at Riley. His shoulders slumped forward for a minute and he looked away, but then he straightened back up with an even gaze that now held back more sorrow than rage.

"First off, yes, I'm a doctor. Specialization in emergency and internal medicine. And I've got dozens of other patients I can give those antibiotics to. I could split them up into two, fifteen-day courses and save two patients with bacterial diseases. You're asking me to keep it all together and use it to save one life. I'm going to need something in return."

"I told you, we can—"

"I've already told you the price, Riley Jay. If you can't pay it, I can't give you the antibiotics."

"Then you'll kill Ian! He's the closest thing I've got to a brother. I can't lose him!"

"I'm giving you the option to save him!"

"By further risking his life and the lives of the rest of my family!"

"Look, that's the deal on the table. Work for me and I'll give you the medication. Otherwise," he stood up and walked over to the door, pulling it open and gesturing outside, "you can take your chances with Command or with Mother Nature. It's your choice."

Riley bit their lip, the salty tang of blood exploding onto their tongue. Some doctor, holding a patient's life hostage. Whatever happened to do no harm?

The Reverend sighed, closing the door. "Fine. Thirty days. You work for me for thirty days. I give you thirty pills. That seems fair to me."

At least the Reverend wasn't asking them to do more than he was willing to do, but he also didn't have a family to risk. Riley did. But they would be willing to take that risk if it meant saving Ian's life, and they knew Sergio and Jen would agree. Riley knew they'd lost the second they'd walked into the room, and the Reverend knew it too. He held all the cards in the form of a pill bottle with thirty capsules in it, and Riley desperately, desperately needed those cards.

"Fine," they spat, refusing to look at the Reverend. "Deal."

The Reverend slumped against the doorframe, a smile coming to his face as he nodded. "Okay then. I'll get my medical kit. Wait for me by the front door."

"I can take the medicine back by myself."

"What? Don't you want a second opinion on a gunshot wound? What kind of a nurse are you?"

The one who didn't want the Reverend knowing where they lived. But as they stood up and looked up at the Reverend, with the half-smile on his face that didn't quite reach his eyes, they knew he'd already anticipated this. He wasn't going to just trust them on their word and hand over the antibiotics without knowing where they were taking them.

That was fine. Riley didn't trust him either.

CHAPTER SIX

Riley watched out the window as the Reverend headed for the back room. No more trucks were rumbling through the streets. Adults were starting to come back out in front of their doors, glancing up and down the street before nodding to each other. Kids' heads peeked out of widows and from behind their guardians' legs before being shooed away.

The man who'd been whistling down the street was standing back out in front of his trailer with a woman whose ebony skin matched his own. She was leaning against the doorframe and holding a baby on her hip. The baby was in a slightly rumpled blue dress, with short braids that almost hit her shoulders. The man was bracing himself against the railing along the small porch outside of the door, accepting silent greetings from the others on the street. He was singing now, a different tune than before. Riley couldn't make out the words of the mournful song, but it also sounded… safe. The danger had passed. People could come back out now.

"Ready to go?" the Reverend asked, settling his backpack onto his shoulders. Riley nodded and stepped back so he could unbolt the door. As they stepped outside, the man's voice became clearer just as his song ended.

The last note floated over everyone as they slowly started to resume their lives outside again. The Reverend beckoned for Riley to follow him, and they stepped out onto the cracked asphalt.

"Raf!" the singing man called, a big grin on his face. "Who's your new friend?"

The Reverend waved as the man vaulted over the railing. The woman laughed and shook her head, walking down the ramp and bouncing her fussing baby on her hip to try and calm her down.

"This is Riley Jay—" the Reverend started, turning toward Riley and raising an eyebrow.

"They," they replied.

The Reverend nodded and continued, "—they're new here in Jericho."

"Saw you just standin' on the road when the soldiers crawled in," the man said, holding his hand out to Riley. "I'm Sam. This is my wife, Yvonne, and my daughter Deborah."

"Hi," Yvonne said, readjusting Deborah on her hip. The baby had stopped fussing and was now listlessly cuddled up against her mother. Riley could see the Reverend's jaw clench as he reached out to take the baby from Yvonne, who sighed and shook out her arms after she'd handed her daughter over.

"How's my favorite niece?" the Reverend asked the little girl. Deborah just buried her face into his shoulder, whining.

Yvonne shook her head as she turned to Riley. "Sorry for snapping at you earlier, but I didn't want you to be caught in the street. Didn't realize you were new here."

"Well, it's not like you had time to explain everything to me politely," Riley replied, unable to keep from watching the baby. They knew a sick baby when they saw one, but they didn't want to offer up that information. Not yet, at least. They needed to know more about Yvonne and Sam.

"So you're the Reverend's… sister?" Riley asked.

Yvonne shook her head. "Not by blood, no. We took in this wandering stranger when he showed up during the Revolution occupation. Somehow managed to convince everyone he was some sort of pastor and not a doctor who was reading the Bible for the first time."

"Hey!" the Reverend said, looking over from where he was rocking Deborah. "My mama made sure my butt was in the pew every Sunday."

"Well none of it must've gotten through your thick skull!"

Sam was laughing his head off at their bickering. "Come on, baby, lay off Raf. Even if he deserves it…"

"Not you too!"

Laughter bubbled up in Riley too, and they tried to smother it behind their hand. A few chuckles broke free, earning them a mock glare from the Reverend. It warmed their heart and reminded them of the banter they had with their friends before the Collapse. Then they remembered that their new "friend," the Reverend, was holding Ian's life hostage, and their heart went cold again.

"Say, Raf, where you off to? Need to check in on Peter, see how he's doin'."

"Yeah we're heading that way. You coming, Yvonne?"

"No, it's almost time for this little princess's nap. Sam knows what to ask," she replied, taking Deborah back from the Reverend. Deborah rested her head against her mother's shoulder with a yawn that made Riley's heart melt. They just couldn't leave without saying something.

"How long has she been sick?" Riley asked.

Yvonne looked up, her eyes slightly narrowed. She glanced over at the Reverend, who nodded with a small smile on his face.

"About a week," Yvonne said. "She started fussing the Saturday before last, then stopped eating and drinking and started running a fever. Raf said it was strep throat and gave her some antibiotics, and she started eating and drinking again, but she just kept fussing and running a fever. Then the rash started a few days ago."

Riley's mind immediately jumped to scarlet fever, a disease that they'd seen a few times in children who hadn't been treated for strep throat. "Can you get her to stick out her tongue?"

Yvonne nodded and stuck out her tongue at Deborah. Deborah stared at her for a few seconds in a mix of confusion and suspicion before poking her own tongue out as well. It was red and bumpy, and still had a white coat on it. Good, that meant Riley had caught it early.

"What antibiotics did you give her, Reverend?" Riley asked, lowering their voice.

"Amoxicillin, 250mg a day," the Reverend replied as the group stepped closer together, throwing glances at the street to make sure there were no lingering soldiers.

"Might need to be upped to 500mg because she's definitely got scarlet fever," Riley replied.

"Scarlet fever!" The Reverend facepalmed, shaking his head. "I should've known. Just never treated it before the Collapse, so I didn't know what to look for."

Sam's eyes had been widening during their exchange, and a grin spread across his face. "Don' tell me you went and found yourself another doctor!" he said, turning to the Reverend.

"Nurse practitioner," the Reverend replied.

"Oh, thank you, Jesus," Sam said. "Especially for somebody that knows how to treat the children. Lord knows we've been hurtin' for that."

"Yvonne, you know where the antibiotics are, grab enough for a week," the Reverend said.

Riley shook their head, "Two weeks if it's already progressed to scarlet fever."

"All right, what they said." The Reverend handed over his keys to the Meeting Space. "I should be back in a few hours. I'm just going to check on a patient Riley has."

Sam put his arm around Riley's shoulders, giving them a brief squeeze. "Come on, Riley Jay! Lemme give you the grand tour of our lovely district."

"What are you talking about? They've already seen all of it!" the Reverend replied. Sam laughed as he leaned over to kiss Yvonne and Deborah. The Reverend broke free from the group and walked down the road a few steps before turning around to raise his eyebrows at Riley. Riley had to swallow what felt like a burning lump of coal in their throat as they moved to follow him.

"Good to meet you, Riley!" Yvonne called as Sam hurried to catch up with them.

"Good to meet you too!" Riley called back, turning to wave. Yvonne seemed like a wonderful person—someone Riley could be friends with. Maybe. They didn't know if they fully trusted anyone who was with the Reverend just yet. But now Riley was in cahoots with the Reverend, they guessed. But it's not like they always trusted their own judgment.

"So, Riley Jay, how'd you get involved with Raf here?" Sam asked.

"Needed some help with my brother. We came to a bargain," Riley replied, glaring at the Reverend. He looked down, unable to meet their eyes. Well, at least he had the decency to feel bad about it. Or at least pretend to.

Sam caught on as well, and he turned to the Reverend. "What's the deal?"

"Actually something that involves you," the Reverend replied, looking up at Sam. "Riley's going to need a radio. They're going to be helping me out."

"I've got more parts comin' in tonight; I should have another radio ready to go by the mornin'."

"Perfect," the Reverend replied. "I'll bring you with me tomorrow so you can get the radio installed after Riley and I do rounds. That is, if Riley doesn't get picked up for work."

They were starting tomorrow? Riley didn't know why that surprised them, but it did. They'd guessed the Reverend would at least let them stay with Ian for another week, especially since they'd be working for him for an entire month. But apparently the Reverend needed help now. Why had they signed up for this again? Oh, yeah, because this was the only way Ian wasn't going to die. Hopefully.

"Say, do you have time to talk to Peter? He's coming up on his next appointment. Right?" Sam asked.

"Not this time. I want to try and get back here before curfew and I don't know how long I'll be with Riley's brother," the Reverend replied. "Just tell Peter I'm trying to find more T, but if I can't find any, we'll have to start tapering him off so he doesn't have severe withdrawal symptoms."

"That'll crush him," Sam said. "Last time he went off T he got really depressed."

"I know," the Reverend said, rubbing the temples of his head. "I'm sorry you're going to have to be the one to tell him."

"You've already had to deliver enough heartbreak these days," Sam said. "I'm glad I can take some of it off your plate."

"Thanks, Sam," the Reverend replied, clapping his hand on Sam's shoulder. Sam responded in kind before heading up to a warehouse and knocking on the door.

"How'd you manage to find testosterone injections?" Riley asked. "Or any type of hormone replacement therapy, for that matter."

The Reverend shrugged, "Luck? Providence? I'm just hoping I can find more before we run out. I don't want Peter to have to go through withdrawal or deal with the dysphoria."

He sighed, shaking his head. "Come on, let's get through the checkpoint before the guard changes."

Riley understood why when the soldier barely glanced at their ID cards and waved them through. Neither the Reverend nor Riley spoke the entire walk through Foxtrot, with the Reverend letting Riley lead the way to the hotel. But Riley had the feeling he could've walked here by himself if he'd had to. Especially when the Reverend headed toward the back entrance instead of walking to the front door.

"I understand if you don't want to tell your family about our little arrangement," the Reverend said. "I'll back you on whatever you want to tell them."

"I don't know how to explain why I'm not getting an entire bottle of pills besides telling the truth," Riley replied, unable to keep the edge out of their voice.

"Just say I'm still trying to get the medication."

"All of them know I'd never start anyone on antibiotics unless I could complete the course." Riley turned and blocked the back entrance to the building, raising their eyebrows. "Do you *want* me to lie, *Reverend?*"

He bit the corner of his mouth and looked away, sticking his hands into his pockets.

Riley smirked as they turned around to open the door. It felt like a small win.

"Good to see you, Rev."

Riley looked up to see Carter heading down the stairs. He reached out to shake the Reverend's hand, and he wiggled his fingers at Riley.

"Good to see you and Riley've met," Carter said. "The Rev's really helpful if you're in a tight spot."

"Well, Riley's actually going to be helping us out for a bit," the Reverend said, smiling again.

"Hey, no kidding!" Carter said. He glanced up the stairs and lowered his voice. "Heaven knows we could use it. I'll let Nozomi know. She'll be thrilled to have someone nearby to consult with if a patient goes sideways. Speaking of which, I've got to run get her more Band-Aids. I'll see you later."

Riley could feel their stomach turn as Carter clapped them on the back as he jumped down the steps behind them.

"The Stephensons are good people," the Reverend said. "You can check in with them if you need anything. Room 315, I believe."

Riley wanted to think of Carter and Nozomi as people they could trust, but right now, all they could think was that they had two downstairs neighbors who could spy on them for the Reverend.

Leading the way to room 406, Riley leaned against the doorframe and knocked three times—their signal that they were with someone else. Hopefully the Reverend was far enough from the door that he couldn't hear the scurrying inside.

They were shocked when Sergio opened the door with Jen close behind him. "Riley! I was 'bout to go look for you," he said.

"When did you get back?" Riley asked. "Carter said you wouldn't be home until dusk."

Sergio shrugged. "Transformer blew at the metal plant, and they sent us all home early without pay."

The Reverend sighed, shaking his head. Sergio looked up at him and then back at Riley.

"You gonna introduce me to your new friend here?" he asked.

"Yeah. This is the Reverend Rafael Jameson, he runs the Meeting Space, and most importantly he has antibiotics."

"Figured you wouldn't bring him back here if he didn't," Sergio said, sticking his hand out. "Sergio, I'm Riley's partner. This is Jen, we've been travelin' together for a while now."

The Reverend shook Sergio's hand with the most winning smile Riley had ever seen on his face. "Lovely to meet you both."

"Good to meet you too, Reverend. What denomination are you?" Jen asked.

"Ah, well, never was officially ordained. I have an MD instead of an MDiv, so Riley figured I could be a second opinion."

Well, he'd invited himself to be a second opinion, but same difference really. What the hell happened to him backing up whatever Riley said?

Sergio took a minute to get it, but finally his eyes widened. "Hell of a cover you've got," he said, stepping back to let them in. "Well, welcome, Reverend. Hopefully you can help us out."

Riley also stepped back and nodded for the Reverend to follow Jen. He glanced between them and Sergio, but did as they suggested. Riley could hear Jen introduce Ian, and Ian say something that caused the Reverend to laugh. But before Riley could follow, Sergio stepped into the hallway and pulled the door partially closed.

"What's the deal you made?" he asked.

How did he always know? "He gives me thirty pills. I work for him for thirty days. He's got a niece who's got scarlet fever and I'm guessing a couple other kids he can't diagnose. Specialty's in emergency and internal medicine, no pediatric experience outside of med school, I'm guessing."

Sergio sighed, "And I'm guessing he's going to give you one pill at the end of every day?"

"How *did* you know?"

"Because you aren't carrying the bottle right now and hurrying to give it to Ian," Sergio replied, kissing them on the forehead. "You're doing the best you can, Riley. And we're better off right now than we were an hour ago."

Riley could tell that Sergio had a million questions and disagreements running through his head, but he had enough sense not to voice any of them right now. Instead he pushed the door back open and let Riley inside.

The Reverend was already by Ian's bedside, a stethoscope hanging around his neck. Ian had woken up, and Jen had exchanged his T-shirt for a tank top so he didn't have to take off his shirt so much. She was hovering over the Reverend, and along with Ian was watching the Reverend put his equipment on the nightstand. As Riley got closer, with Sergio right behind them, they saw that Ian's eyes were a little more focused.

"The ibuprofen seems to be doing a good job," the Reverend said. "Riley's got some stronger stuff, but I'd rather we hold off on using it unless we absolutely need to. I'm assuming you confirmed his lungs were clear yesterday."

Memories of being held at gunpoint and forced to throw their stethoscope to the soldier filled Riley's head. "Lost it in Revolution territory," they managed to choke out. "Had to go off his breathing best I could. He hasn't struggled at all, except for exhaustion."

"Which is to be expected," the Reverend said, putting the earbuds in his ears. "BP cuff's with your stethoscope, I'm assuming?"

"No, lost that a few months before the stethoscope."

"Well, I've got some backups in the Meeting Space you can use. They're not ideal, but they'll get the job done." He turned back to Ian with a comforting smile. "I'm going to check your heart and your lungs. The stethoscope might be a little chilly."

"Hope so," Ian said. "It's too hot out!"

Riley could feel some of the stress roll off their shoulders at how much stronger his voice sounded. A decent night's sleep and more pain meds had done him some good, and now the antibiotics would do the rest. The Reverend chuckled as he pressed the end of the stethoscope to Ian's chest and moved it around.

"Chest is clear, heart rate's high but strong, which is to be expected," he said. "I'll get his BP if you want to change out the bandages, nurse."

Riley nodded and headed for the sink to scrub up. Sergio remained where he was, leaning against the wall with his arms crossed so the Reverend would have to go around him to get out the door. Riley caught his eye for a moment as they tried to scrub the grime out from under their fingernails. He seemed more relaxed than they felt, but they knew him well enough to know it was just a façade.

"Jen, can you unzip my med kit for me?" Riley asked as they headed back toward the bed. Jen nodded and reached for where it sat at the foot of the bed, but the Reverend stopped her.

"I've got some gauze and tape you can use instead," he said. "Don't want you depleting your supplies."

"Much appreciated," Riley replied as they hopped up on the bed beside Ian so they wouldn't interfere with what the Reverend was doing.

"Did you check his medical license?" Ian asked. "I mean, I think he knows what he's doing, but I'm not an expert."

"If he had his medical license, I'd be very impressed. Mine probably expired a year ago."

The Reverend snorted as he pumped up the BP cuff. Riley steeled themself as they ripped off the tape as fast as they could. Ian winced, jerking his arm out of the Reverend's grasp.

"Hey! I'm trying to get an accurate BP reading here!"

"Sorry, Doc," Riley said. They could see the Reverend look up in surprise, but he just shook his head and bent back over the BP cuff. The nickname had just slipped out, but Riley could tell he found it irritating. Good. He'd have to live with it.

Gingerly, Riley peeled up the bandage and tossed it in the Ziploc bag they were using as trash. The pus levels had gone down, but the red streaks were as bright and angry as ever.

The Reverend sucked air through his teeth. "Yeah that's… that's definitely infected,"

"Hence why we need antibiotics," Riley said.

"Got 'em right here, I'll give Ian one once I've got a good reading," the Reverend replied.

When Riley looked up, they saw Jen furrow her brow. She tilted her head in question, and Riley shrugged, turning back to Ian. He was looking between the Reverend and Riley. They could tell he was confused, but Riley was sure he didn't think anything was up. He seemed completely relaxed as Riley cleaned the wound.

"So, Reverend, have you been in Jericho long?" Ian asked.

"Since shortly after the Collapse," the Reverend replied as he removed the BP cuff from around Ian's upper arm. "I was traveling when it happened and I ended up getting stuck here. What about you all?"

"Just got here. We were living in Philippi."

The Reverend raised his eyebrows, looking up at Ian. "You're a long way from Revolution territory, my friend. How long did you live there?"

"Not entirely sure," Ian replied. "Maybe up to a year?"

"That's a fair bit of time," the Reverend said, pushing himself up and turning to Riley. "Your stitches are incredible, by the way. I'm guessing you were from a place that allowed nurses to suture."

"Luckily, yes," Riley replied as they leaned back to allow the Reverend to take a closer look at the wound. "Saved a couple of lives, I'd like to think."

"Well you definitely saved Ian's here," the Reverend said, smiling at Ian. "His BP's perfectly fine, I was still expecting it to be a little lower at this point. And the infection's not too bad. Just keep it clean and the antibiotics should clear it up. Speaking of which—"

He reached into his pocket and pulled out a small pill bottle. "Jen, can I trouble you to get a glass of water?"

"Of course," Jen said, jumping a little as she hurried to get a water bottle.

"Thank you, ma'am," the Reverend said, turning back to Ian as he shook out a pill onto his palm. "Well, I think you're in good hands with Nurse Riley here. I'll check in on you tomorrow night and see how you're doing, make sure the antibiotics are doing what they're supposed to do."

"Appreciate it, Reverend," Ian said, sticking out his hand.

"Oh please, all my friends call me Rafael."

Friends? Is that what they were now? Well, at least Ian and the Reverend seemed to be as Ian's face broke into one of the biggest smiles Riley had seen on him in a while. And that was saying something.

"Well don't be a stranger, all right?" Ian said. "I'd like some reassurance now and then that RJ's not making up that they used to be a nurse."

The Reverend laughed. "No, they're definitely not. They're pretty damn good if I say so myself."

It took everything Riley had to not roll their eyes. They could tell when someone was trying to butter them up, and it wasn't going to work. Not this time.

"Do you want to stay for dinner, Rafael?" Jen asked as she handed a glass of water to Ian. That was unusual; normally Jen insisted that any guests stay for a meal. She'd given the Reverend too much wiggle room to get out of it, which he took.

"I appreciate the offer, ma'am, but the sun's getting low. I need to get home before curfew," he replied, packing up his equipment.

"I'll see you out, Doc," Riley said before Sergio could open his mouth. He glared at them, which they ignored as they escorted the Reverend to the door.

"You've got a good family, Nurse Riley," the Reverend said as he shouldered his backpack.

"Yeah, I'm pretty lucky. And I'd like to keep them all around," Riley replied, crossing their arms.

"Well, then, I'll see you bright and early tomorrow morning," the Reverend replied. "And when we're done, I'll come back with you to give Ian his next dose."

"What, you don't trust me to carry one pill? What do you think I'll do? Split it in half? I'm not an idiot, Doc."

"No, you're not," he said, lowering his voice. "I just want to check up on my patient. That's all."

"He's my patient!"

"Look, you're helping treat my family. I'll help treat yours in exchange," he replied. "Unless you really don't need the second opinion? I saw how much your hands shook when you took off the bandage and how steady you were when you put a new one on."

Their hands had been shaking?

"You're scared. You've got every right to be," the Reverend went on. "At the very least I can put your mind at ease a bit." He opened the door and stepped out into the hallway. "Soon as you can after reveille. Good night, Nurse."

"Good night, Doc."

The Reverend turned and walked down the hallway, humming to himself. Riley let the door fall closed behind him before stepping forward to lock it.

Their hands hadn't been shaking, and he knew it. He just wanted an excuse to come back. And Riley couldn't figure out why.

CHAPTER SEVEN

The next morning, right after reveille, Riley and Sergio retrieved their backpacks from behind a warped, rusted dumpster. Riley had the medical kit, while Sergio had combined his and Riley's survival bags into one kit that he slung onto his back. The family argument last night still rang in Riley's head. They'd explained the situation to Jen and Ian, and both of them agreed the arrangement was slightly unfair, but they were much more sympathetic to the Reverend's desperation than Sergio had been. Jen still wanted the Reverend to hand over the entire pill bottle.

"Then what reason would Riley have to go back?" Ian had asked.

"To pay off the debt!" Jen had replied.

"What reason would he have to trust that they'd actually follow through?"

"Well, what if he can't come back and give you the medication? What then?"

"He seems like a smart guy. He'd figure something out."

Riley wasn't surprised that Ian was on the Reverend's side, even though his life was on the line. He'd always thought the best of people, leading to mixed consequences. Riley hoped this would be one of the better times.

Sergio grabbed Riley's hand and pulled them into the street. Loud, methodical bootsteps crunched past the two of them, and Riley stared down at the soldier's feet. Every combat boot that passed was black and shiny as if it had been dunked in pen ink. Not a scuff or fleck of dirt could be seen. They didn't look up until the boots were gone.

"Have you noticed more soldiers are out today?" Sergio said.

Glancing around, Riley saw another squadron of soldiers on the sidewalk across the street, marching the other way.

"We've been here for what, three days? We don't know what's normal and what's not yet," Riley replied. "Come on, honey. We've got to get to the Meeting Space."

The rest of the trip was silent as Riley led Sergio back to the checkpoint between Echo and Foxtrot. Nobody was there except for the soldier, who came out of the concrete box as Riley and Sergio approached. Damn it, he probably wanted to search the backpacks. Riley scrambled for an explanation for what was in the medical kit, but they couldn't find one.

Damn it, damn it, damn it!

The soldier stepped up, a few inches taller than Sergio, so he towered over Riley. He had a bright red scar that slashed from his cheekbone down the right side of his mouth before ending on his chin. The wound had clearly been cauterized, not stitched or bandaged. Riley wondered if the soldier had cauterized it himself.

"Good morning, sir," Sergio said in a forced casual tone.

"IDs," the scarfaced soldier replied. The last inch of his lips on the right side of his face remained frozen and oddly smooth. Definitely cauterized, Riley couldn't see any stitch scars.

Riley had already pulled their ID out of their pocket and handed it over to Scarface. He scrutinized Sergio's ID first, squinting at the photo before looking back up at Sergio.

"You sure you weren't picked at reveille this morning?" he asked.

"No, sir, I was not."

"You sure? You're a lot healthier than most people I've been seein'."

What the hell were these questions? They all but grabbed your arm and dragged you into the truck if you were selected. There was no way you could get away.

"No, sir. They didn't pick me. Otherwise I'd be there instead of here."

Scarface narrowed his eyes, and Riley's heart lurched into their throat.

"You'd do well to keep that sassy tongue of yours in check," Scarface growled. "Otherwise someone might try to tear it out."

It felt like the bravado of a power trip, at least, Riley really hoped it was. But they weren't entirely sure that Scarface wouldn't follow through on his threat. Or face consequences if he did so.

Sergio swallowed back whatever he was going to say and looked down at the ground. Riley stepped closer, pressing their arm against his, hoping it was somewhat comforting. Scarface slid Sergio's ID under Riley's, squinting at the photo before looking back up at them. He stared at them for a good long minute, but Riley couldn't tell if he was trying to come up with something to ask them, or if he was just trying to intimidate them. Either way, Riley refused to break his gaze now. Not after he'd threatened Sergio.

"I'll have to run these," Scarface said, keeping his eyes on Riley's for as long as he could as he turned away and headed for the checkpoint building.

Riley let out a breath they didn't know they'd been holding as the soldier headed into the concrete box and picked up a black, corded telephone hanging on the wall. If he was focused so much on the IDs, maybe he wouldn't ask about what was in the backpacks.

"That cut wasn't treated correctly," Sergio said. "Even I can tell that."

"No, it definitely was not," Riley replied.

"Guess I assumed all of the soldiers got good medical care from the Command."

So had Riley. Lower-ranked soldiers must be part of the tier system too. Riley didn't know why they'd assumed soldiers wouldn't be subjected to it.

Scarface slammed the phone back onto its hook and slid the two IDs out from underneath the glass window. One of the IDs fell on the road.

"Be back before curfew," he said.

Sergio grabbed the ID off of the window and glanced at it before handing it to Riley. When he straightened back up, rubbing the dirt off his own ID, Scarface flicked the switch to allow the gate to raise. Riley could feel Scarface's eyes on their back as they and Sergio walked through.

The street hangouts that had been going yesterday had turned into what Riley guessed was a black market. The tool rental stall was back, staffed by the same teenage boys as yesterday. Another stall was just a wooden board laid between two stacks of chipped concrete bricks with piles of rags on it in various states of filth. An older woman sat on a crate next to it, clutching a wooden walking stick as she eyed a group of children playing catch a few feet away.

Another stall a few feet down the road had rigged up a signboard to hang on the wall of a warehouse above a wooden table that reminded Riley of tables from their elementary school. A variety of dishes were set out, some with chips and cracks in them. The man standing behind the table was talking with a woman who had a small pink bowl in her hands.

The man's voice drifted to Riley's ears as they and Sergio walked by. "...all right, I'll take the bowl in exchange for the cup set, if you can look after the kids the next time the wife and I both get picked up at reveille."

The woman seemed to agree, but a shout from across the street blocked out her words. Riley turned to see two older teenage boys squaring up. A group of kids and teenagers crowded around them. The steps of the trailer behind them had a variety of plastic buckets on it, with a sign propped up on the bottom step that said "Carry water for 5¢." A few men from farther down the street were running toward the gathering crowd.

"Take it it's the building with the black cross on it?"

Riley looked over to see Sergio pointing down the alley next to the trailer at the Meeting Space. Nodding, they led the way toward the building, skirting the crowd and ducking between the trailers. They managed to make it to the other side without getting pulled into the gathering mayhem.

"Hey! Riley Jay!"

Riley turned to see Sam jogging down the ramp from his trailer, Deborah on his hip. Even from this distance, Riley could tell that she was much perkier, looking around instead of keeping her head on her dad's shoulder.

"Morning, Sam!" Riley said as he walked up beside them, trying to ignore the shouts coming from the other street.

"Mornin'! Who's your friend here?"

"This is my partner Sergio. Sergio, this is Sam and Deborah."

"Hey Sergio, nice to meet you, man."

Sergio grinned as they shook hands. "Good to meet you too."

"How's Deborah doing?" Riley asked, waving at the baby. She smiled a little, hiding her face in her dad's neck. Riley had never been more relieved to see a baby smile.

"Well the Reverend got her started on the amoxicillin last night, still fussed most of the night but seems to be a lot better this mornin'."

"Can I check her rash?" Riley asked. Sam nodded, so Riley stepped forward and carefully pulled up the back of Deborah's shirt. They had to squint to make out the rash, the redness had definitely started going down overnight. And unlike yesterday, Deborah protested and tried to swat at Riley's hand.

"Sorry, little Debbie," Riley said, putting her shirt back down quickly. "She's definitely going to be fine. Just keep going with the amoxicillin and I'll check on her in a week unless anything comes up earlier, in which case let me know."

"I definitely will. And speakin' of medicine, I've got your radio ready to go. I'm lookin' after Debbie this mornin' while Yvonne gets some blood samples from patients, but I'll swing by this afternoon before curfew and get it set up for y'all."

Riley could hear footsteps coming up behind them, and by the way Sergio tensed, he could hear it too. But instead of looking around he just said, "Radio?"

"It's a little 'welcome to Jericho' gift," the Reverend said as he stepped up behind them. Deborah looked up and reached for him, and he took her from Sam. "We use the ham radio to communicate in the medical network, and the shopkeepers use it to facilitate the delivery of goods and such. Then we have a normal broadcast radio where Sam serves as a mighty fine DJ in the evenings, which I think is why most people want one nowadays."

"Aw, I do okay," Sam said with a sheepish grin. "Think I finally got it set up so I can play the piano live instead of having to rely on CDs and vinyls."

"Wonderful!" the Reverend said, bouncing Deborah on his hip. "Well the sooner you can get the radio to the Foxtrot hotel, the better."

"I'll get it over just soon as Yvonne's back to look after the baby," Sam said. "Don't really wanna take her out when she's sick, especially when it's gettin' hot out."

"She's looking better this morning, at least," the Reverend said, handing Deborah back to Sam and turning to Riley. "You ready to head out?"

"Uh, I still need that stethoscope and BP cuff-"

"Right, right, I've got them right here." The Reverend swung his backpack off his shoulder and balanced it on his knee as he unzipped it. Pulling out a black stethoscope wrapped in a gray blood pressure cuff, he handed it over to Riley. Both were in better condition than they expected.

A sharp, repetitive beep emanated from the trailer. "Might be Yvonne calling in," Sam said. "Good to see you Raf, Riley Jay, and good to meet you Sergio."

"You too," Sergio replied. The Reverend nodded as Sam hurried inside the trailer, and then he turned to Riley and Sergio.

"Let's get going. I promised the Kader family we'd visit them before noon, and Charlie district's a ways away."

Plodding along behind the Reverend, Riley was surprised to learn that they were going to be leaving Echo. "I thought all of your patients were in Echo or Foxtrot district," they said.

"There's seven districts and only Alpha and Bravo don't have civilians in them," the Reverend said. "Alpha's got all of the Command's VIPs, generals and officers and such. With how much we're able to skim from them without them noticing, they've got medical treatment out the wazoo. They don't need us. I've thought about trying to get into Bravo to treat some of those soldiers, though. Seems like Command restricts their medical care too although I can't figure out why. They've certainly got the resources for it."

Riley thought of Scarface at the checkpoint. They felt a little sorrier for him, until they remembered his threat to tear out Sergio's tongue.

"What about the other districts? How many patients do you have in them?" Riley asked.

The Reverend shrugged, "Quite a few in each of them. Fortunately I have volunteers in each district, former EMTs and medical assistants and the like. People that survived the Revolution purges and weren't important enough for Command to press into service. The district volunteers serve as contact points. Word of mouth is a powerful thing; soon as someone comes down with something, they'll hear real quick from their neighbors that it isn't a good idea to register for medical care, especially if they're struggling to get by on the rations they have. Somebody'll let the district contact know, and they'll pay the person a visit. Then they'll radio me; most of the time they're able to handle it and I just have to send a runner with medication and supplies. Other times I have to make the trek myself. If they're bad enough, I might bring them back here to the Meeting Space to keep an eye on them—Yvonne helps me out with that when I have to make calls."

Riley thought about offering up the pickup truck to help deliver supplies and transport people, but something about the way Sergio still looked at the Reverend told them he wouldn't agree to it. Plus almost nobody drove in the roads unless you were a Command soldier driving a transport or Jeep, as far as Riley could tell.

"I thought you said most families here have radios," Riley said.

"Not right away, of course, we need to make sure we can trust them," the Reverend replied. "Most of the time we wait a month or so to see how they settle in. If someone proves themselves trustworthy, Sam hooks them up. Otherwise we limit contact, keep our distance unless there's serious trouble."

"Why're you trusting us so fast, then?"

The Reverend didn't reply. The fight a few streets away died down, leaving a thick silence behind. Riley already had a good idea of what the Reverend's answer would be, though. Desperation.

"What district are we heading to again?" Sergio asked.

"Charlie, but we'll have to go through Delta to get there," the Reverend replied. "Got a call last night from Hasan that his son Kamal is sick. He thinks it's chicken pox. And there's a couple of other families with kids I want Riley to take a look at."

"How old is Kamal?" Riley asked.

"Just turned three, he was born a few months after the Collapse. The hospital he was born at had already run out of the chicken pox vaccine so he never got it. I'd been searching for some for him and Deborah and the other babies, but most of the vaccines are gone or expired now..."

There wouldn't be much Riley could do past an actual diagnosis and treating for symptoms, but it would be something.

"Did you tell them to keep him inside and away from other children?" they asked.

"They started isolating him the minute he started getting sick."

Good, hopefully there wouldn't be an outbreak then.

The three of them came up to the checkpoint, and Riley held their breath. But the soldier merely glanced at the ID cards before waving the group through. It was getting close to noon, so he must be ready to go off-shift. Ducking under the bar as it rose up, Riley walked a few steps before realizing the Reverend and Sergio had veered to the right. They jogged to catch up, and Sergio reached back to take Riley's hand.

Delta district looked a lot like Echo, with similar black market stands and people milling about in the streets, but it felt less crowded. There were also a lot more buildings with two or three stories although the upper floors were dark. For good reason too, they were starting to crumble. Riley was a little afraid that a chunk of concrete might come down on their head any moment. But that didn't stop them from slowing down in front of one stall that seemed to be selling gauze and medical tape.

The Reverend grabbed their shoulder and shoved them forward. "Made a mistake and trusted some people with supplies that should not have been trusted," he said in a low voice. "We need to move fast. This entire district is under the control of a… less-than-savory character. Besides, I want to get through the Delta-Charlie checkpoint before the guard changes."

The Reverend and Riley caught back up with Sergio, who put his arm around Riley's shoulders as the three hurried on. Riley kept their eyes on the dirty asphalt as the group wove through the narrow streets to the checkpoint. Sergio nudged Riley and pointed out the soldier only a few yards away marching toward the checkpoint. The soldier at the checkpoint noticed too, and he barely glanced at the three IDs that had been passed to him before handing them back and waving them through.

"That was lucky," the Reverend said, glancing back at the checkpoint as the two soldiers traded places. "Dealing with a soldier new to his shift can ruin your entire day."

Riley would bet money that Charlie district had been a residential area before the Collapse, given all of the town-houses and duplexes squished up against each other. However it still had black-market stalls up, people milling about, and children running around in the streets.

"The two days after a district raid are the best market days," the Reverend said. "Smallest chance of another raid."

"What about all the soldiers patrolling around?" Riley asked, thinking back to the squadron of soldiers they'd seen in Foxtrot.

"Have you seen any soldiers here? Or in Echo?"

"We just got here. I hadn't noticed anything."

"That's fair. Point is, they're short on manpower, so they only patrol Golf and Foxtrot districts on a regular basis," the Reverend said. "They rely on the threat of random raids on Charlie, Delta, and Echo to keep order."

"Why Golf and Foxtrot?" Sergio asked.

The Reverend shrugged. "We've tried to figure it out, but like most things with Command, we can't. There's really no difference as far as we can tell, besides the type of buildings. Probably just drew the short straws."

That had to be it. Riley couldn't see much of a difference between Foxtrot and all of the other districts they'd been to so far, besides the fact that Foxtrot might have a slightly smaller population. Maybe.

"The house should be right up here," the Reverend said, stepping over a pile of broken wood pieces. "The family had to move a few months ago, the last home got flooded out in a rainstorm… ah, here it is!"

They'd arrived at a small, run-down duplex with tarps covering windows and shingles missing from the roof. The exterior was spotless however, with a three-foot clean perimeter around the building as if the ash and trash scattered about was scared to come any closer. The Reverend stepped up to the duplex closest to them and knocked on the door.

"Hasan? Nabila? It's Rafael. I've brought the friend I was telling you about."

The door opened and a teenage girl with dark, tanned skin and bright brown eyes peeked her head out as she adjusted her sky blue hijab.

"Reverend!" she said, pulling the door fully open and stepping aside. "Dad told me you were coming. He and Rami got work today, and Mom went to help the Lowerys with their stall since Mr. Lowery also got work."

"Oh, good, the Lowerys have been hurting for cash for a while," the Reverend said, taking the lead inside. "Aisha, this is Riley Jay and their partner, Sergio. Riley, Sergio, this is Aisha."

"Nice to meet you," Aisha said, nodding to them as they all stepped inside. "Kamal's down for a nap. Normally he's up by this point but he's been sleeping longer than usual."

"He's not waking up and fussing?" Riley asked.

"No, but it takes a while to get him to fall asleep."

Riley frowned as they followed her down the hallway toward the bedrooms. It was pretty small, so Riley turned back to Sergio and gestured toward the living room to tell him to stay there. He nodded and stepped back as Riley and the Reverend followed Aisha into the bedroom. Before Riley could step inside the Reverend stopped them with a hand on their shoulder.

"I want to see how you work on your own if I'm going to trust you with my patients," he said. "Just let me know if you don't have anything you need in your medical kit."

Riley nodded, trying to swallow the stress ball in their throat as they ducked past the Reverend and into the room. A king-sized bed was in the middle of the room, with a small toddler with feathery black hair and the same skin tone as his older sister lying on it. He was curled up on his side, his eyes squeezed shut, with one small fist tucked under his chin. A beige blanket lay on the bed a few feet away, leaving Kamal shivering.

"He was just kicking off the blanket earlier!" Aisha said as Riley knelt beside the bed.

"Hey there Kamal," they said. "My name's Riley. I'm going to give you a quick checkup. Okay? I heard from your sister that you don't feel that well."

He opened his eyes and immediately began to whine while looking around the room. Aisha pushed past the Reverend to the other side of the bed. She said something soothing in a language Riley didn't recognize as she pushed the hair out of Kamal's eyes and wiped the boogers away with a scrap of cloth. Riley squinted in the dim light at Kamal's hairline, realizing there were small bumps. Kamal whined loudly, pulling away from his sister.

"Aisha, is there any way you could roll up the tarp and get more light in here?" Riley asked.

"Of course," Aisha said, hurrying to the window. She pulled on a strand of twine and the tarp rolled up, letting soft sunbeams stream in. Now it was a lot easier to see the red blotches that spread down Kamal's face and onto his neck. He fussed, turning away from the sunlight. Aisha immediately put the tarp back down.

"Where did you first notice the rash?" Riley asked.

"In his hair, why?"

Riley looked back at the Reverend, who was standing in the door watching everything. He closed his eyes and shook his head. They both knew what that meant, especially since it was a rash and not individual spots.

"Hey, Kamal, can you stick your tongue out? Like this!" Riley opened their mouth and stuck their tongue out toward their chin, wiggling it to try and get him to laugh. He didn't. But he did slowly poke his tongue out and open his mouth a bit. Grabbing the penlight, Riley pointed it in his mouth. And just as they expected, small, blue-tinged white spots dotted the insides of his cheeks.

"Ok great job, buddy! You can put your tongue back now." Riley slurped their tongue back inside their mouth in one last attempt to get him to laugh. They did get a small smile as he put his tongue away and hid his face in the pillow.

"Koplik's spots," they called to the Reverend as they unzipped their backpack to see if they had any vitamin A.

"What does that mean?" Aisha asked, heading back to the Reverend. "Is it serious?"

Riley looked up to see the Reverend putting a comforting hand on Aisha's shoulder. "It means he has measles. It's one of the telltale signs," he explained softly. "It is pretty serious, but fortunately we have access to all of the things we need to treat it."

Riley managed to find the last bottle of vitamin A, half-full, and pulled it out alongside the Ziplock bag of toys they kept in their own compartment. They'd started collecting toys shortly after the Collapse, meaning to give them to patients. Of course, that was before Revolution started killing doctors and nurses, but by that point it was force of habit.

Selecting a fairly chunky toy truck, they put the rest of the toys away and zipped up their backpack before slinging it to their back.

"Hey, Kamal. Do you like trucks?"

His eyes shot open. Riley held the fiery red truck out to him, and he eagerly took it, rolling onto his back to hold it up in the air.

"Kamal, what do you say?" Aisha scolded.

The "thank you" that came out of his mouth was raspy, and he coughed as soon as he was done talking. Riley's heart ached. He was such a sweet kid. For some reason the sick kids were always the hardest for Riley to take care of. At least with children who'd been abused there was a person, a system Riley could direct their anger at. It was really hard to be angry at something you couldn't see.

Patting Kamal's shoulder, Riley nodded for the Reverend and Aisha to step back into the hallway. When they got to the door, they turned to see Kamal asleep, one chubby little fist holding the truck. Riley smiled in relief as they closed the door as quietly as they could.

"I'll run you through treatments in the living room," Riley said, leading the way back down the short hallway. Sergio was standing by the door, shifting from foot to foot and glancing out the window once in a while.

Riley turned to Aisha. "The most important thing for you to do is to keep his fever down, keep him quiet, and keep fluids in him. Whatever he's willing to drink and whatever you can get, give it to him. Reverend, do you have kid's Tylenol?"

"We have some," Aisha interrupted. "From the last time he had a fever."

"Great. One teaspoon every four to six hours, but don't give it more than five times in a twenty-four-hour period. Also, here are some vitamin A tablets; break them up into whatever food you can and make sure he eats it. It'll help. Five tablets a day for the next week, doesn't all have to be at the same time."

"We're working on getting Riley hooked up to the radio network; we'll broadcast out their call sign tonight once Sam's done installing their radio," the Reverend said. "Then you can call in case anything changes."

Aisha nodded. "Thank you, Reverend, Riley Jay. I'll let you know if anything does change."

"He's going to be fine, Aisha," Riley said. "He's doing all right, and people were surviving measles long before we had a vaccine."

Aisha nodded again, but Riley could tell there was no comforting her. She kept glancing back down the hallway toward where Kamal was sleeping, and her foot hadn't stopped tapping since the second they'd gotten into the living room.

"We need to head out," the Reverend said. "Good to see you, Aisha, even under these circumstances. You know where to find me if you need anything."

"Good to see you too, Reverend."

Aisha saw them out the door, but as soon as the door had closed, Riley could hear her hurrying back to Kamal.

"She's a good sister," the Reverend said, "and you're a good nurse. How did you know what measles looked like, though?"

"I treated two babies who had it," Riley replied. Sergio took their hand and squeezed it.

"We need to get moving," the Reverend said, looking away toward the center of Jericho. "I want you to see a few more patients."

The rest of the morning was a blur as Riley followed the Reverend from townhouses to trailers, all in varying states of cleanliness and with varying amounts of bullet holes in the sides. The only thing Riley clearly remembered was the Revered taking back a sling he'd loaned to a man who'd strained his shoulder working a shift in the factory. No one talked very much except with the patients and the patients' parents, and the Reverend and Riley would debrief after every house. Sergio found himself a job taking notes of what each patient had been diagnosed with and medications they'd been given.

"Thanks for keeping track of that," the Reverend said as they headed back to the Meeting Space. "Normally I just try to remember it all and then write it down when I get back."

"You need a better system," Riley said as the three approached the checkpoint. The soldier waved them through without even glancing at their IDs. Riley followed the Reverend through, their stomach twisting. This was new. What if the soldier shot at them for not showing ID?

The Reverend glanced back at the checkpoint, biting the inside of his cheek. "Yeah, I do need something better, especially since I'll be keeping track of your patients as well as mine," he said. "I've been trying to keep medical records as best I can, but I don't have the time to organize them, especially when it's all in code. Actually…do you think Ian would want to help out with organizing the files? Or Jen?"

Riley glanced over at Sergio, who was shaking his head. "You'd have to ask," Riley said, turning to face the Reverend's back again.

"Think I will. Speaking of which, how's Ian doing? Did he sleep okay last night?"

"Yeah, the ibuprofen and antibiotics are helping a lot," Riley replied. "Definitely better then when we only had elderflower to treat Sergio's fever back in Philippi."

"Hey, don't knock it. It worked!" Sergio said.

The group walked up to the Meeting Space, where Sam was leaning against the doorframe talking to a thin, sunburned man with a faded black baseball cap, sitting on the bottom of the two steps that led up to the door.

"Afternoon Sam, Thomas," the Reverend said, stopping on the sidewalk. "What's going on?"

"Just tryin' to pass the time," Sam said, grinning at Riley and Sergio. "How's everyone doin'?"

"Just holding on and doing the best they can, same as usual," the Reverend replied. "How're you doing, Thomas?"

Thomas shrugged, uncrossing his arms and legs and pushing himself to his feet. "I'm doing all right, I guess," he said. "I've got to get going, Ev's going to be expecting me for dinner soon."

"Good to see you, Thomas," the Revered said as the man trundled off down the road, his hands in his pockets. The four of them watched him go, and then the Reverend turned back to Sam.

"He trying to break in?" the Reverend asked Sam in a low voice.

"Sure was," Sam replied. "Lookin' for anythin' to keep him runnin' I expect."

The Reverend sighed and shook his head. "Who lives up in that area again? Shaun and Tamika?"

"Yeah, they're two doors down. I'll have them check in on the family; they've taken in Evelyn and the kids before when he's gettin' dopesick. And Harry's stayed with him before. I'll give him a call too."

"Let me know if Harry's going to need help. I can at least get him Thomas's records so he knows the history."

"Sounds good, sounds good," Sam replied. "Hey, can we talk inside for a bit? Was about to head out to Foxtrot and I have a feelin' y'all can help me with somethin'."

He threw his duffle bag across his back as the Reverend let them in to the Meeting Space. Sam headed for one of the dimly lit corners, far away from any windows. He set the duffle bag down on the ground and unzipped it to reveal the parts for what Riley was sure was a ham radio.

"I've got it partially assembled, so it should only take me 'bout an hour to get it finished," Sam said. "How much can you fit in your bags?"

It took some finagling, but the four managed to fit the radio pieces under bandages, medical equipment, clothes, and food rations. Sam borrowed bits from each of their bags to fill out his duffel bag.

"All right, shall we go two at a time?" the Reverend said.

"Makes the most sense. It's the least suspicious, 'specially with four backpacks" Sam said. "How 'bout I take Riley Jay on ahead so they can guide me, and you and Sergio come on in 'bout fifteen minutes?"

"Wouldn't it be suspicious if Riley and I went back through the checkpoint without each other and instead with new people?" Sergio asked.

"It's a new dude. Guard changes at six," Sam replied. "It'll be less suspicious if you two split up since you live in Foxtrot and we're in Echo."

As much as Riley didn't like it, it made sense. So with a glance at Sergio, they nodded their consent.

"All right, let's hit the road then! See you soon, Raf, Sergio."

Sergio pulled Riley in for a quick kiss while the Reverend clapped Sam on the back as everyone headed for the door. The Reverend pulled it open to let Sam and Riley out, but he stopped Riley with a gentle hand on their shoulder before they could follow Sam.

"Here." He handed over the sling he'd gotten earlier. "See if you can fit this to Ian. I'll give him a full checkup when I get there. Stay safe."

"Thanks. You too."

Sam was waiting in the street, and he waved behind them to the Reverend and Sergio as the two set off down the road.

"So how long you and Sergio been together?" he asked.

"Over two years we think," Riley replied. "Met on the road a few months after the Collapse. What about you and Yvonne?"

"Oh, we met at one of my shows through a mutual friend," Sam said, his grin becoming much softer and somewhat shy. "Eloped a year later since her parents weren't thrilled 'bout me. Then Deborah came along right before the Collapse."

Riley couldn't imagine having a baby as the world was falling apart around them. "Were you from Jericho... or whatever this place was called?"

"No, we're from farther out east," Sam replied. "Heard rumors that the west wasn' hard hit. Turns out it was only that—rumors."

"We heard them too," Riley said. "Well, I heard it from Sergio. We were trying to get out west when a Revolution caravan picked us up."

"Sweet Jesus. We were in one of those. That's how we got here."

"Which was before the Reverend, right?"

Sam nodded, "He wasn't with a caravan. Patrollin' Revolution squad picked him up all on his lonesome and dragged him in. Interrogated him for a day then dumped him on the street in front of our trailer. We took him in. Told us he was a pastor at first, but when Yvonne came down with the flu he told us the truth pretty quickly. That's when he started treatin' everyone on the down low, takin' any payment they could give, even if all they could give was a smile."

"Huh," Riley said as they watched a mother herd four kids into a warehouse across the street. A low rumbling that shook the ground heralded the arrival of a Command transport vehicle. Riley stepped back as it crawled by, making sure not to run into Sam.

"You get used to it," Sam said, watching the transport as it turned a corner. "So, I'm guessin' you agreed to work for Raf in exchange for somethin'?"

Riley nodded, mentally steeling themself to keep their voice even. "Antibiotics. My brother got shot on the road and the wound got infected. Reverend gives me a pill every day I work, and I need thirty pills to make sure the infection goes away and stays away."

"Sounds about right," Sam said. "'Specially since you've got a skill set he desperately needs. He's not good with kids."

"Deborah seems to like him," Riley said.

"Oh, sorry, should've said he's not good with diagnosin' and treatin' kids," Sam said. "He gets along with them just fine. Yeah, it don't surprise me he drove a hard bargain once he found out who you were. Especially since there was a little girl, Lily, who passed away 'bout a month ago. Raf couldn't figure out what was goin' on for the life of him, and he took it hard when she didn' make it."

And then Deborah had gotten sick, and the Reverend hadn't been able to figure out what was going on with her, and then Riley had come along...

Riley was starting to have more sympathy for the Reverend, and they didn't like it. The question that had been poking around in the back of their mind came bursting forward, refusing to be ignored any longer.

Would Riley have done any different if they'd been in the Reverend's situation?

"Eyes up, Riley Jay. Here comes the checkpoint."

The soldier was walking toward them, his gun in his hands. "IDs."

Riley and Sam pulled them out of their pockets and handed them over. They remained silent as the soldier walked back to the shack, but as soon as he was inside Sam starting humming under his breath. Riley didn't recognize this song either, but it had a soothing melody. They were disappointed when he stopped as the soldier came back.

"Unzip your backpacks."

Riley froze. Sam nudged them with a small nod. They took it as a sign that it would be okay. Standing on one foot and balancing the bag on their thigh, Riley could feel the radio parts pressing against them. They could feel their heartbeat speed up as they fumbled to unzip the main pocket of the backpack. The soldier stuck his nose in and prodded at the contents with a wooden stick. Riley tried to keep breathing normally. They glanced over at Sam who at first looked unfazed, but Riley could see his Adam's apple bob as he swallowed while watching the soldier.

After a long minute, the soldier stopped snooping around in Riley's backpack and moved on to Sam's duffel bag. Sam had set it on the ground and unzipped it, standing above it with his hands in the pockets of his jeans. The soldier gritted his teeth as he bent down and began poking around in the duffel bag, but he quickly straightened up, pressing his hand to his lower back. Riley had to hide their smile.

"You're good. You can go," he said, handing back over their IDs. "Be sure you're home before curfew."

"Thank you, sir," Sam said, winking at Riley. Neither one bothered to zip up the backpacks before hurrying through the checkpoint

"Their belts make it hard for them to bend down, and the heat means they can't kneel on the road," Sam muttered as the two stashed IDs and zipped up backpacks. "So if you put your stuff on the ground for them to look at—"

"—they won't look as hard."

"Exactly," Sam said. "Now, where's this hotel of yours?"

CHAPTER EIGHT

Riley rapped three times on the door, leaning against the doorframe of their hotel apartment.

"Y'all got a nice place," Sam said, looking down the hallway.

"Yeah, we got lucky," Riley replied as the door opened to reveal a wide-eyed, frowning Jen.

"Well you're home early. I figured you'd be skirting curfew trying to see all your new patients," she said. "Who's your new friend?"

"Sam Lakewood, ma'am," Sam replied, setting his bag down and holding out his hand. "I'm a friend of Raf's—I mean, the Reverend. I'm here to set up some equipment Riley here's gonna need to help him out. Plus, I think it'll provide some much-needed entertainment."

Jen shook his hand, smiling at him. "Well, anything to break the boredom! I'm Jennifer Smith, but you can call me Jen. Come on in. Please pardon the mess. We're still trying to get everything arranged."

She stepped back to let Sam in, but before Riley could follow, Jen grabbed their upper arm. "Where's Sergio?" she whispered.

"Coming with the Reverend right behind us," Riley replied. "We split up so that if one pair got detained, Sam would only lose half the radio parts."

"Radio?" Jen's eyes were wide with excitement.

"Radio."

A slow smile spread across her face. "Lord, I didn't even think it was still around!"

The apartment somehow felt warmer, lighter when Riley walked in. Sam was standing over Ian, holding his hand in a handshake.

"You seem to be doin' a lot better," Sam said. "'Least compared to how Raf was describin' you yesterday."

"Yeah, yeah, I'm feeling better," Ian replied with a small smile. "So, what're you here to do?"

"I'm here to build a radio," Sam replied, heading back over to where he'd set his bag down next to the desk.

"A radio?" Ian said, sitting up a little straighter. "For us to listen to music and such?"

"Somethin' like that, but good luck gettin' any good stations," Sam replied with a chuckle. "Mainly, this is so people can talk with y'all, 'specially so families can get in touch with Riley."

Jen had come over at this point, her hands on her hips. "I hope you're not planning on making more of a mess in my living room."

Sam laughed, shaking his head. "Oh no, ma'am, I promise, I'll leave everythin' just as clean as it was when I came in."

"Well, in that case, let me know if I can help. I may not know much about radios, but I know how to hold things and hand them to people."

"You're my favorite assistant already!"

Riley turned away, pressing their hand to their mouth to hold back a chuckle, but they nearly lost it when Ian caught their eye with a repressed smile on his face.

"When'd you say Rafael and Sergio were going to get here?" Ian asked as Riley walked over to stand next to him.

“Should be ’bout fifteen minutes behind us,” Sam replied before Riley could open their mouth. “Riley, do you happen to have the resistor?”

“The what?”

Sam laughed, which caused them all to laugh along with him. “All righ’, let my favorite assistant help me. You got a patient to treat.”

Riley gladly handed their bag over to Jen, pulling out the sling and materials they needed to clean the stitches. “Does this mean I’m your second favorite assistant?”

“No, it means you’re my favorite nurse!”

Riley had to laugh as they turned back to Ian. Ian was grinning now, shaking his head with a small chuckle.

“How’re you feeling?” Riley asked, pushing back his hair to press the back of their hand to his forehead. He felt a lot cooler than yesterday. Thank goodness.

“Like I told Sam, better than yesterday,” Ian said, reaching up with his uninjured arm to muss up Riley’s hair. He was fully sitting up in bed, dressed in a white button-up shirt. Riley helped him unbutton it so they could take a look at the wound. Same green puss and same red streaks from yesterday, but if Riley squinted, they could swear the lines were starting to recede. Maybe.

“I thought it would look better,” Ian said.

Riley could hear the worry in his voice as they began to clean the wound. “It’s going to take a few days for the antibiotics to fully kick in. I’m just happy it doesn’t look worse.”

They turned when they heard the *snick* of a key in the lock and then Sergio opened the door. “Oh, good, you made it!” Sam said. “One of you has the battery and I need it.”

“Battery?” Jen echoed. “I thought this was going to be an electric radio.”

"It is, the battery's just for when the power gets shut off at night."

The Reverend pulled out the stethoscope and BP cuff from his backpack before handing it over to Sam. Slinging the stethoscope around his neck, the Reverend smiled at Ian. Riley could see the exhaustion in his soft, caring grin. Ian smiled wider than Riley had seen in a while, and Riley felt their shoulders relax at his happiness.

"How're you doing, Ian?" the Reverend asked.

"Better then yesterday, I think," Ian replied. Riley heard the note of annoyance at being asked the question so many times, but they were sure the Reverend couldn't pick up on it.

"Good, that's good to hear. Mind if I take a look at it?"

Ian nodded, and the Reverend gently pushed back his shirt to get a better look at the stitches. "It's looking okay," he said, looking up at Riley. "I'll re-bandage it if you want to get him some water?"

Riley nodded and headed for the kitchenette. Sergio was already there, and he passed them a bottle of water.

"How was the walk over?" Riley asked.

He shrugged, "Didn't talk much. Wanted to know what I did before the Collapse. Told me about Sam's kid."

Riley glanced over their shoulder to see Ian and the Reverend laughing. "Apparently he couldn't figure out what was wrong with a different child a few weeks ago. The child didn't make it."

Sergio shook his head. "Explains why he played hardball with you."

"Yeah."

"He's still playing with Ian's life."

"I know. I don't like it either."

"Hey, Riley! Do you have the water yet?"

Riley tossed the water bottle to the Reverend, who nodded in thanks. Sergio put his arm around Riley's shoulders as they leaned back against the counter, watching the other pairs work. Sam had gotten the radio assembled a lot quicker than Riley thought he would, keeping Jen laughing the entire time with his jokes and stories. The Reverend was re-bandaging Ian's wound and fitting him with the sling, having given him the pill Riley had earned that day alongside more pain medication. The two of them were talking in low voices, and at one point Ian looked up from his sling to give the Reverend a sweet smile that Riley had never seen on his face before.

"Aaaaand done!" Sam said, throwing his hands up in the air. "Think y'all are ready to go!"

"Wonderful!" the Reverend said, helping Ian up from the bed so they could walk over and look at the radio. Riley and Sergio also meandered over, Sergio keeping his arm around their shoulders.

It was an unassuming light brown box, made out of scraps of plywood, but it was emitting static. The right side looked like a normal radio, while on the left was a ham radio with a pair of headphones hanging off of it. Sam was sweeping through the frequencies on the ham radio, holding a radio microphone in his other hand. After a minute he pressed the button to turn on the microphone.

"Thunder, this is Shockwave. Come in, Thunder."

The static crackled and a voice came through loud and clear. "This is Thunder. What's crackin', Shockwave?"

"Just testin' a new setup. Thank you for your assistance."

"No sweat. Signin' off."

Sam hung up the microphone on a hook he'd screwed into the wall and threw up his hands. "Works like a charm! Raf and I'll get y'all your own codenames once we get home.

Raf's got his own system of names for the medical network while I take care of everyone else. We gotta check our books and make sure we're not doublin' up on names."

"It's amazing," Ian breathed, his eyes raking over the radio. "I used to work in radio. Kind of. I was a journalist, did radio spots for my paper's affiliate station. It was always a lot of fun!"

The Reverend took a step back so he could look Ian in the face. "You were a journalist?"

"Yeah i-in the capitol."

Sam and the Reverend stared at Ian. Riley looked over at Jen, who was rubbing her thumb and ring finger raw. Ian had only talked in detail about his time as a journalist pre-Collapse once, when he, Riley, and Sergio had gotten rip-roaring drunk one night. It'd ended with him sobbing in Jen's arms. The next morning he hadn't remembered anything. Riley didn't remember much either, but his cries of pure anguish still echoed in their ears.

"Ian, I might just have a job proposal for you," Sam said. "But we can talk more 'bout it later. Raf and I here have to be gettin' back to Echo. Thank you so much for your help, ma'am, made everythin' go a lot quicker."

"It was my pleasure, Sam," Jen said, shaking Sam's hand. He kissed the back of her hand, and Riley could see the blush on Jen's cheeks. They turned away so nobody would see them smile, but as they did so they caught the Reverend's eye. He was also trying to hide his smile and failing. Riley felt a grin break out over their face.

The Reverend winked at them, grabbing his medical kit. "I'll see you tomorrow, Riley."

"See you tomorrow, Doc."

The Reverend sighed, and this time Riley didn't try to hide their smirk. The rest of the goodbyes were hurried as Sam and the Reverend headed out the door.

"Tune in to 104.1 at eight p.m. to hear my concert!" Sam said as they walked into the hallway.

"We will!" Jen replied as the door closed. The Reverend was waving as Sergio closed the door; Riley waved back before realizing he was looking behind them at Ian.

Just as Sam requested, at 8 p.m. everyone gathered around the radio. Looking around at their family, Riley saw everyone more relaxed and happier than they'd been in a while. Ian was sitting in the metal chair, turning the dial to find the channel. Jen was sitting on the loveseat, resting her chin on her hand, watching Ian. Sergio and Riley were sitting on the edge of the bed, Sergio's arm back around Riley's shoulders. Riley rested their head on his shoulder as smooth jazz rippled into the apartment.

"This is it!" Ian exclaimed, turning to grin at the rest of them.

"It's so clear," Jen said, shaking her head in awe. "Wonder how Sam does it?"

"CD? Vinyl record?" Riley guessed.

"Makes the most sense," Jen replied as the music stopped and Sam's voice rang out over the radio.

"Gooood evening, Jericho! This is Shockwave coming to you live, and that was 'So What' by the man himself, Miles Davis. Now I hope y'all'll allow me to indulge myself for a minute. Been a long time since I was able to play for an audience."

The sounds of the piano were more muddled than the last song had been, but Sam's joyful personality shone through the static. Pure soul music flowed into the blues that swung back into jazz. Sam was singing over the piano, but in the static they couldn't make out the words. It didn't matter; it was music and it was beautiful. Riley's feet were tapping, but they could feel tears threatening to fall out of their eyes.

Sergio nudged them, and they looked up to see that there were tears in his eyes as well. Taking their hand, he pulled them to their feet and put his other hand on their waist. Riley slid their hand onto his shoulder and they began to step-touch.

"Aww, how cute!" Ian said, fluttering his eyelashes while Jen chuckled.

Sergio also laughed, gesturing with his head toward Jen. "Dance with the lady. Will ya?"

"Oh, yeah, of course!" He hopped to his feet and comically bowed in front of Jen. She laughed as she offered him her hand, which he used to help her to her feet.

A kiss on their temple caused Riley to look up at Sergio again. His smile was so relaxed and loving, softer than Riley'd ever seen it. All of his kisses, hugs, and caresses had a tinge of worry behind them, desperation, as if he knew each touch would be their last. This was the first time in Riley's memory that all of that was gone. When they kissed, all Riley could feel was love.

"Ian!"

Riley and Sergio broke apart to see Jen swatting Ian's shoulder. "That is the third time you've stepped on my toes! Riley, can we switch dance partners?"

Riley and Sergio couldn't stop laughing at the sheepish look on Ian's face and the indignant-yet-amused look on

Jen's. Riley was about to quip that they needed their toes for tomorrow when three quick beeps emanated from the radio.

"Someone's calling in," Jen said as Ian slid into the chair and turned down the radio.

"Valerian calling Elderflower, come in Elderflower."

"Sounds like the Reverend," Sergio said. "I'm guessin' you're Elderflower, Ry."

"Guess so," Riley replied. Taking the microphone that Ian offered them and holding onto the back of Ian's chair, they pressed the talk button. "This is Elderflower. Go ahead Valerian."

"Good, you caught on. Shockwave's assigned call signs to everyone else, too. Your partner's Wildfire, your brother is Blizzard, and your mother is Windstorm."

Riley clicked on the mic. "Got it, Valerian. Anything else?"

"Yeah. If Blizzard's up to it, Shockwave would like for him to come with you the day after tomorrow. Something about a project he thinks Blizzard can help with."

Riley looked over at Ian, who shrugged. "Don't have anything else going on. Besides, I'm feeling a lot better."

Sergio rubbed his chin, and Riley heard the scratching from his stubble.

"He's in," Riley said, not meeting Sergio's eye.

"Good to hear. You stay safe tonight. See you tomorrow afternoon. Good night Elderflower, Blizzard, Windstorm, Wildfire."

"You too. Good night."

The ham radio went quiet, and Ian turned back up the radio. Sam was playing slow piano music, speaking over it.

"Y'know, I recently learned about a kinda plant called an elderflower. It's some powerful stuff, reduces inflammation, makes you less tired, real healin' stuff. Well we got some elderflower in a few days ago, and boy is it great for kids! Just fifty-eight grams can cure them of anythin'. Course for adults, we still recommend sixty-two grams of valerian. Should be able to get your hands on it pretty easy. Just like how I'm about to play y'all out for the night. Good night, Jericho, and sweet dreams. You'll hear me back here at the same time tomorrow night. Until then, keep your head up."

The piano music got louder, playing a soothing melody that Riley realized he'd been whistling that morning. They looked over to where Jen and Sergio had sat down on the loveseat, staring up at them.

"Guess you're in business, Nurse Riley," Jen said. "We'd all better get to bed then so we can all get to work tomorrow."

The power shut off. Glancing outside Riley saw that all the other buildings had gone dark. Apparently the nighttime blackout had come early tonight. Fumbling for each other's hands, Sergio led the way to the door and into the other room.

"Good night Ian, Jen!" he called.

"Good night you two!" Jen replied.

Fortunately they'd left out a few candles on the uneven nightstand in their room in case this happened. Riley lit one as Sergio fumbled for the box that had their clothes in it. The room didn't have a bed to go with the nightstand for some reason, so they were sleeping on a mattress on the floor. But they did have a full-sized couch, an armchair, and a coffee table—all faded and all banged up.

"Here," Sergio said, chucking a gray T-shirt at them. Riley barely managed to catch it before it could hit the candle.

"Could you please not set the building on fire?" they said.

"Sorry," Sergio replied, yanking off his T-shirt. "I trusted your reflexes."

Riley exchanged their clothes for the T-shirt Sergio had thrown at them and slid between the sheets. They'd shower in the morning when the power came back on. Sergio changed into a ragged pair of gym shorts and plopped down on the mattress next to Riley.

"What's up with you?" Riley asked.

Sergio's shoulders heaved with a large sigh. "He gave you a code name and told people to contact you," he said. "That don't sound like someone who only wants you to work for him for thirty days."

Riley reached out to rub his back. Sergio flinched as soon as their fingers brushed his skin.

Shit. "Sorry, honey."

"It's all right. "

He turned around and slid under the sheets as well. Propping his head up on his elbow he looked up at them, "You don't have anythin' to say?"

"About what?"

"'Bout the Reverend making you a full-time employee."

Riley sighed. They didn't want to have this conversation. They just wanted to sleep.

"Look of course he wants me to work longer for him," Riley said. "But the deal was thirty days. He's getting thirty days. Sam'll just make another announcement in a month saying I'm out."

"You actually gonna get out, though?"

Riley looked around the room, watching the shadows dance on the walls. "Y-yeah, I'll get out." It didn't feel like a lie, but it didn't feel like the truth either.

"I don't want you to get hurt," Sergio said.

"I know. I don't want you to get hurt either."

Sergio patted their pillow, and Riley slid down to rest their head on it. He pushed their hair out of their eyes and caressed their cheek.

“Do you trust the Reverend?” he asked.

Riley didn’t know how to answer that. It’d only been a few days, but he’d held to his word and had done a good job with treating Ian. And he’d kept them out of trouble so far. And all in all, he seemed like a good man. Maybe a little too closed off, maybe a little too untrusting, but Riley couldn’t fault him for that.

“Baby?”

“Huh?”

“I need to know if you trust him. Otherwise, we’ll pack up right now and I’ll get you out of Jericho. We’ll find somewhere else.”

Riley seriously doubted that they could get out of Jericho. The Command seemed just as likely to let them leave as the Revolution had been. But the determined look on Sergio’s face assured Riley he’d tear down the gates with his bare hands if it meant getting them out. But leaving meant putting Ian in danger without the antibiotics. Unless he was suggesting…

No. Sergio would never abandon Ian and Jen.

“Riley!”

““What?”

“You don’t trust him.”

“It’s only been a few days, Sergio! But he hasn’t led us wrong yet. And he’s held to his word. He hasn’t given me a reason not to trust him.”

“Yet! Do you want to give him the chance to let you down?”

“Do you want Ian to continue to get antibiotics?”

Sergio sighed in frustration. He wrapped his arm around Riley and pulled them closer as they tucked their head under his chin. He pressed a kiss to the top of their head and began rubbing their back.

Riley could feel the desperation in his touch.

The next afternoon Riley found themself torn away from doing inventory with the Reverend and instead setting the leg of a four-year-old boy named Jack. The little boy had screamed at the top of his lungs the entire time, leaving his dad Ben frazzled and heartbroken. Kate, the medical contact for Delta, had escorted Riley and the Reverend there and had led the way out of the house once everything was done.

"Thanks for dropping everything to come help. I've splinted enough bones in my lifetime, but that leg was something else," Kate said as she closed the door to the small townhouse. She'd been an EMT before the Collapse, went by "Peppermint" over the radio, and was the only person the Reverend trusted to provide medical care and distribute medication in Delta. As a tall, heavy-set woman with fierce blue eyes, flyaway gray hair and soft wrinkles, she looked as if she'd either scare the sickness out of you or laugh it away.

"Keep a close eye on it. I'm worried about infection," Riley said as the small group hurried down the steps to the dirt below. "He'll never regain use of that leg, not if it's broken in two places, but I don't want to risk amputation unless we have to."

"I'll check on them every day," Kate said. "Maybe round up a couple of the teens to watch after the kid so Ben can get work."

"Make sure they're trustworthy," the Reverend said, scanning up and down the road. It was mostly empty in the heat of the day with people lounging in open doors or other patches of shade as they kept an eye on their stands.

"Now, Rev, you know I always do," Kate replied, folding her arms. "Everything's been quiet on the whole anyways."

"Mark hasn't been snooping around?" the Reverend asked.

"Not lately, hasn't been harassing the stall owners either."

"Maybe he found a better stream of revenue."

Kate laughed, low and husky, as she walked out to the middle of the street. "Well, I'm going to go check on the Bennetts. See how the dad's doing. Look after yourselves. All right?"

The Reverend and Riley waved as she set off deeper into Delta district.

"Come on, we need to get you home before the sun goes down," the Reverend said, setting off in the opposite direction.

Riley followed him. "You want to just give me the antibiotic for today? That way you don't have to double back right before curfew?"

"No, no, I'll go with you."

Did he really not trust them with just one pill? Riley was about to argue when the Delta-Echo checkpoint came in sight. The soldier guarding it barely glanced at their IDs before waving them through.

"Really, really wish I could store more medical supplies here," the Reverend said as soon as the checkpoint had disappeared behind the horizon. "The soldiers really don't give a shit."

"Why can't you, then?"

"Mark and his cronies. They've got a tight control on Delta, keep taking 'taxes' from stalls in order to 'protect' them, the whole deal. Kate manages to keep them away from her and her stock for the most part, but she's found supplies missing before, so I can't store much more with her."

"That's a shame."

Turning the corner, the Reverend threw out his arm to stop Riley.

"Ow! What..."

"Shh!"

Riley choked as they saw a trailer surrounded by six soldiers with a Humvee sitting on the street right in front of it. A short, burly man and a taller woman were in handcuffs, being held against the car by two other soldiers. The door to the trailer swung open, and a soldier came out with a manila folder tucked under one arm and a black backpack in his other hand.

"Shit!" the Reverend said. He grabbed Riley's arm and yanked them behind a warehouse.

"What? What's going on?" Riley asked, pressing their back against the brick wall. The Reverend did the same. He gritted his teeth as he banged his head back against the wall.

"That's Harry and Brenda's house," the Reverend said. "Harry's looking after Thomas for me while he goes through withdrawal. I gave him a copy of Thomas's medical records, and I'll bet money that the soldier who just came out of the house had the records and Harry's medical kit."

"Th-the records are in code, though, right?"

"Yep."

"A code Harry can break."

"He won't give it up. He's tough. He can take whatever those soldiers can throw at him. Besides, even if he does, Command'll only have that one file."

"Not if Harry says you have the other files. Or if Command raids the Meeting Space."

"I know. I know!" the Reverend hissed. "We've got to move those files. Jen told me you'd take them."

"It's too close to curfew, we wouldn't make it across the checkpoint in time," Riley said. "Besides, if Harry tells the soldiers who you are, we're screwed anyway."

The Reverend shook his head. "He wouldn't do that."

The two jolted when they heard the sound of slamming car doors and the roar of the Humvee's engine. Their throat and chest felt tight as they listened to the engine and the sound of boots on pavement grow softer and softer. Once everything was quiet, the Reverend took off his backpack and pulled the antibiotics out of a side pocket.

"Here, get home, and stay there," he said, pressing a pill into their hand. "Only take calls in Foxtrot, stay out of the other districts. I'll call you if it's safe to come tomorrow."

"What if you can't get the antibiotics to us tomorrow?" Riley asked.

"Then Sam will. I promise, Riley. You'll get what you need. Now go on. I'll call you tomorrow."

CHAPTER NINE

When Riley stumbled back up from reveille the next morning, they found Ian already dressed and sitting at the radio desk. Jen was still in her bed, another mattress on the ground, covering her head with a pillow.

Riley yawned into their hand. "You stayed up. I'm shocked."

"Rafael called. He says it's fine to come to Echo, but there's a sick kid who needs help here first," Ian said. "Kit's apparently got more information and we should check with her."

Riley was shocked. "He's okay? He didn't get picked up?"

"No. Apparently everything was more quiet than usual last night."

This wasn't right. At the very least the Reverend should've been questioned. Maybe Harry had been able to withstand whatever interrogation techniques they'd thrown at him?

"Hey, remember Sam asked me to head to Echo district with you today?" Ian said.

Right. Shit. "Look, Ian, I'm not sure if you should come with me, not after what happened yesterday."

"But nothing happened, and Rafael says it's safe to go to Echo. Come on. I've been cooped up here for days now. I want to get out!"

"Well, that's going to leave Jen alone for the day," Riley said. "Sergio got picked up for work. So if Jen's okay with that..."

"Maybe I'll actually get a decent nap for once," Jen grumbled from under her pillow.

So after Riley cleaned and re-bandaged Ian's wound, thankful that the swelling had gone down and the pus had disappeared, they led the way outside. Ian stared at the squadron of soldiers marching by as they made their way up to the sidewalk.

"That's normal," Riley said, nudging him down the sidewalk. "Just stay out of the way."

Ian stumbled forward like he was pulling his feet out of mud and they set off down the street. He wasn't wearing the sling because Riley didn't want him to be a target because of it. Either people would think he was in with the Command, or a Command soldier would realize he hadn't been to the medical center. So Ian was left holding his arm stiffly against his body, wincing whenever he stepped down too hard.

The two made it to the grocery store without running afoul of any power-happy soldiers. Kit looked up as the bell rang, echoing through the store.

"Hey! Hi Riley!" she called. "Who's your friend?"

"Hey Kit," Riley replied, already exhausted by her way-too-chipper attitude for this early in the morning. "This is Ian. Ian, this is Kit. She runs the store."

"Nice to meet you, Kit!" Ian said, sticking out his hand. Kit reached over the counter and shook it.

"You're looking a lot better than how Riley here described you a few days ago," she said. "What can I do you for? You need more pain meds?"

"Uh, no, the Reverend hooked us up," Riley said. "He wanted me to check in with you about a sick kid?"

Kit's eyes shot wide as she grinned. "Knew it."

"Knew what?"

Kit glanced out the grimy store windows. "That you've got professional medical training. C'mon, what is it? You another doctor to knock the Reverend down a peg?"

"Wha-? N-no, I-I was a pediatric nurse practitioner," Riley replied, glancing around the store to confirm that it was empty.

Kit shrugged, "Just as good. He's not as confident with kids, hence why he's sending you to the Honey family. Mom's Sarah, and she's got two kids, Veronica and Oliver. Oliver spiked a fever yesterday, and Sarah was in here trying to get Tylenol but she didn't have the money. I can't take any from the stock without payment, so I called the Reverend, and he told me he'd send you. Now here you are!"

"Yeah, great. Where's the Honey family live?"

Kit passed over a piece of paper with directions scribbled on it. "Thanks," Riley said, sticking it in their pocket. "We need to go."

Kit stepped back and put up her hands. "Yeah, go. I'm sorry for keeping you for so long. Let me know how the little guy is, huh? He's a real sweetheart."

Riley and Ian jogged to the boy's house. Fortunately it was nearby, fortunately Oliver was almost four years old, and fortunately the fever didn't feel too high. They could breathe a little easier when they left the Honey household with a few cans of mushroom soup as payment.

"So are we going to Echo now?" Ian asked as soon as he stepped onto the sidewalk. Riley sighed and nodded, leading the way east. They could tell Ian was trying not to stare at the buildings as they passed, but he snuck a few too many glances for people not to notice.

Riley felt the rumbling first, the ground shaking beneath their feet. Ian swatted their shoulder, and they looked up at him to see his eyes wide and his jaw open.

"Wh-what the fuck?" he said, his voice strangled.

Riley turned their head to see a massive gray monster of metal and rubber and diesel. The tank screeched as it completed its turn onto the road they were on, knocking a chunk of concrete out of the building on the corner. It stopped for a second, the turret with the long gun barrel attached scanning the road. Riley's stomach flipped as they braced themself for pure hot fire to be shot out of the tank. The turret whined to a halt, the gaping maw of the barrel pointing straight at them and Ian.

"*Run!*" Riley yelled.

Ian grabbed their hand and yanked them up the road.

The few other people in the tank's path scattered. Riley and Ian ran for an alley a few feet ahead and ducked into it alongside another man in a sharp black blazer and horn-rimmed glasses.

"I-Is this normal?" Ian asked as the metallic scraping and clanking grew louder.

"No!" the man replied, pushing his glasses up on his nose.

Riley wondered where he'd managed to get glasses in such good shape as the tank rumbled by. Dust and dirt swirled through the air in its tracks. Riley squeezed their eyes shut, trying not to breathe in the grit hitting their face. The rumbling and screeching faded away, leaving a silence that rang in Riley's ears.

"What the hell was that for?" the man yelled as Riley opened their eyes.

"You all right?" Riley asked, even though he looked in a lot better shape than they were with his blazer, horn-rimmed glasses, and more than a few pounds to spare.

"Do I look all right?" the man snapped. "This is my best blazer, and now it's stained to hell!" He looked Riley and Ian up and down before shaking his head. "Then again, I'm doing all right compared to some people."

Riley could feel the fury rise in their chest as he walked out of the alley and headed toward the direction the tank had come from.

"Interesting person," Ian said as the two of them stepped back out into the street. Riley realized the man was heading right for the Alpha-Foxtrot checkpoint. Unlike the other district checkpoints, this one had a wooden sign saying "Alpha-Foxtrot." Barbed wire surrounded the guard tower, and the gate was a swinging chain-link fence with more barbed wire on top.

"How the hell did he manage to get a blazer and glasses?" Riley asked.

Ian shrugged. "Honestly, I'm not sure I want to know."

"Might have something to do with the fact he's heading into Alpha."

"Y'know, it just might."

"Come on, Echo checkpoint's this way."

The two snaked their way toward the checkpoint, following the painted arrows with "E" splashed in the middle of them. As the two of them turned the corner, Riley froze, and Ian nearly tripped over them.

"What?" he asked.

"Th-that's not normal," Riley replied.

Four soldiers manned the checkpoint. Two were standing in the little concrete shack, and the other two stood in the middle of the road blocking the gate.

"Great. My first day out and nothing is normal," Ian said.

None of the soldiers seemed particularly on edge as one of them checked over Riley's and Ian's IDs. The two were let through fairly easily although Riley could feel one of the soldiers' eyes on their backs as they headed deeper into Echo district. The anxiety simmering in their stomach started to bubble a little more. It rose to a boil when they got further into Echo district and didn't see any of the stalls they expected. People were huddled in small groups on the sidewalks and on the doorsteps of trailers and warehouses. Some nodded in greeting now, maybe with a small wave, but everyone was silent, watching, waiting for something.

What the hell was going on?

"So, where's the Meeting Space?" Ian asked, breaking Riley out of their thoughts. He was keeping his voice low.

"We're almost there," Riley said, stepping closer to him so they didn't have to raise their voice. "And I thought you said you needed to go to Sam's place?"

"Uh, I thought we were going to the Meeting Space first?"

"Wasn't planning on it... but Sam's trailer's right across from the Meeting Space. We can stop in if you want the Reverend to look at your shoulder for some reason."

Riley couldn't keep the tinge of bitterness out of their voice. Did Ian not think they did a good enough job because the stitches had gotten infected? He'd never asked for a second opinion before...well, mainly because they couldn't find anyone to give one...

"Oh! No, no my shoulder feels fine," Ian said. "I just wanted to say hi, y'know?"

Really? I mean, I guess they've been getting along pretty well...

Riley didn't trust themself to do more than shrug and keep going. But when they turned the corner and saw the Meeting Space in the gap between Sam's trailer and his neighbors, they saw Sam sitting on the front steps. The Reverend was leaning against the doorframe, surveying the road, alive and well and not being interrogated. When his eyes landed on the two of them, he broke into a wide grin. Relief swept through Riley, and they couldn't help but return the smile.

"Well, well, well, look who's up and moving around," the Reverend said, hopping around Sam to get to the street. "How're you feeling, Ian?"

"Feeling p-pretty good!" Ian replied, grinning up at the Reverend as his voice went up about a half-octave. "H-how are you doing?"

What the heck was that voice change? Riley side-eyed Ian just as Sam strolled up to the party.

"Hey, Ian!" he said just as the Reverend was about to reply to Ian. Glancing up and down the road he lowered his voice, "How would you like to put your journalism skills back to work?"

"What?"

The Reverend raised an eyebrow, frowning as he looked over at Sam. "What are you thinking?"

"What am I thinkin'? I'm thinkin' Ian's perfect for that news show idea we had!"

"I was joking!"

"I wasn't!"

"Might want to keep it down," Riley said, glancing down the street where a squadron of soldiers had just turned out from a side street. They could feel everyone in the group tense, especially the Reverend and Sam. Command soldiers didn't patrol Echo district. Well, until now.

"Yeah," the Reverend said. "We can talk more inside."

"Uh, you three go on ahead, I want to check on Deborah if that's okay," Riley said, looking at Sam.

"Yeah, go for it. Yvonne's got her in the trailer," Sam replied.

"Thanks," Riley replied. They clapped Ian on the back. "Don't do anything dumb without me."

"Course not," Ian replied, grinning as Riley jumped down the steps and ran across the road.

They reached the top of the ramp to Sam and Yvonne's trailer and was about to knock on the door when they realized Ian hadn't mussed up their hair like he normally did. Turning around, they saw the door to the Meeting Space close as the squadron of soldiers marched in lock-step down the street.

Deborah's fever had finally broken. She'd been playing happily on a quilt on the floor and had been vocally disappointed when her mom picked her up and forced her to have a checkup on the couch. Riley chuckled at Deborah's little temper tantrum, especially when it stopped the second she was placed back on her quilt.

"She has a lot of opinions," Yvonne said as she shook her head, smiling. "I don't know what I'm going to do once she starts talking."

"That's a little over my pay grade," Riley replied. "You still good on Tylenol?"

"Yes, and antibiotics. How long should I keep her on the Tylenol?"

"Keep her on it for tonight so she sleeps okay, and then you're probably okay to stop it tomorrow."

"And if her fever comes back, start it up again?"

"Exactly."

Shouts echoed up from the street, unintelligible but close by. Riley stuck their head out the window to see a transport in the middle of the road with about a dozen civilians in the back. Two soldiers jumped up into the truck bed and began shoving people out of the truck. The people were jumping out over the sides or climbing over the closed truck gate, stumbling to their feet and staggering onto the sidewalks and into the alleyways. Some were clutching their arms or shoulders where they'd been struck. As the last man was still dangling off the side, the transport coughed to life, spitting black smoke before speeding off. The man dropped to the ground, rolling away from the wheels. A younger man and woman doubled back, getting him to his feet and escorting him into a nearby alley.

Riley looked up to see Ian, the Reverend, and Sam in the doorway of the Meeting Space, also watching the scene. The Reverend caught Riley's eye and jerked his head down the road toward the checkpoint.

"I'll see you soon, Yvonne," Riley said, heading for the door.

"Yeah, I hope so."

Riley jumped over the railing of the trailers' steps, dropping the few feet to the ground. Ian and the Reverend were saying goodbye to Sam, and Riley waved to Sam as they headed down the road. Sam threw back a two-fingered salute as he walked across the street back to his trailer.

Ian and the Reverend jogged up to Riley's side. "You coming with us, Reverend?" Riley asked.

"Yeah. We managed to hide all the medicine and supplies, but I need to get Jen the records now."

Riley nodded as the group turned the corner onto the street where the checkpoint was. "Hey, Ian, what was the project Sam wanted you to help with?

"It's really cool, actually!" Ian said, glancing around and keeping his voice low as they hurried on. "Sam wants me to put my journalism skills to use and start doing news reports."

Riley expected him to continue, but he stopped walking as he looked back down the road. Realizing that the Reverend had fallen behind, Riley turned to see the Reverend staring past them, his mouth open.

"Were there six guards when you came in?" the Reverend asked.

Riley frowned. "Six?"

Ian slapped their shoulder, forcing them to turn around. Sure enough there were six soldiers—two on the side of the gate closest to them, two on the other side of the gate, and two in the shack.

"Th-there were four this morning," Riley said.

The Reverend took a deep breath. "Well. Let's see what happens."

The group approached the checkpoint and were met by one of the guards in the road. "IDs."

He took Ian's and Riley's, but the second he saw the Reverend's ID he handed it back. "We've been ordered not to allow anyone outside their home district. You're free to move about within Echo."

"Oh," the Reverend said. He and Ian glanced at each other. "Can I have a minute, then?"

The soldier shook his head. "We've been ordered to get everyone back to their districts as quickly as possible as well. You have until we finish running their IDs. Stay in the road."

The Reverend's jaw clenched as he watched the soldier walk away. "Ian, switch backpacks with me," he muttered, taking it off his shoulders. "Get the files to Jen. The rest of antibiotics course's also in there in one of the side pockets. I'll call you tonight and we'll talk logistics."

"Raf, what's going on?" Ian asked as he did what the Reverend said.

“I’m not sure,” the Reverend replied, shouldering Ian’s backpack. He swallowed and glanced behind them. Riley could hear the soldier’s footsteps crunching on the asphalt. He put his hand on Ian’s shoulder and looked at both him and Riley. “Be safe. Keep your heads down. I’ll visit once all this blows over.”

“Raf—” Ian started, but the soldier cut him off, thrusting his ID back into his hand.

“Get moving. Don’t leave your home once you get there,” the soldier said, shoving Riley’s ID at them.

The Reverend squeezed Ian’s shoulder as the soldier broke them apart, shoving the Reverend back. Riley ducked under the gate that was still rising up before noticing Ian wasn’t following them. He was still standing in the middle of the road, staring at the Reverend. The Reverend was staring back at him.

“Go on, Ian. It’s all right,” he said with a small, forced smile.

Riley stepped forward to take Ian’s arm, but the soldier got there first. He shoved Ian back into Riley, and they nearly fell onto the pavement.

“All right, we’re going. We’re going!” Riley yelled, grabbing Ian’s arm and yanking him through the gate. They chanced a glance behind them and saw the Reverend with his hands up, moving back down the road.

The two jogged back to their house in silence, dodging military transports and squadrons of soldiers. A mechanical voice wound up into a loud, screeching wail.

“Attention, citizens, the district checkpoints are closing. Please return to your district immediately. Attention, citizens, the district checkpoints are closing. Please return to your district immediately.”

Rounding the hotel and ducking into the back door, Riley yanked the door shut while Ian bent over with his hands on his knees, trying to catch his breath.

"What is going on?" he panted.

Riley didn't know what to think. The nausea was back to simmering in their stomach, but they couldn't tell if it was from anxiety or from running in the heat.

"I don't know," Riley replied. "I-I was hoping this was normal, but after those records getting taken yesterday, and the way the Reverend was acting today..."

"We need to tell Jen and Sergio," Ian said.

"Yeah, we do," Riley replied.

Ian led the way up the stairs. Reaching their apartment, he went to unlock the door, but the door wouldn't open.

"Why would the deadbolt be turned?" Ian asked, banging on the door. Riley heard scuffling as the door lock snicked open and Sergio stuck his head out.

"Get in," he said, grabbing Riley's hand and pulling them inside. Ian jumped in after, and Sergio slammed the door shut before locking the deadbolt.

"Where's the Reverend?" he asked as he turned back around.

"Why did you have the deadbolt turned?" Riley asked. "And why are you back so early?"

"Sent us home early. When I got back soldiers were in the hallways. One knocked on the door sayin' that the district checkpoints were shut and we should think about stayin' home tonight."

"That's why the Reverend's not here. The soldiers wouldn't let him through the checkpoint," Ian said.

"Shit. Did he give you the antibiotics?" Sergio asked.

"He said he did," Riley replied, unzipping the side pocket. Sure enough, a little orange bottle was in there with identical pills to the ones Ian had been taking.

"Did he also give you the medical files?" Jen asked from the loveseat.

"Think so," Riley replied, handing the bottle to Ian and unzipping the main pocket. It was full of manila envelopes stuffed with off-white pages. On top of the pile was a small, faded red notebook with a scrap of red ribbon sticking out from between its pages. Flipping it open to the bookmark, Riley ran their finger down the cipher column. Each letter in the alphabet had a corresponding pair of numbers.

"Oh, this is going to be a pain to decipher," Jen said, taking the book from Riley.

"Yeah, have fun with that."

"Oh, no, you're helping me too. All of you are helping. Family project!"

Riley, Sergio, and Ian groaned. "Can we at least eat dinner first?" Ian asked.

"It's four o' clock. We have at least two hours before dinner. Come on. It'll be fun!" Jen said as she headed back for the loveseat.

"You just said it was going to be a pain!" Sergio said, following her.

"It's going to be both!"

Riley seriously doubted it as they started to follow Ian back to the living area. They stopped when they heard voices and footsteps outside the door. Getting up on tiptoe they peeked out the peephole to see two men standing at the apartment door across the way.

"...can't believe they didn't send us back immediately after the district checkpoints closed," one man said.

"Well, you gotta keep the city fed, the soldiers clothed, and the metal flowing," the other replied.

"Guess you're right."

"Riley, you coming?" Ian asked.

"Y-yeah, I'm coming," Riley replied, stepping back. Their mind raced as they stared at the door. Sergio must've been working in a different factory. That was it. Maybe the two were just assuming that all three of the factories had worked a full day.

"Riley! Come on, don't miss out on the fun!" Sergio said.

"Coming!"

Riley turned back around to see Sergio sitting on the end of the bed, one arm out toward them. Ian was sitting on the ground, pulling the files out of the backpack while Jen was back on the loveseat, flipping through the notebook.

Riley smiled, hurrying to sit next to Sergio. They leaned their head on his shoulder, trying to ignore the churning in their stomach as they waited for Jen to tell them what to do.

Riley groaned as they woke up to the sunlight hitting their face. They tried to turn over to get away from it, but Sergio tightened his grip around their waist.

"Where're you trying to go?" he asked, his voice still thick with sleep. "It's the weekend. We don't have reveille."

"Trying to get away from the sunlight." Riley couldn't get their lips or tongue to move properly, so they were sure it came out like gibberish. Sergio chuckled, pressing a kiss to the back of their neck.

"But it's good for vitamin B."

"Vitamin D."

"Same thing."

"No..."

"Okay, fine." He kissed the back of their neck again and held them tighter. Riley was just about to relax back into sleep when a banging at their door made them and Sergio sit straight up.

"Riley! Raf's calling in!"

Ian was at the door between their rooms. Sighing in relief, Riley called back, "Okay, I'll be there in a minute!"

Sergio groaned. "Can't he let us sleep in one day?"

"Who, Ian or the Reverend?"

"Both!"

Riley chuckled, crawling out of bed and tossing Sergio's sleep shirt at him. He responded by chucking back their pajama pants, which they pulled on before finding their tank top. Checking to make sure Sergio was decent before opening the door, they headed into the other room.

Jen was still in bed with the pillow over her head, and Riley assumed Ian'd already tried to get her up this morning. "Good morning, Jen!" they called as they headed to the radio.

"Morning," Jen replied, muffled under the pillow.

Ian was sitting in front of the radio with the headphones on and the mic in his hand. He grinned up at Riley, passing over the mic and reaching up to plunk the headphones over their ears.

"Thanks," Riley said as they pressed the mic button. "Valerian, this is Elderflower, over."

"Elderflower, good to hear from you. Have you heard from any families needing your help yet?"

"Not yet. Have you?"

"No. I think people are still in shock, trying to figure out what this all means. They've got a squadron at every checkpoint from what we've heard. Blizzard's going to check it out for Shockwave."

Riley's heart stopped. Ian investigating whatever the heck Command was doing did not seem like a good idea. He could end up in the wrong place at the wrong time and put them all in a world of trouble. At least they could probably convince Ian to let Sergio go along as well.

"Got it," Riley replied. "So, what's our plan?"

"I'll handle my home district. You handle yours. Anyone outside we'll have to handle over the radio."

It wasn't much of a plan, but it was something. Riley was thankful the Reverend wasn't expecting them to try and cross heavily guarded district borders. Maybe they could still toss medication over the border if… no. Way too dangerous. If Riley was caught, they were sure the Command would not only interrogate them, but Sergio, Ian, and Jen as well. And they didn't want the chance to compare Command interrogation methods to Revolution ones.

"Okay, that sounds good."

"How much medication do you have?" the Reverend asked.

"I was going to inventory it this morning."

"The correct answer was 'hopefully enough.'"

"I thought that was implied."

The radio was silent for a minute, and Riley imagined the Reverend was laughing, or at least chuckling.

"All right, maybe it was," he finally said. "Just stay safe and watch your back. We'll debrief any calls you have tonight, but let me know if you need a second opinion before that."

"Yeah, I'll keep in touch."

"I will too. Also, if Blizzard is still there, can you put him back on?"

"Yeah, he's right here."

Ian hadn't moved out of the metal chair the entire time. Riley plopped the headphones back down on his head and put the mic in his hand before heading to the front closet to retrieve their med kit.

"What did the Reverend say?" Sergio asked.

"We're sticking to our home districts and just doing radio calls to everyone else," Riley replied. "Best we can do."

Sergio's shoulders relaxed as he sighed. "Okay, good. You going to head out soon?"

Riley shrugged, "Haven't gotten any calls yet. Granted, I'm not sure any calls can get in because *somebody* won't get off the goddamn radio!"

"It'll beep if someone is trying to call in on the medical line," Ian called back. "I'm on our personal talk channel!"

"Glad someone knows how to use that thing," Sergio said.

"Bet Ian would teach you if you asked."

"If he could get off long enough for me to ask..."

"All right, I'm off. I'm off!" Ian said, taking off the headphones and throwing up his hands.

"Good, now can you all go talk in the other room?" Jen asked. "I was up late reorganizing those medical files and I would like some sleep, thank you."

Riley, Sergio, and Ian glanced at each other, and then Ian led the way into the other room. Sergio gently closed the door behind him.

"How long has the insomnia been back?" he asked in a low voice.

"Last night was the first night," Ian said, folding his arms. "Raf said to check with Kit to see if she had melatonin, but she didn't reply when I called."

"I'll swing that way when I get a call out," Riley said, turning to Sergio. "How much money do we have?"

"Six bucks," he replied. "Hopefully it's enough."

"Sam's going to pay me in goods for my investigative work. Maybe I can ask him to pay in melatonin if he has any?" Ian said.

"Oh, good," Sergio said. "Wasn't expecting him to pay you."

"Do you think I would've agreed to do something without some sort of payment in return?"

Sergio refused to meet his eyes. Riley thought of the multiple times back in Philippi where Ian had gone missing for hours to help out another family without telling anyone.

Ian sighed and rolled his eyes. "Hey, those were one-off times! I never agreed to help anyone out long term without anything in exchange."

That was true. Sergio was about to say something when the radio in the other room beeped.

"Whose bright idea was it to put the radio in my room?" Jen called out.

"Because that's where the desk was," Riley replied, heading into the other room. Putting on the headphones, Riley glanced over at Jen, who still had her head under the pillow. They kept their voice down as they turned on the mic.

"This is Elderflower. Who is this?"

"This is Oak, I live in four-two-twelve-two. My daughter fell and cut her leg, we've stopped the bleeding but we have nothing to bandage it and keep it clean. Can you help?"

Riley did the math on one of the scrap pieces of paper they kept by the radio for this purpose. Subtract the first two numbers to get the block, multiply the second two to get the housing unit. Block Two, HU Twenty-Four.

Running through the list of things they'd need in their head, they clicked the mic on. "Yes, I can help. I'll be there in twenty minutes. Are you able to clean out the wound with soap?"

"We have dish soap, is that all right?"

"Dilute it, three parts water to one part soap. Use the cleanest cloths you have. I'm on my way."

The little girl with the cut leg, Lila, was the first child in a whirlwind of sick and injured children over the next few days. Between dodging trucks, squadrons of soldiers, and the odd tank, Riley had to navigate worried parents and fussy kids. Most of the kids had chronic illnesses and injuries that parents wanted someone with pediatric experience to give a second opinion on. Riley had to confirm to three too many parents that no one could do anything except keep their children as comfortable as they could when they inevitably started to decline. Riley had never been good at this part—parents crying. All of the comforting words they could think of sounded cliché. They always just settled for handing over some tissues and waiting silently until the family either railed at them or thanked them. Those emotions they could work with.

The last family, Henry's family, thanked Riley fairly quickly. The Reverend had told them the same thing a few months ago, so they were prepared. As they did at every patient's home, Riley used their radio to call back to their home and see if anyone else had called in for help.

"Nope, you're in the clear," Ian said. "Plus the sun's about to go down, and I think curfew's going to be strict tonight."

He wasn't wrong. As Riley walked home in the cool fall evening, they swore they had to step into the street for more soldiers than usual. Most of the soldiers glared at them as they jogged by, but the lead soldier of one squadron stepped into the road in front of them as they tried to pass.

"Let me see your ID."

Riley stumbled back and stared at the soldier, not comprehending what she'd just said.

"ID, now!"

Riley jumped, their hands shaking. They nearly dropped their ID on the ground as they passed it over. The soldier squinted at the ID in the dying light, looked back up at Riley, looked back down at the ID, and then looked up at Riley as she chucked the ID to the ground. Riley scrambled for it but then froze, afraid that they'd just opened themself up to having the butt of a gun come down on their back. But the soldier was already walking away toward her snickering squad mates.

Riley finally managed to snatch the card out of the road, stuck it back in their pocket, and ducked down an alleyway so they didn't have to follow the soldiers. Their heart pounded as they walked along, and no amount of deep breaths would make it calm down. They could feel their face burn with shame and fear. Another half-mile or so and they were coming up on the backside of the hotel. Wondering why they didn't take this route all the time, they hurried inside the building and sprinted up the stairs and to their apartment.

Unlocking the door, Riley expected to find the rest of their family in the room, but nobody was there. Riley could see through the cracked glass door that Ian and Sergio were sitting out on the balcony. Dropping their medical kit and kicking off their shoes, they hurried outside. As they passed the bed, they realized that the desk and radio were gone.

Freezing for a second, they pushed forward and yanked the balcony door open.

"Hey," they said, not realizing they were out of breath until they tried to talk.

"Riley! You're home!" Ian exclaimed. Sergio reached out and grabbed their hand, pulling them down for a kiss.

"Hi," they said, kissing Sergio. "Where's Jen? Where's the radio?"

"In the other room and in the other room," Ian replied. "I figured out how to hook up the radio, so I moved it to your room so you'd get woken up by the beeps instead of Jen."

"Gee, thanks."

"No problem! Jen's in there now talking with Raf and updating the medical records for the day. She's going to want your notes I bet."

Notes? Riley never took notes, they just memorized everything. Realizing that probably made them worse than the Reverend and his scrawled notes in Jen's eyes, they made a mental note to write out actual notes in the future.

"You want to join us?" Sergio said. "Kit gave Ian some beer when he swung by the grocery store earlier for the melatonin."

"Sure, I will in a minute, I need to talk to Jen first before I forget everything."

Ian and Sergio gave each other knowing looks, and Riley rolled their eyes. They had enough problems without Ian and Sergio harping on their failure to actually write shit down. Kissing Sergio on the cheek and running their hand through Ian's hair, Riley turned and shut the balcony door behind them.

Heading into their room, Riley stopped at the door.

"...wish I could've taken a tour around all the districts so I'd have a better idea of where everyone lives."

Jen looked up and waved her fingers at Riley while intently listening to whoever was talking—Riley assumed the Reverend.

"Yeah I guess that's true," Jen said after a minute. "Well, Ri-I mean Elderflower's finally back, so no need to send out that search party. I'll let you talk to them."

"Hey! I was back before curfew!" Riley whispered.

Jen chuckled, passing over the headphones and getting up from the chair. Riley plopped down into it as Jen headed into the other room.

"Evening, Valerian," they said, thankful they no longer sounded breathless.

"Evening, Elderflower," *the Reverend said.* "How're you feeling?"

Riley took a deep breath, trying to figure out how to answer that. They finally settled on, "I'm okay."

"You talk to the Redwood family?"

"And the Dandelion, and the Peony family," Riley said. "They all wanted second opinions."

"That's fair," the Reverend replied. "I should've warned you about them, but I thought I'd be able to go with you on your first visit. Are you equipped to do palliative care?"

"No, unfortunately, but they didn't ask for anything. Yet."

"Greenhouse will be able to help you when the time comes. They've hopefully set aside enough medication for the families."

"It'd be more helpful if she could set aside more Tylenol or other pain medications," Riley said.

"We've tried before, but Command seems to have a really tight grip on it for some reason. Greenhouse got in trouble a few months back for changing the numbers, so she's been extra cautious with when, what, and how much she sets aside."

Riley wondered what had happen to Kit, but they honestly didn't really want to know. Whatever it was, it hadn't left any visible scars that Riley could see.

"Makes sense."

"Yeah."

They fell silent, but for some reason it didn't feel awkward. Maybe the radio was just mediating their discussion.

"How do you keep it all from getting to you?" the Reverend asked.

Was he asking for advice? It didn't sound like it. More like he was encouraging them to process everything. Nobody had given them permission to do that in a while. It was always about where the next meal was coming from, where to get more currency, where to get new shoes for Jen…

"Elderflower? You still there?"

"Yeah, still here, just thinking."

"Gotcha."

Riley had wanted a hint as to what the Reverend was looking for, but he was too smart to give them one. "Uh, well, I… I guess I just file it away and move on. You do the best you can for who you can with what you have."

"Yeah. Yeah, ain't that the truth."

"How do you process everything?"

"Prayer. Lots of prayer. Sometimes all you can do is do your part and pray for a miracle."

Apparently his Reverend disguise wasn't that much work after all. "Guess so."

"Well, Shockwave's about to do his evening broadcast, and I'm sure you don't want to miss that. Speaking of which, is Blizzard going to be doing his first report after the show?"

"Not sure. We'll both find out in a bit."

He was. During his broadcast, Sam let the people know what ham radio station to tune into if they wanted to hear the news of the day. Ian flipped through his script over and over as the last song played.

"Hey, can someone hold the mic button down?" he asked, looking up at Riley and Sergio. "I need to be able to flip through this."

"I've got you," Riley said, sliding past Jen to the corner that the desk made with the wall. Taking the mic off of its hook, they waited until Ian switched off the radio and tuned the ham radio to the correct station. Taking a deep breath, he nodded at Riley, and they pressed down the button.

"Good evening everyone, this is Blizzard with the news. Our top story tonight is something I'm sure you are all aware of. The district checkpoints have been closed for four days. There has been no official explanation for why this has occurred, which has left room for plenty of speculation. Given that we are still free to move about our districts, it seems as if Command is only concerned with inter-district communication and travel. Also, the sudden nature of the shutdown suggests an immediate security risk they wished to mitigate. This could be related to the records of a medical network taken five days ago, especially if Command has evidence there is more to the operation. Now, dear listeners, I'm not confirming there is. I'm not confirming that there's even a network. But it could explain why they shut the checkpoints down as fast as they did."

It made sense. Prevent people from moving in between districts so they could isolate Echo, the only place where there was proof of illegal medical activity. Riley was thankful the Reverend had managed to get the records out.

"This could also explain the reports from Charlie and Golf districts of an increase in troop transports entering Jericho with soldiers and leaving empty, alongside increased shipments of supplies. It is very possible that Command is increasing troops in preparation of a sweep of establishments suspected of being tied to this network, so stay safe out there, folks. We will, of course, bring you more updates as we know them."

Riley didn't want to think about how they determined "suspicious" establishments. They made a mental note to figure out the best hiding place for the radio.

"In other news, the ammo factory is nearing completion. Once it is finished, they are expected to hire around twenty permanent workers with thirty other day labor positions open. Speculation abounds that Tier Two will again begin to be called out for potential day labor positions. The last time reveille included Tier Two individuals was eight months ago before the canning factory burned down."

There used to be a dedicated canned food factory? Riley tried not to think about how much bigger the rations would be if it was still around.

"Well, folks, that's all the news we have for tonight. If you have any tips for stories, be sure to contact me on this channel. I'll be back here tomorrow night, but until then, stay safe and stay vigilant."

Riley let go of the mic button and stretched out their thumb as they hung the mic back up on its hook.

"Well, that went better than I thought it would," Ian commented as he switched off the radio.

"You were wonderful, Ian," Jen said, patting him on the back.

"Yeah, good job stringin' all that together," Sergio said.

“Thanks,” Ian said, yawning and resting his head on the radio.

“All right, we all need some sleep before whatever adventures tomorrow,” Jen said. “Good night, Riley, Sergio.”

“Night,” Riley replied as Ian pushed himself up and followed Jen to the door. But just as Jen’s hand touched the doorknob, the radio beeped. Riley grabbed the mic and stuck on the headphones. Jen and Ian continued on into the other room as Riley answered.

“This is Elderflower, go ahead.”

“This is Valerian, is Blizzard there?”

“Uh, we’re heading to bed now, but y-yeah he’s still up.”

“Oh, never mind then, sorry about that. Can you have him call me tomorrow when he gets a chance?”

“Yeah, I-I’ll let him know.”

“Thanks, Elderflower. Good night.”

“Good night, Valerian.”

CHAPTER TEN

"Attention, citizens. Jericho is now in lockdown. Remain in your homes unless ordered otherwise. Attention, citizens."

Riley was yanked out of sleep by the droning mechanical voice. Sergio rolled off the mattress, the floor creaking as he hit the ground. Squinting through the darkness, they saw him pull the curtains aside to peer out into the night.

"They've got two soldiers stationed in front," Sergio said. "And a truck is driving around blasting that message."

"Wh-why couldn't they have waited until m-morning?" Riley wondered, their tongue thick in their mouth.

"Disrupt our sleep, make us more compliant," Sergio replied. "Form of psychological warfare."

He let the curtains fall closed and crawled back into bed. Riley shivered when he lifted up the blankets and flinched at his icy hands. It'd gotten so much colder in the past few weeks since the district borders had been slammed shut.

"Attention, citizens. Jericho is now in lockdown. Remain in your homes unless ordered otherwise. Attention, citizens."

Tendrils of anxiety unfurled in Riley's gut, lashing against their chest. It felt like they were weighed down by an iron blanket. All they wanted was to be able to sleep, but that wasn't going to happen. Their brain was full of swirling ash and fire, their thoughts both unintelligible and all too clear and frightening.

The radio beeped, and Riley was relieved they had something to take their mind off the nonsense in their head and on the street. Stumbling out of bed, Riley fumbled for the headphones and the mic.

"Th-this is Ri-E-Elderflower," they stuttered.

"...Elderflower?"

"Y-yeah. Who is this?"

"Is your entire family there?"

"Yeah, I th-think so."

"Check!"

Startled, Riley dropped the headphones and mic and felt their way toward the door.

"What's going on?" Sergio asked.

Riley ignored him as they pushed the door open and squinted into the other room. "Ian? Jen?" they said, their voice finally getting under control.

"Yeah, we're up," Ian groaned.

"Okay," they said, relief doing little to ease the tension in their chest. Leaving the door open, they hurried back to the radio.

"Yeah, everyone's here, we're all okay. Just exhausted."

"Well that's to be expected."

Riley finally registered that the Reverend was talking to them. "Valerian, what's going on?"

"I'm not sure. Jericho's never been under a city-wide lockdown. It's always been one district at a time, and only for a few hours. Everyone's house here in Echo has been swept, and several families have had people taken as well. I'm checking in and getting a list of who's missing."

Riley's heart jumped into their throat. "Did they find anything where you are?"

"No, nothing. They just interrogated me for a bit, trashed the place, but didn't find anything. Call me tomorrow when you wake up and we'll talk more."

"All right, stay safe, Valerian."

"You too, Elderflower. Give everyone else my love."

The line went dead.

"Was that Raf?" Ian asked, leaning against the doorframe. Sergio set candles out on the table, lighting them with his cheap blue lighter.

"Yeah, it was," Riley replied. "Wanted to make sure we were okay, but he had more families to call. Meeting Space got searched and he got interrogated, but the soldiers didn't find anything. Told us to call him tomorrow morning when we wake up again. Said to give everyone his love."

"There had to be more than that," Jen said. "Even in this light I can tell you're as pale as a ghost."

Riley looked up into her concerned eyes. The reality of what the Reverend had so casually said broke them down in full force, and they could feel the lump in their throat threatening to burst. "He said some people had been taken."

Sergio swore under his breath, but Riley couldn't tell what he said. "Is Raf okay?" Ian asked.

"It sounded like it," Riley replied. "Just worried and scared, like the rest of us."

"Attention, citizens. Jericho is now in lockdown. Remain in your homes unless ordered otherwise."

The metallic voice—it had to be a recording—grated on Riley's nerves. And it seemed to screech more and more as time went on although they could be imagining it.

"Come on. Let's sit down," Jen said, gesturing to the couch and armchairs. "I'll warm up some broth and we can play cards until the racket stops."

"Think the cards are in the other room," Ian said. "I'll grab them."

Riley slowly sat down on the couch and stared at the flickering candles. They felt completely numb with exhaustion. Sergio sat down next to them and wrapped his arm around their shoulders.

"It's okay, baby," he whispered, kissing the top of their head. "We'll get through this. I promise."

His words did nothing to ease the tightness in their chest.

Ian came back in a few minutes later with the deck of cards. Unwrapping the rubber band, he asked, "Texas hold-'em or blackjack?"

"How about go fish?" Riley replied. "Since, y'know, we don't have any money to gamble with."

"You're boring."

"You telling me that blackjack's interesting without cash?"

Ian shrugged, and they all laughed half-heartedly. When it died out, the mechanical voice scraped in Riley's ears again.

"Attention, citizens. Jericho is now in lockdown. Remain in your homes unless ordered otherwise. Attention, citizens. Jericho is now in lockdown."

Riley woke up the next morning to find themself back in bed with Sergio's arm wrapped around them. Lifting their head, they saw Ian sprawled out on one of the armchairs. Jen was curled up on the couch with a blanket and pillow from the other room. Riley wondered how she was able to sleep with Ian snoring right next to her ear.

Sergio pulled them back down, burying his face in the back of their neck. Closing their eyes, Riley realized the droning mechanical voice was gone. In fact, no sounds were coming at all from the road below. It felt like the silence after a fresh snowfall.

"Please tell me you're not getting up right now," Sergio whispered.

"Mm, still deciding," Riley said, snuggling back against him.

The recliner squeaked. "Oh good, you're awake," Ian said, yawning.

"For the moment. Thinking about going back to sleep," Sergio replied.

"RJ up?"

Riley didn't want to get up, but they were also pretty sure that they wouldn't be able to fall back asleep. "Maybe."

"You guys are lazy," Ian said.

"Blame Command."

"Can all of you shut up?" Jen said. "I'm trying to get my eight hours!"

"Might want to go to the other room to do that," Ian said. "We're going to need to call Raf soon."

Jen sighed, kicked off the blanket, grabbed her pillow, and trudged into the other room. Ian jumped out of the armchair as soon as the door closed and hurried for the radio.

"Hey, give me a minute to wake up," Riley said, rubbing their eyes.

"You've already had a minute!"

He had them there. Riley groaned as they pushed Sergio's arm off of them and rolled off the mattress. Sergio turned over, grabbing Riley's pillow and putting it over his head.

Ian claimed the chair in front of the radio. Riley pulled the headphones out of the headphone jack before stretching, trying to get their cramped muscles to wake up. Ian keyed up the Reverend's channel and clicked on the mic.

"Valerian, this is Blizzard and Elderflower, over."

No response. Ian looked up at Riley, his eyes wide with panic.

"It's going to take a minute," Riley said, putting their hand on his shoulder to calm him. "He might be talking to someone else. Just give it a minute and then call again."

Ian tapped his fingers on the desk, keeping the mic in his hand. After about thirty seconds he clicked the mic on again. "Valerian, this is Blizzard and Elderflower. Are you there?"

The line was silent. Ian went to radio again, but Riley stopped him. "Give him a chance to respond!"

Sure enough, the radio crackled to life a few seconds later. "This is Valerian. Sorry, Blizzard, had someone on the other line. You doing all right?"

Ian's shoulders slumped forward in relief. "Yeah, yeah, I'm fine. We're all okay here. You all right?"

"Yeah, I'm okay. We're missing about twenty-three people, though. Including Peppermint."

"Shit," Ian said. "I'm sorry, R-Valerian."

"Yeah, me too."

The line went silent for a few seconds before the Reverend said, "You said Elderflower was there. Right?"

"Yeah, they're listening right now."

"Ok, so they heard that. Elderflower, did Peppermint ever call you?"

Riley took the mic from Ian. "Yes, last week. She needed help with the Spruce family."

"Did she ever give you any hint as to whether she was working with anyone else?"

Riley racked their brain, trying to remember any hint that Kate might have given them about anybody they might be training. "No…no I can't think of anyone, and she didn't have anyone with her when we visited her before all this mess," they said. "I can try calling the Spruce family and see if Peppermint brought anyone with her when she visited."

"Yeah, if you can do that, that would be great. Just to give the people in Golf someone to call for minor things. Then if there's anything major they can be redirected to us. I'm pretty sure we're about to be slammed with panicking people now that they can't get medical care."

"Yeah, my worry is trying to get medicine to people."

"I don't have a good answer for you. Maybe a way will make itself clear."

"Yeah, I hope so," Riley replied. "I'll let you know if I think of something."

"Please do. Well, I've got a couple other families trying to contact me, so I'd better see what they need. We'll talk more tonight. Is Blizzard still there?"

Riley handed the mic back to Ian. "Yeah, I'm still here," Ian said.

"Okay, good. I'm sorry we didn't get to talk more. I'll call when I get a chance. Stay safe, Blizzard, Elderflower. Let me know if you need anything."

"Stay safe, Valerian," Ian replied as the line went dead.

It felt like Riley was trying to walk through the deep end of a swimming pool the next day. Most of the time they were glued to the radio, calming panicked parents and giving advice on bumps, scrapes, and runny noses they prayed wouldn't turn into serious infections. Every time the line went silent, they tried to stand up, stretch, and walk around. But no matter how much they moved around, they felt claustrophobic. All they wanted was to walk out the front door. And given how much Sergio was pacing,

Riley knew he felt the same way. Without being able to go out and help Riley, or even get work through reveille, they knew he felt useless.

"Here's some more notes, Jen," Riley said, handing over some scraps of paper. Jen was sitting on Ian's bed, the medical files neatly arranged in a circle around her, writing up files on Riley's new patients.

"Goodness, how many people are going to call you today?"

"Great question," Riley replied as the radio began beeping. Hurrying back into the other room, they didn't realize Sergio had followed them until they felt his hand on their shoulder as they slid on the headphones.

"This is Elderflower. Who's calling?"

"This is the Poplar family. I've got a five-year-old son who's been coughing for the past three days and it's getting worse. We thought it was all the dust from the tanks and military transports, but everything's quiet today and he's still coughing."

Riley pursed her lips, "Does his cough sound wet or dry?"

"Wet, definitely wet."

"Could be he's still trying to cough up all the mucus his body produced trying to protect against the dust," Riley said. "And believe me. We want him to cough it up. If you can, get some steam going and have him breathe it in from a safe distance to loosen the mucus."

"Kind of like we were treating croup?"

"Exactly like that. Do it maybe twice a day, and give it another few days. If it keeps going or turns into a dry cough, give me another call."

"Sounds good. Thank you, Elderflower."

"No problem. Stay safe."

"You too."

The line went dead, and Riley turned back to the notes they'd pulled from the medical files about the families in Golf that the Reverend had been treating and that he was sure Kate had been doing follow-ups on. None of the families Riley had managed to call so far, including the Spruce family, had seen or heard of an assistant to Kate. But just as they were about to call the next family, the radio beeped.

"This is Elderflower. Who is calling?"

It was a pattern Riley would repeat for the next week. Get up in the morning, answer radio calls, take notes for Jen, shove food into their mouth when necessary, listen to Sam's broadcast in the evening, answer more radio calls, fall into bed and toss and turn all night. Everything started to blend together, only broken by the variation in Sam's music selections in the evenings. Ian couldn't even keep doing his nightly news broadcasts because the radio was tied up with medical calls. So he was left to re-read the few books they had and sit out on the porch with Sergio, playing cards and drinking the last of the beer in the fridge.

"Can't you have specific office hours?" Ian asked, plunking dinner down in front of Riley. Canned mushroom soup with frozen meatballs, half heated because the power had been shut off early. Riley really hoped lockdown would be lifted soon so they could get some actual decent food. Jen could only do so much.

"Might radio Sam and the Reverend and ask for that," Riley said, rubbing the temples of their head. "Otherwise I might be up all night too. Also, can I have a spoon?"

"Shit, sorry."

Riley took their bowl over to the coffee table when Sergio and Jen came into the room with their dinners. Ian joined soon afterward with spoons for both him and

Riley. Somehow, choking down the food in the candlelight together made it taste better. Or, at least, the conversation between bites took Riley's mind off of how bad it tasted. Or looked.

"Can't believe you haven't gotten a call this entire half hour," Ian said, glancing over at the radio as if he'd jinxed it.

"Everybody else must be making dinner," Jen said. "I'll take your dishes."

"RJ, can I hop on the radio with Raf?" Ian asked as Jen stacked their bowls and headed into the other room.

"You just talked with him this morning. For over an hour."

"Yeah, but…I've got more I want to talk about."

"Like what?"

"Just stuff, Riley! Can I use the radio or not?"

Riley's eyes went wide at his use of their full name.

"Y-Yeah, but tell me if it starts beeping. I need to answer it."

"Thanks!" He scampered over to the desk, plunked down, and slipped the headphones over his ears.

Riley and Sergio turned to each other, and Sergio raised his eyebrows. "What was that?" Sergio mouthed. Riley shrugged, pointing toward the door to the other room. Sergio nodded, and Riley followed him out of the room.

"Want to get some fresh air?" Sergio asked.

"Yeah, sounds wonderful." Thank goodness for balconies, especially ones that came with two lawn chairs.

"You want something to drink?" Sergio asked as he settled into one of the porch chairs.

"You and Ian haven't drank all of the beer yet?" Riley said, looking back into the apartment as they sat in the other chair.

"Oh, no, I meant water."

Riley swatted at him. "You're an asshole."

Sergio dodged the swat, laughing. "Do you seriously want water or something?"

"Nah, I'm good."

The sun was starting to set, blood-orange against a purple sky and pink clouds. It was ethereal, and almost distracted from the soldiers stationed in front of every building. Across the street, they could see one soldier standing directly in front of the door to a converted storefront with the other pacing the length of the building, his gun in his hands. Riley was sure their orders were to shoot on sight if anyone tried to leave.

The blanket covering the window moved, and a small head poked out. It was immediately snatched away. The solider standing behind the door turned his head toward the window and then said something to the soldier pacing on the sidewalk, who laughed.

"Thank goodness we managed to get a hotel room and not a storefront," Sergio said. "I'd hate to have a soldier right outside our home."

"Yeah," Riley said. "Wait… did you actually check?"

"What? N-no?"

Riley pushed themself out of their chair and ran for the front door.

"What is it, Riley?" Jen asked.

Riley got on their tiptoes to look through the peephole. Nobody was there!

Riley felt a huge wave of relief rush through them, until a person walked into view with an olive-green bucket helmet, a cammo uniform, a flak jacket, and an assault rifle in their hands. He stopped in front of Riley's door and leaned in toward the peep hole. Riley ducked down, their heart racing and their stomach churning. After a few seconds they could hear muffled bootsteps moving away.

"Riley?" Jen asked, peeking around the corner from the kitchenette. "What's wrong? You're as white as a ghost."

Riley looked up at her and tried to answer, but they couldn't form the words to express how violated they felt.

They couldn't help but continue to peek out the peephole every hour they were awake for the next week. Sergio and Ian did the same while Jen stayed as far away from the door as possible. She'd asked early on if they could cover up the hole with something, but Sergio and Riley were sure that would cause more problems than it would solve.

"They might think we're hiding something and ransack the place," Sergio explained, and Jen had to agree.

So they were left to tiptoe around their own home, trying to stay out of sight of the door, and play the radio low at night so the soldiers wouldn't hear. During one of these sessions their ham radio crackled to life.

"Elderflower, this is Valerian. Are you there?"

Riley reached over Jen's head to grab the mic and headphones. Awkwardly sliding on the headphones, they clicked on the mic. "This is Elderflower. What's up?"

"I need your help. We have a measles outbreak in Echo."

What? The Kader family had been the only family they knew of that had measles, but that was over a month ago.

"What do you need?"

"Tylenol, any fever-reducing medication, I've used up all mine. These kids are burning up. We managed to sneak them all to the Meeting House during the guard change, but…I don't know how much longer they're going to hold on."

"How many kids are we talking?"

"Twelve. There's probably going to be more over the next few days."

Twelve kids! "I-I don't have enough Tylenol for all of them."

"I know, but we're in luck. Sort of. Greenhouse is supposed to deliver your rations tomorrow morning, she's going to slip in some medication. Then you'll need to get it to me."

"What? How? How the hell do I even get out of the building?"

"I don't know. Greenhouse may be able to help you more. I wish I didn't have to ask you to do this. I wish I could tell you to wait until after lockdown is lifted, but I have no idea when that could be and without your help these kids aren't going to make it."

Riley had never heard the Reverend sound so defeated or desperate. For a second they thought about not replying, unplugging and disabling the radio, and forgetting that the Reverend had ever called. There was no way they could make it into Echo, deliver the medication, and get back to Foxtrot and into their building without being discovered. It would have to be a one-way trip until lockdown was lifted. If lockdown was lifted…

"Elderflower. Please. I can't tell you to do this, but I can beg you. Please."

Twelve kids. No way in hell were they going to leave them to die.

"We're more than even after this. All right?" Riley said.

"Yes, of course. I'll owe you. I'll see you soon, Elderflower. Stay safe."

"You too. You want to talk to Blizzard?" The two had talked every night for the past week for hours, to the point where Sergio and Riley had started sleeping in Ian's bed and Ian was sleeping in theirs.

"…yes, but I've already been away too long from the kids. Give him my love. Will you? And the rest of the family, of course."

"Yeah, of course," Riley said, shaking their head at Ian, whose face fell. "I'll let you get back to them. Good night, Valerian."

"Good night, Elderflower."

Riley hung back up the mic and headphones. "What's wrong?" Ian asked.

Riley could barely hear him over their racing heart. "Reverend's got twelve kids in the Meeting House who all have measles and high fevers, no help, and no medication to try and keep it down."

"Oh sweet Jesus," Jen said, pressing her hands to her cheeks. "Those poor babies!"

"Why'd he call you?" Sergio asked. "You're stuck here in Foxtrot with us. There's not much you can do."

"Kit's got the medication the Reverend needs," Riley said, not meeting his eye.

"And you're going to get it to him," Ian finished, his eyes widening.

"That's the idea."

"No," Sergio said with Jen shaking her head behind him. "It's too dangerous. How the hell would you even get out of the building with the soldiers patrolling the corridors and standing in front of all the doors? Why would the Reverend expect you to do that?"

Riley opened their mouth to reply, but Ian beat them to it. "Because he's got no other options?"

"Why can't Kit do it?"

"She's delivering rations tomorrow. That's how she's getting me the medication," Riley said. "But outside of that she's watched closely because she stores the rations. If she disappears for days, they're going to notice."

"Days?" Sergio said.

Shit. "Look, making the trip there is going to be dangerous enough. Might as well wait lockdown out at the Meeting Space."

"If lockdown ever gets lifted."

"I-it has to, eventually," Riley replied although now they really couldn't ignore that thought. "At the very least the Reverend's going to need my help for a few days until we get the kids well enough to be sent home."

Sergio ran his fingers through his hair, shaking his head. "You can't go. It's too dangerous."

"And if I don't go, twelve kids are going to die!"

"That's not your problem. It's the Reverend's!" Sergio said. "Look, Ian's already completed his course of antibiotics. You don't have any reason to help the Reverend anymore. Especially if he's telling you to take on a suicide mission!"

"Raf wouldn't tell Riley to do something like that!" Ian said.

"He just did!"

"Ian's right. He asked. He didn't tell me to do anything," Riley said. "He's leaving the choice up to me."

Sergio's anger deflated, replaced with confusion and worry. "And you're actually considering going?"

"It's Riley's decision, Sergio," Jen said.

Sergio looked back and forth between Jen and Riley, finally settling on Riley. They couldn't meet his eyes.

"Who's to say those kids won't die even with the medication?" Sergio asked. "Do you trust the Reverend that this isn't a Hail Mary? That he isn't risking your life for something that probably won't work?"

Riley's brain froze. It was another question that had always been in the back of their head, through working with the Reverend, and lately during their evening debriefs that would turn into long talks about anything and everything until Ian begged for his turn on the radio. The two actually got along well, especially now that the Reverend wasn't holding the antibiotics over their head to get them to work. But how disposable was Riley? Would the Reverend be willing to throw them away on a Hail Mary?

They tried to find a small crumb of the mistrust they'd held for the Reverend, but nothing was there. He'd held to his word and had quickly turned over the antibiotics when it became clear he wouldn't be able to give them one every day anymore. And Riley had seen how desperate he was for help, especially with the kids in Jericho. And honestly, Riley didn't know if they would've done any differently if they'd been in his place.

"Riley!"

They snapped out of their thoughts and looked up at Sergio. Riley knew he wouldn't understand if they told him everything. "He's not going to risk me and my skill set for something he doesn't think will work. Especially when it's so rare and valuable, and when he played so dirty to get it."

Sergio sighed and nodded. "That's a good point. But I'm—"

"—not going with me because two people are more likely to be caught than one," Riley finished.

They'd never gotten such a "fuck you" look from Sergio before, but that was only because they were right and he knew it. "Fine. All right. But you're going to call us the second you get to the Meeting Space. All right?" he demanded.

"I think that's Jen's line."

"*Right?*" Sergio glared at them.

"Yes, I will call you the second I get to the Meeting Space."

"Good," Sergio said, stalking out of the room. After a minute they could hear the balcony door bang open and shut.

"What the hell's gotten into him?" Ian said. "Does he really expect you to sit by and let twelve kids die when you can do something about it?"

"No, he doesn't," Riley said, biting the corner of their mouth to keep from crying. "He's just mad we're in this situation in the first place."

Jen had walked over to Riley's side by this point and gently pulled them into a hug. "That's exactly right," she said, rubbing Riley's back. "He just needs some time on his own to cool off."

Riley buried their face in Jen's shoulder, returning the hug. They only looked up when Ian mussed up their hair.

"Come on, RJ," he said, offering up a weaker grin than usual. "You want to play cards or something for a bit?"

Riley debated. They wanted to go after Sergio, but Jen was right. He needed to cool off. "Sure. You want to join us, Jen?"

"No," Jen replied, letting Riley go and smoothing out their hair again. "I think I'm going to go ahead and turn in for the night. It's been a long day, and I'll need to be up early tomorrow to debrief with Rafael. Have a feeling I'm going to be doing up records for all those kids."

Riley nodded, giving Jen her nightly kiss on the cheek. Ian did the same, and Jen headed into the other room, closing the door behind her.

"For what it's worth," Ian said, pulling them in for another hug, "I'm glad you're going to help Raf."

Riley tried to reply, to say they were happy to be helping too, but they couldn't lie. They weren't happy about it. They were just trying to escape the crushing guilt of not helping. But in trying to escape the guilt, anxiety had started bubbling up in their gut again.

How the hell were they going to survive this?

CHAPTER ELEVEN

Sergio came back a half-hour later, suggesting that everyone turn in. Ian clapped Sergio on the back and mussed Riley's hair before heading into the other room. As he passed the radio Riley saw him give it a long glance before shaking his head and closing the door behind him.

"Weird to be going to bed before the power's off," Riley said, switching off the light.

"Weird to actually be sleeping in our own bed," Sergio replied, pulling off his shirt. "Ian's slept in here, what, five of the past seven nights?

"Something like that," Riley replied, fumbling back through the shadows to their bed. They'd barely slid under the sheets when Sergio reached out and wrapped his arm around them, pressing his forehead to theirs. Riley was sure he was going to say something, but instead he just kissed them and scooted up to rest his chin on top of their head.

Riley was surprised when they woke up the next morning to the sun hitting their face. They'd been sure they would be unable to sleep. Sergio was already up, leaning over the coffee table with his back to Riley.

"What're you up to?" Riley asked, trying to get past the scratchiness in their throat.

Sergio jumped and turned around, holding Riley's survival daypack. "Just making sure your pack is up to date.

Figured you might need it expanded a bit if you're going to be gone for...a few days."

"Yeah... yeah, thanks," Riley said, rubbing their eyes.

"You want me to pack your green T-shirt or your gray one?"

Riley knew they'd have to check to see how many days he'd actually packed for. "Both."

Sergio closed his eyes and took a deep breath before putting both shirts in the backpack and zipping it up. "Okay, I think you're good to go," he said, climbing back into bed and wrapping his arms around Riley. They didn't know the next time they would be held by Sergio, so they tried to ignore the stress boiling in their gut and the impulse to go check their backpack and instead enjoyed the moment.

"You know, nobody would blame you if you didn't go," Sergio whispered.

"I'd blame myself."

He kissed the back of their head and didn't reply. Riley couldn't get any of their muscles to relax. But they also didn't want Sergio to stop cuddling them. But they wanted to make sure they were prepared...

Ian made the decision for them when he knocked on the door. "Riley? Sergio?"

"What is it?" Riley asked, while Sergio groaned and buried his face in the base of Riley's neck.

"Jen's made pancakes."

Pancakes? How the heck had she managed to throw together pancakes? Sergio jumped up and Riley quickly followed, throwing on their clothes and hurrying into the other room.

They weren't exactly the pancakes Riley remembered from before the Collapse, but they were delicious. They only wished there was maple syrup to top it off. They were able to eat half of it before the excitement wore off and they were unable to take another bite. Ian finished their plate.

"You all packed for your adventure?" Jen asked, sitting down on the end of Ian's bed as Sergio collected the plates.

"Think so," Riley replied, pushing themself off the floor.

"Well you'd better go check, and make sure you leave room for some snacks," Jen replied.

With the way she was acting, Riley could almost pretend as if they were just going on a hike for a few days. But then they caught sight of Sergio's pale face and Ian's smile that was just a little too wide and stiff. So Riley nodded, hurrying out of the room to inventory their backpack. As they thought, Sergio hadn't put nearly enough in. Stuffing in a few more changes of clothing, Riley zipped up the backpack, hid it and their jacket in the closet, and headed into the other room.

"Did Raf call last night?" Ian asked.

"No, otherwise I would've told you," Riley said. "He's got his hands full with those kids. I'll make sure he talks to you when I call back."

Now Ian's grin was genuine. "Thanks, RJ."

"Domestic Security, open up!"

Everyone glanced at each other. Riley stepped up to the door. Looking through the peephole they saw two soldiers standing behind Kit, who was holding two bags and looking down at the ground. They unlocked the door and pulled it open.

"I need to see everyone's ID cards," one of the soldiers said.

Riley scrambled in their pocket, thankful they'd just put on yesterday's pants, and handed it over to the soldier on the right. They turned around to call to everyone else, but Sergio was already right behind them, with his, Ian's and Jen's cards. The soldier lined up the cards on his clipboard, ran his pen down the other side of the page, and nodded at Kit. "They're good."

Kit nodded and handed over the two bags, looking up at Riley for the first time. Her teeth were clenched, eyes burning with anger. Riley forced their face to remain neutral as Kit glanced at the bag now in Riley's left hand.

"Thank you," they said, stepping back. Sergio took the ID cards back from the soldier and closed the door as quickly as he could. Letting out their breath, Riley hurried to put the rations on the counter and dig through them to find the medication. But a hand on their shoulder made them stop.

"Wait," Sergio whispered, looking toward the door. Ian followed his gaze while Jen frowned at Sergio. Nobody moved until they heard the distinct sound of muffled footsteps walking away from the door and disappearing.

"Okay," Sergio said, and they tore into the bags. The bottles of Tylenol were buried in a bulk bag of rice, along with a carefully folded square of paper.

"Guard change is at midnight," Riley read. "Best time to get over the fence is right before midnight between the last patrol passing the fence but before the first one sets out. But how am I supposed to know the time out there?"

"With this, I guess," Ian said, pulling a watch out of the rice bag. "She thought of everything."

"That she did," Riley said, taking the watch and putting it on as Sergio took the paper from her hands.

"I'd give it at least forty-five minutes to get into Echo, and thirty minutes to get to the Meeting Space," Sergio said. "Means you should leave around 10:45."

Riley wondered why the hell they'd gotten up so early, and it became clear that everyone else had the same idea.

"Why don't we all go back to bed for a few hours?" Jen said. "Then we can do last-minute preparations, check in with Rafael and make sure Riley's actually still needed, and..."

"Yeah, sounds good," Sergio said, putting his arm around Riley's shoulders. Riley followed him back into their room to lay awake for a few hours, mentally tracing the paths they could take to the fence between Foxtrot and Echo and praying there weren't too many soldiers along the way.

"No, I can't see any soldiers guarding the back door. They don't even patrol back here since there's just a concrete wall on the other side. You're in the clear."

Riley let out a huge sigh of relief at Nozomi's words before clicking the radio mic on again. "Thanks, Licorice."

"Good luck, Elderflower. You'll need it."

Hanging up the mic, Riley turned and nearly smacked into a black, woolen beanie that Ian was holding out to them.

"Here, take this. You'll need it."

Riley took the hat from him. "You're just turning me into a burglar. Aren't you?"

"If it helps, then yes," Ian replied. Riley grinned, pulling the beanie on and tucking their hair up into it.

"Looks good," Ian said, trying to match Riley's grin but failing. Riley could feel their own grin slide off their face. The two stared at each other, but then Ian pulled Riley into a hug. His shoulder didn't seem to be hurting him anymore, and for that Riley was thankful.

"Please stay safe, RJ," he said, pressing his forehead to the top of their head. "We need you to come home."

"I will," Riley replied, squeezing him tightly before letting him go.

Jen was next to give them a hug. "I managed to fit another two water bottles in your backpack, just in case."

"Thank you, Jen," Riley replied, kissing her cheek. "I'll be careful. I promise."

"I know you will be," Jen replied, returning the kiss and pressing both of her hands to Riley's cheeks. Tears were in her eyes, which made the knot in Riley's stomach tighten. But they forced themself to smile, kiss her cheek again, and then turn to head for the front door. Sergio had been standing there for the past half an hour, watching for the soldier to pass by.

"At the rate he's crossing, he has to be checking the stairwells," Sergio said. "We'll give it sixty seconds once he passes, then you haul ass for the other stairwell. Watch for other soldiers checking the stairs. Stick to the alleys and backstreets. Find that place on the fence that doesn't have barbed wire on the top and go over there. Don't try to fight through the wire. And call as soon as you get to the Meeting Space!"

"I will," Riley said as Sergio peered closer at the peephole.

"All right he just passed, sixty seconds." He stared at Riley, grabbed their face, and pulled them into a long and desperate kiss. Riley tried to lean into it, tried to enjoy it, but in the back of their head they were counting down the seconds until they had to run. Sergio must've been too, because at twenty seconds he pulled away.

"Stay safe and come back as soon as you can."

"I will," Riley said. "I will."

One last kiss and Riley was out the door. The hallway was pitch black, but Riley's eyes adjusted quickly from the dim light of their apartment. Trying to balance speed and sound, they hurried for the stairwell, fumbled for the knob, and pushed it open. Sliding through to the other side, they pushed it closed as quietly as they could and held their breath. Any second they expected the door to burst open and for a hand to grab their shoulder. They strained for the sound of quick bootsteps, but everything was quiet.

Taking a deep breath to calm themself, Riley set off down the stairs. At every door they stopped and pressed their ear to it, trying to hear if anyone was coming. At the door that led to the second floor, they did hear muffled bootsteps. They pressed themself against the wall next to the door so it would hide them when it opened. Holding their breath, they squeezed their eyes shut. The door opened. Silence. The door banged shut and the footsteps stomped away. Letting their breath out, Riley hurried down the last flight of steps to the back door.

They really hoped Nozomi was right about the absence of a patrol as they creaked open the door. Straining their ears Riley listened for any nearby footsteps. All they could hear was the screeching rumbles of a tank that was hopefully far away.

Sucking in the brisk night air, Riley slipped outside and headed for an alley behind the building that would lead them in a straight line to the fence. Wincing as their feet crunched on the gravel, Riley made their way to the line of buildings at the start of the alleyway and crouched beside a stack of pallets. They could see lights bouncing on the main road, but the beams fell short of Riley's hiding place.

Each of those lights had to be a soldier. With the power out and a dim moon, that was the only way the guards could see. And that made it a lot easier for Riley to see them. Grinning, they gave the alley one last glance and set off.

They couldn't bring themself to run. That was a good way to run directly into trouble. They settled for a crouched speed walk, pausing at every alley intersection to look both ways for lights before crossing. After a while they couldn't tell how far away from their home they were, and they couldn't tell how close to Echo they were. All they knew was to crouch, move, freeze, and hide when they saw lights. But they were confident if they continued down this alley they'd get to Franklin's house. The house was right next to a section of the fence that didn't have barbed wire on it—unless the Command had found the supplies to repair it. They really hoped the soldiers hadn't.

After another…minute? Ten minutes? Large headlights beamed across the alley ahead of them. Ducking down behind a rusted empty water barrel, they peeked out and saw the chain-link fence in the beams. The headlights of a Humvee driving by flashed up to the top of the fence. Luckily, there was still a sizable gap in the barbed wire. Riley hoped they could squeeze through. The Humvee drove past, then another, and another.

Riley hoped their luck wasn't about to run out now.

They counted to twenty and made a break for the fence. There was no way they could climb this silently, Riley just had to be as fast as possible and hope they were far enough away from the checkpoint so nobody would hear. A few feet away from the fence Riley jumped, trying to get as much height as they could.

Riley didn't get as high as they wanted to—they were out of practice—but it was a couple less feet to climb. They scrambled up, relying on their arms to pull themself up since they couldn't get a good foothold. Riley's chest squeezed and squeezed as they pulled themself higher and higher. Their feet slipped out from under them. Pain shot through their fingers. Out of the corner of their eye they saw pinpricks of light bouncing in the distance. They were running out of time.

Adrenaline pumped through their system. Riley yanked themself up to the top of the fence. They threw their legs one after the other over to the other side. They couldn't see the ground in the dark. How far down was it? Ten feet? Fifteen? They leaned forward, but something tugged them back. Their backpack was caught on the barbed wire.

Shit. Fuck.

Riley squinted, trying to make out where the snag was. There! Gritting their teeth, they tried to thread their hand through the barbed wire. Pain radiated up their arm. The wire had sliced through their hand. They twisted away, yanking the backpack free. The headlights were bouncing closer and closer, the beams threatening to capture them.

Riley grabbed the top of the fence with their non-injured hand. They found footholds and turned to face the fence. Taking a deep breath and cradling their injured hand against their chest, they jumped back.

They were weightless, swallowed up by the void. Slamming into the ground, they threw themself into a roll. They staggered to their feet and headed for the closest alleyway. Nothing else hurt, must've been a good landing.

"Movement! Noise! Over there!"

ShitshitshitshitSHIT!

Wrapping their injured hand with the end of their jacket sleeve to get pressure on it, Riley darted for a thin space between two warehouses. Taking off their backpack and holding it in their non-injured hand, they slid in. They shimmied to the center of the alley-like space so no flashlight beams would accidentally hit them. But if the soldiers checked between the buildings, they were toast. All they could do was hold their breath and hope they wouldn't be found.

Voices floated up through the night: "Did you see where they went?"

"No, I just saw someone drop from the top of the fence!

"You sure they dropped on this side of the fence?"

"Course I'm sure! Look at that splot there. Looks like blood. Doesn't it?"

"Yeah, sure enough, must've gotten cut on the wire. Let's call the patrol and take a look around."

Shit. Backup. Of course.

They inched their way to the other side of the alley. The street was completely dark. Riley was thankful that their theory was right. The soldiers were only guarding buildings that were occupied. They hoped they remembered correctly which buildings were occupied and which weren't.

Riley wove their way through the back alleys of Echo. Every time their feet crunched on gravel or slipped on ash, they'd freeze and hold their breath, afraid someone had heard. But no flashlights spotted them. They kept moving.

After a few more minutes, Riley managed to position themself a block or so down from the Meeting Space. No one lived in these warehouses anymore, given that they were mostly charred rubble. Crouching behind melted steel beams, they counted… a lot of flashlights. Riley racked their brain, trying to remember if people lived in the buildings behind the Meeting Space. If not, they could try to sneak in the back door. If so, uh, distract and hope for the best?

Riley had no clue how they'd managed to even make it this far with their miserable excuse for a plan.

Darting across the road, Riley slipped into another alley. They moved from warped dumpster to scorched crates as they approached the street where the Meeting Space sat. Peeking out, they didn't see any flashlights down near the Meeting Space. Glancing the other way, they choked at the sight of two fat headlights.

Jumping back, Riley held their breath, afraid someone had seen them. But there were no shouts, no sounds of running. They gingerly poked their head back out again. The headlights weren't pointing toward them. The truck was up closer to the fence pointing down the crossroad. It had to be one of the patrol Humvees, parked so the soldiers could help search for Riley. They would have to chance that nobody was sitting in the truck.

Taking a deep breath, Riley took off down the street. They stopped at every alley entrance, checking to make sure the flashlight beams didn't travel through the alley. As they got closer to the Meeting Space, they had to force themself not to get complacent. Press back against building, check alley, check behind them, move fast.

Finally they landed behind the building next to the Meeting Space. They could hear footsteps crunching closer, so they slid back into the nearest alley. Cautiously peeking their head around the corner, they watched the soldier stride around the building. When the soldier disappeared, Riley checked the alley and ran to the door, which was boarded up. Well, there went their brilliant plan out the—window!

Stepping back, Riley looked to see if a window was near the door. Nope. But the window to the Reverend's office was just around the corner. Peeking around, they saw the soldier disappear around the building and two faint flashlight beams across the street. Now or never.

Crouching, they snuck to the window and straightened up. It was closed. Getting on their tiptoes, Riley threaded their arm through the jagged hole in the window pane and fumbled for the latch. Their fingers brushed against it. They inched themself higher on their tiptoes. After a few more seconds of grasping, they sprang the latch. Yanking their arm out, they tore their jacket on one of the shards of glass.

Riley inched the window high enough to squeeze through. Tearing the backpack off of their shoulders, they dropped it on the ground inside the dark room. It thudded louder than a bass drum beat. Bootsteps on the asphalt stopped and then got louder and faster. They were out of time.

Gritting their teeth, Riley grabbed the windowsill with both of their hands. Pain flashed through Riley's injured hand. They yanked themself up and squeezed through the window. Their feet hit the ground. When everything went quiet, they couldn't hear the bootsteps anymore. They pressed themself against the wall under the window and held their breath, squeezing their eyes shut. They couldn't fail now. Not when they'd just gotten here!

The bootsteps started up again, crunching on the dirt that coated the alley. Riley could hear them growing louder and louder. Every part of them was squeezed so tightly, suffocating them. Not today. Not today. Not today.

The footsteps hesitantly moved away. Riley let out their breath as quietly as they could, trying to keep their breathing even and slow so they wouldn't hyperventilate. As the footsteps got quieter and quieter, Riley could feel the stinging in their hand grow stronger and stronger. Clenching their teeth, they pushed themself to their feet.

Creak.

Riley jumped as the office door inched opened, throwing their hands up. A beam of light poked into the room. The door widened, and in the split second before the light hit their face, Riley saw the Reverend.

"Only me!" they whispered.

"Riley!"

The light dropped, and before Riley could fully comprehend what was happening, the Reverend pulled them into a tight hug.

"You're okay," he gasped. "You're okay!"

Riley could feel all of the stress and tension flood out of them as they hugged him back.

The Reverend gave Riley gauze, tape, and a flashlight so they could bandage their hand while he started administering the medicine to the kids. Riley could hear him talking to what sounded like two other adult voices, so they didn't feel as guilty taking their time and making sure their wound was cleaned out and the bandages were secured correctly. They were about to head out to help when the Reverend opened the office door.

"How's your hand?" he asked, setting the flashlight on its end so it lit up the room better.

"Still stings, but that'll hopefully go away in a minute," Riley replied, examining their handiwork.

"Yeah." The Reverend pulled the chair out from behind his desk and spun it around so he could sit on it backward. "Aisha's setting a cot up for you in the back room. Figure you'd be in no rush to make the return trip."

"You figured correctly," Riley replied. "So Aisha's here?"

The Reverend nodded. "And Rami, her older brother. They got caught in Echo district when lockdown was called, and instead of trying to make it all the way back to Charlie before dark, they came to me. They've been very helpful at keeping the kids calm and taken care of."

"How many kids do you have here now?"

"Ten. We lost two."

Fuck.

"You did the best you could, Riley. Had you gotten here any later… well, we would've lost a lot more."

True, but it didn't make Riley feel better. They glanced over at the Reverend's radio and realized they hadn't called back home yet.

"Shit, is your radio working?"

"Yeah, call home and tell them you're all right," the Reverend said, pushing himself up off his chair so Riley could take it.

"You got a minute? Ian misses you."

"Uh, y-yeah, I think I can spare a minute. Long as you can cover for me out there."

"Yeah, of course. I was planning on letting you sleep for a while," Riley said, taking his chair.

"You're an absolute angel sent from heaven."

Riley laughed as they clicked on the mic. "This is Elderflower calling in. Wildfire, Blizzard, Windstorm, are you there?"

The radio stayed silent. Riley's stomach churned. What if one of the soldiers had identified them? What if they hadn't gone after them but their family? What if Sergio, Ian, and Jen…

The radio crackled to life. "This is Wildfire. I…Ri…"

"I'm okay. I made it just fine."

"Thank God. I love you," *Sergio said.*

"I love you too."

The radio went silent. Riley didn't know what else they could say. Clearly neither did Sergio because the next voice on the radio was Ian.

"Good to hear you, Elderflower," he said, sounding a little choked up.

"Good to hear you too," Riley replied, "but I have a feeling I'm not the person you really want to talk to." They got up from the chair and passed the mic to the Reverend.

He eagerly took it. "Blizzard this is Valerian. You still there?"

Riley couldn't make out exactly what Ian said, but he sounded elated. Grinning, they grabbed the backpack and flashlight and headed into the main part of the Meeting Space.

It was always scary when sick kids didn't fuss. Ten sick kids not fussing was absolutely terrifying. Riley could only hope it was because the medication was starting to kick in and lowering their fevers so they could sleep.

The room was lit by a dim electric lantern and two flashlights, one of which was standing on its end while the other was moving around. Riley could see Aisha in the light of the lantern and her flashlight. She looked up as the door opened and gave Riley a nod. The other flashlight was moving toward them.

"You must be Riley Jay," the man said, sticking out his hand. He was tall and thin with dark brown skin, brown eyes, and thick black hair that was buzzed short. "I'm Rami. Good to finally meet you."

"Good to meet you too," Riley said, shaking his hand. "How's Kamal doing?"

"Back to his happy little self, thanks to you."

"Think there was a miracle or two involved in there as well," Riley replied. "Hopefully we'll get a few more miracles for these kids."

"I pray we will," he said, looking over the rows of children sleeping on sleeping bags, thin mattresses, and piles of blankets. "Want me to join you for your rounds?"

"No, thank you. Get some rest. You must be exhausted."

"That is an understatement," Rami replied. "Try to convince Aisha to get some sleep too. Will you? She's slept less than me."

"Of course."

Yawning, Rami gave Riley a small wave and headed toward a back room. Riley made sure to keep the flashlight off the faces of the kids as they made their way over to Aisha's side.

Aisha stood up as they got close. "You got here at just the right time."

"Yeah, I'm thankful I made it," Riley whispered. "How's everyone doing?"

"The medication's making sleep come easier."

"Thank goodness, sleep is the best thing for them right now," Riley said. "Speaking of which, I can take over. Go get some rest. Won't do us any good if you get sick too."

"Guess you're right," Aisha said, brushing off her jeans. "I set a cot up for you next to mine in the back room. Let me know when you need me to take back over."

"I will," Riley replied, knowing there was no way they were grabbing her first with how bloodshot her eyes were.

Aisha trudged off to the back room, leaving Riley alone in the main room with a bunch of sleeping, sick kids. After a quick round to make sure all of them were still breathing, Riley plopped down in a folding chair that was on the edge of the group, next to the Reverend's office door. Leaning back, they rested their head against the wall. They could hear his low voice, presumably still talking to Ian. Riley couldn't help themself; they strained to hear what he was saying.

"...come see you as soon as lockdown is lifted. I promise. I love you."

Riley's heart stopped. They were smiling, but their stomach was also flip-flopping with guilt for listening in. They weren't surprised, but...why didn't Ian tell them?

CHAPTER TWELVE

Riley did not know how to ask the Reverend about what they'd overheard. Fortunately, there wasn't enough time to talk with so many crying kids with sore throats and fevers. Rami managed to rig up a humidifier tent with plastic sheets, an electric hotplate, and a saucepan that he rotated around the kids whenever they had power. Aisha made sure everyone had enough fluids, concocting the most delicious drinks they could to encourage the kids to drink them. And the Reverend and Riley kept track of the medications and the kids' vital signs. The kids' fevers went down and their sore throats improved once the Tylenol did its thing. Soon, the evening conversations turned from keeping the kids alive to getting them home.

"Jacob's the farthest away. He lives near the edge of the district," the Reverend said as they scarfed down a rice dish Aisha had managed to throw together. "I really don't know how we're going to get him home."

"Yeah, especially since he's not going to be able to run that far and he's too big to be carried," Riley replied.

"I could probably fireman carry him," Rami said.

"Stealthily?" Riley asked.

"...that's harder."

"Maybe we can get the parents to help," Aisha said.

"Good idea. But how?" the Reverend asked. "If we ask them to come get their kids, we run the risk of them getting caught and then nobody to look after their kids. And I'm sure all our luck was spent with getting the kids and Riley here."

Aisha sighed in frustration. "I know, but I don't have any other ideas."

"Neither do I," the Reverend replied. "Think the best we can do right now is sit tight and hope lockdown will be lifted soon."

Crying swelled up from the main room and Riley went to see what was wrong. After comforting a fussing Molly, Riley made their rounds to the other kids. For the first time, none of their foreheads felt feverish. Jeremiah even felt well enough to follow Riley around and talk their ear off. His prattle was music to their ears.

Ten out of twelve kids made it. Riley could almost count that a win.

The Reverend, Rami, and Aisha cheered when Riley delivered the good news. "Guess our next biggest worry is keeping ten kids entertained," Aisha said.

"I will take that problem over ten kids having measles," the Reverend replied.

"Yes, and hopefully we won't have that problem for much longer," Rami said.

Unfortunately, Rami was wrong. A week later they were scrambling to come up with toys and games for the older kids while constantly cuddling the little babies. Rami turned out to be a genius with calming down the older kids while the Reverend could soothe a screaming baby in under a minute.

"And you're telling me you didn't have *any* aptitude for pediatrics?" Riley said as the Reverend cradled a one-year-old Luca.

"Look, I'm good with kids. I'm not good about examining and diagnosing them. I like it when my patients can tell me what's going on instead of screaming."

Riley knew what he meant. As much as they loved working with kids, it was incredibly difficult when they constantly tried to squirm away and complained loudly when you tried to get them to eat more. Every night when they got on the radio with their family, their bones ached with exhaustion.

"This'll be over soon, baby," Sergio said soothingly, and Riley knew he was saying it as much to himself as he was to them.

"I know, but I'd like sooner to come a lot faster," Riley replied.

"Me too. I miss you."

"I miss you too."

Riley rested their face on their hand, blinking back tears. What they wouldn't give to be home with him and Ian and Jen again.

The Reverend came into the office, and behind him Riley could see the lights had been turned off in the main space. "I have to go, honey. I don't want to wake the kids up. I love you," they said.

"I love you too. See you soon."

Riley turned off the mic and hung up the headphones, vacating the chair so the Reverend could slump into it.

"I don't know how much longer we can keep doing this," he said, plunking his elbows on his desk and hiding his face in his hands.

"I'm surprised we've done it this long," Riley replied.

"I'm trying not to think about that." The Reverend glanced at the radio. "Did you talk to Ian?"

"He said hi before Sergio got on, but not really."

"Oh," the Reverend said, looking back up at Riley. "He wanted to tell you something. Guess he decided against it."

"Did he want to tell me that you two are a thing?"

The words were out of their mouth before they could stop them, and a wave of relief and fear flowed over them.

The Reverend froze, his eyes wide, his mouth falling open. "H-how…?"

"I-I overheard you talking a few nights ago," Riley said, regretting saying anything. "I'm sorry. I'd started suspecting, but I should've waited for Ian to say something."

"Okay, okay, okay," the Reverend said, chuckling. "Well, now you know, I guess. I figured you might've been catching on, so I was trying to encourage Ian to tell you tonight since he's essentially your brother. Guess he got cold feet."

"Guess so," Riley said. "Still, I'll act surprised when he eventually tells me."

"Much appreciated," the Reverend said. "You… you okay with that?"

Were they okay with Ian dating the man who'd used his life as a bargaining chip? Riley's logical side said no, of course not, who would be okay with that? The Reverend was a *doctor.* He'd sworn an oath to do no harm. By threatening to withhold the antibiotics, he'd threatened to do harm unless Riley put themself in harm's way.

But what if he had just handed over the antibiotics and let Riley go, knowing they were a pediatric nurse? Was he then doing more harm since he had a way to help those kids and he didn't take it? But it wasn't his fault those kids were hurt and sick from diseases and conditions they'd been able to cure before some *stupid* soldiers decided to storm into the capitol and massacre all of the governing party's legislators. The decision to bargain had been his.

"Do you regret bargaining with his life?" Riley asked, finally meeting the Reverend's eyes.

He looked past them, toward the door that led to ten kids who were sleeping soundly without fevers that threatened to burn them alive.

"I regret I had to do it in the first place," he said.

They could accept that answer.

"Attention, citizens. Jericho is now out of lockdown. You are allowed to leave your homes unless ordered otherwise. Attention, citizens. Jericho is now out of lockdown."

Riley bolted upright, blinking through their sleep-blurred eyes. "Wh-what time is it?"

"Sun's just come up," Aisha said from the window. "Command waited until curfew was over to announce it. We can go home! We can get the kids home!"

She ran out the door into the main space before Riley could stop her. The sounds of fussing and crying grew louder, and Riley could hear Aisha and either Rami or the Reverend consoling the kids. Rubbing the sleep out of their eyes, Riley rolled off of the cot and threw on their jacket before joining them. Aisha was bouncing Patrick on her hip while Rami had scooped up Emilie and was tossing her into the air. Thomas, a small three-year-old with very pale skin, bright blond hair and dark green eyes, staggered toward Riley while big tears rolled down his cheeks.

Riley scooped him up and wiped away his tears. "Is the noise too loud?"

He nodded, wiping his nose with the back of his hand. "I want Mommy!"

"Mommy's going to be here soon to pick you up," Riley replied, walking closer to Aisha and Rami. "Where's the Reverend?"

"Still in his office. I heard the radio going off," Rami said. "It is probably parents calling in to ask about their children."

"Hopefully the Reverend is telling them to come get them," Riley said. "I'm about ready to sleep for two weeks."

"Tell me about it," Aisha said.

A pounding at the door made everyone jump. The kids cried harder. Rami took Thomas from Riley as they ran for the door. Unlocking it, they cracked it open and peeked out. A harried man with light brown skin, dark brown eyes, and black hair that was sticking up in a jagged mess stood in front of them.

"Hello. My son, Neil. Is he here?"

Riley blanked on all the kids' names. The Reverend put his hand on Riley's shoulder and opened the door wider.

"Arjun, yes, your son is fine. He's still a little weak from recovering, but he's okay. He's right over here—"

Arjun burst into tears, and Riley jumped out of his way as he barreled inside. The next few hours were a swirl of crying children, crying parents, and the Reverend, Riley, Aisha, and Rami trying to calm them all. The Reverend had already told the Wilsons and the Martins that their sons had died. Neither family could claim the bodies since preserving them was impossible. Instead, they'd given the Reverend permission to hide the bodies in dumpsters for the soldiers to take away, so Command wouldn't find out about the children hiding in the Meeting Space. Riley tried to not to think about what had happened after that.

Finally Thomas's mom took him away, only leaving baby Amanda, who was sleeping peacefully in the Reverend's arms.

"Have you heard from her parents?" Rami asked.

The Reverend shook his head, pressing his lips together.

"Dad said there were...rumors, of people disappearing," Aisha said.

"Some people were taken right when the strict lockdown was called," the Reverend said. "Haven't heard of anyone since then. Rami, do you know where the Sanderson family lives?"

"I think so."

"Check the house. See if anyone's home. I expected Emma to be one of the first people here."

Rami nodded and took off. The door clanged shut after him, and Amanda cried out. The Reverend began bouncing and shushing her.

"Reverend, if you don't need me anymore, I'm going to let Mom and Dad know we're all right," Aisha said. "In person."

"Of course, go. Thank you so much for your help, Aisha. I don't know how I can repay you."

"You've already helped us so much. This is just making us even," Aisha replied. After grabbing her backpack from the back room, she gave Riley a hug before heading out the door.

Riley waited until they were sure she was gone before turning to the Reverend. "You think her parents were taken?"

The Reverend looked down at the baby who was back to sleep. "I... I think it's likely. Mac's been openly critical of the Command, and if Emma tried to stop the soldiers in any way..."

Riley looked down at the tiny baby. "Wh-who's gonna take her, then?"

"I honestly don't know," the Reverend said. "Emma has a sister in Charlie district, but they're estranged. I don't know if she would take Amanda."

"It's worth a try?"

The Reverend was about to reply when the front door banged open. Riley whirled around to see Sergio staring at them with Ian just over his shoulder.

It took them a second to realize it was *actually Sergio* and not some hallucination caused by missing him desperately and a lack of sleep. Still, they weren't entirely sure he was actually real until he pulled them into his arms and kissed them.

Riley never wanted to leave him again. Ever. He was warm and safe and… and… just everything Riley needed right now. And Sergio seemed just as willing to never let them leave again, grabbing their hands and pressing his forehead to the top of their head after they broke apart.

"You're okay. You're okay," he said, kissing the top of their head. "People were being dragged out of their apartments last night after we hung up. We had to hide the radio in case they broke in so we couldn't call you and see if you were okay. Jen was freaking out and ordered us to go get you as soon as we could…"

He pulled them back into a hug, and Riley rested their head on his chest. They doubted Jen was the one who had told them to find Riley; they were pretty sure Sergio had sprinted out the door the second it'd been safe to do so.

Opening their eyes, Riley saw Ian lean back from the Reverend, his palms resting on the Reverend's cheeks. The Reverend looked absolutely shocked, but a smile was spreading across his face. Ian said something that Riley couldn't quite catch, but whatever it was made them both laugh.

Ian leaned back in to steal another quick kiss from the Reverend, and Riley looked away. They didn't want to say anything until Ian said something, but if he was straight-up kissing the Reverend in front of them, he might just want them to get the hint…

The door burst open and Riley and Sergio broke apart to see Sam and Rami standing in the doorway.

"Raf, we've got a problem," Sam said.

"Mac and Emma are gone?"

"And the Jacobsons, and the Okoros, and the Lebeds, and the—"

All families that had received medical care from Riley or the Reverend.

"Everyone? Including the kids?" the Reverend asked.

"Everyone!"

Riley heard what Sam had said, but they didn't believe it. Even with everything the soldiers had done, somehow Riley hadn't believed they would actually *kidnap* children. Why was it always so much worse if kids were involved?

"Do you know where they were taken?" Ian asked.

"I'm guessin' the prison in Bravo district," Sam said. "That's where most people get taken."

"Is that prison big enough to hold everyone?" the Reverend asked.

"Do we really know how big it is?" Sam asked. "How deep underground does that thing go?"

"What do we do?" Rami asked.

"Easy. We march on over there and let them know we ain't goin' nowhere until they release everyone," Sam said.

"What if they just throw us into prison too?" Rami asked.

"That's a risk we gotta take," Sam said. "Otherwise they may never release those families."

Would going change anything, though? Riley looked over at the Reverend, who was nodding his head in agreement.

“We’re not prepared, though,” he said. “We don’t have time to soak bandanas.”

“We’ll stay for as long as we can,” Sam replied. “At least it’ll be something.”

Riley and Ian looked at each other, and Riley could see their confusion mirrored in Ian’s face. Time to soak bandanas? For what?

“Ian, put out some calls over the radio. See who we can get together,” the Reverend said.

“Send them to the Echo-Bravo checkpoint. We’ll march from there,” Sam said. He looked out over everyone else. “Y’all coming?”

“No,” the Reverend said, walking over to Riley and handing them Amanda. “You need to stay, Riley. If we both get arrested, the entire network falls apart. If anyone gets seriously hurt, I’m sending them back to you.”

Riley wanted to tell him no, that they’d go, because they knew he was more important to the network. He started it, he designed it, he knew how to run it. But they couldn’t bring themself to switch places with him. They didn’t want to risk being arrested and getting hurt any more than they already were. So they took the baby and nodded. The Reverend looked up at Sergio, and when Riley glanced back, they could see he was shaking his head.

“I need to go back and get Jen. We’ve left her alone for long enough already,” Sergio said, coming up beside Riley and wrapping his arm around their shoulders. Riley didn’t want him to leave, either to get Jen or to go with the Reverend and Sam. They just wanted him to stay put for once. But they also didn’t want Jen to be alone, especially since people had been kidnapped. So as everyone got ready to leave, Riley tucked Amanda into her makeshift crib and kissed Sergio good-bye.

“I’ll be back soon,” he said, pulling them in for a hug, kissing the top of their head. “Stay inside until I get back.”

They both knew inside wasn’t any safer than outside, but just hearing it made Riley feel better. So after one last kiss, Riley watched from the doorway as he headed off with Sam, the Reverend, Rami, and dozens of others who’d gathered around as Sergio and the Reverend had been saying their goodbyes. After the group turned the corner, Riley stepped back into the warehouse and quietly closed the door so it wouldn’t wake up the baby or disturb Ian at the radio.

“I think I should go,” Ian said, stepping down onto the bottom step in front of the door.

“The group’s only been gone for half an hour,” Riley said. “Nobody’s going to come back ’til close to sunset, probably.”

“What if everyone’s been arrested?” he asked, glancing around to make sure no soldiers had overheard.

“Someone would’ve gotten away,” Riley said, but they weren’t entirely sure if they believed it.

“Guess so,” Ian replied, sounding like he had exactly as much faith as Riley did. Riley stepped back to allow Ian back inside. It was so quiet now since Rebecca and Irene Paulson had come by to take Amanda. They’d been sent by the Reverend and had been good friends of Mac’s and Emma’s. But since the radio was silent, that left Riley and Ian nothing to do.

Which made it really, really hard not say anything to Ian about the Reverend.

“RJ? You okay?” Ian asked as he collapsed in the Reverend’s chair, kicking his feet up on the desk.

"Yeah, I'm fine. Why?" Riley asked as they sat down across from him, hoping they hadn't answered too quickly.

"You seem on edge," Ian said. "Like, there's you with anxiety, and then there's you when you're trying to keep something hidden. You're definitely keeping something hidden."

That was all the permission Riley needed to blurt out, "IsawyoukisstheReverend."

"What?"

"I saw you… kiss the Reverend."

Ian's eyes went wide, but he shrugged. "So?"

"The Reverend said you wanted to tell me you two were together."

"I did, but… I didn't know how. A good time never came up. Like I didn't just want to blurt out in the middle of dinner, 'Hey! I'm very bi and Rafael's very hot and also we love each other!' Y'know? So… I guess now you know."

"I guess so," Riley replied, unable to keep the grin off their face.

"So you're…okay with it?"

"Of course I am," Riley said. "Goodness knows you've been putting up with Sergio's and my couple shenanigans for way too long. Guess it's time for you to get back at us."

Ian laughed as the radio crackled to life. "Windstorm calling Valerian. Come in, please."

Ian leaned over and grabbed the mic. "This is Blizzard, Windstorm. I've also got Elderflower here with me."

"Blizzard! Are you all right? Are Elderflower and Wildfire all right?"

"Yes, I'm all right and Elderflower's all right, but Wildfire went back to get you and we haven't heard from him yet. Is he with you now?"

Static burst through the radio before Jen said, "What? Repeat that?"

"I'm fine. Elderflower's fine. Is Wildfire with you?"

"He's not here. You said he was supposed to come get me?"

"Yeah, that's what he said he was going to do," Ian said, looking nervously over at Riley.

"Well, where else would he have gone?"

Ian took a deep breath. "A group of people went to see about getting the families who were taken released. Wildfire might've gone along with them."

"What! Why the hell would he do that?"

"I don't know."

Riley didn't have a good answer to that either. They honestly didn't believe that Sergio had gone with the group to Bravo. They were pretty sure what had happened, but they didn't want to admit it to themself, or Ian and Jen.

"Well, I'm going to head out your way. I'll leave a note for Wildfire when he shows up. I'm sure he just got pulled aside to help Greenhouse or something."

Riley let themself believe that as Ian said, "All right, stay safe. We'll see you when you get here."

"See you soon. Love you, Blizzard, Elderflower!"

Ian put the mic up to Riley's mouth, who forced themself to say, "Love you, Windstorm!"

Now Riley had yet another person to worry about. They paced back and forth in the main area of the Meeting Space, trying to work off all of the anxious energy that kept building inside of them. Ian stayed on the radio, trying to reach anyone in Bravo district who could tell them anything about what was going on. All they could learn was that a sizeable group of people was standing in front of the prison, surrounded by soldiers. That did not put either Ian's or Riley's mind at ease.

"What are the soldiers going to do?" Ian said, leaning against the doorframe of the Reverend's office and crossing his arms.

"I have no clue," Riley replied. "Hopefully nothing too bad."

Wave after wave of anxiety crashed over Riley as they paced, and it didn't abate when Jen showed up at the door. She immediately pulled both of them into a long hug, which did nothing to make Riley less anxious either.

"Well, I need to get started on dinner, I'm sure everyone's going to be very hungry when they get back," Jen said. "Riley, do you want to run across the street and ask Yvonne if she and Deborah want to join us for dinner?"

"I think Raf normally goes over there for dinner," Ian said. "There's not a real kitchen here, just a hotplate and an icebox."

"How does he live like that?"

"Great question," Riley replied before Ian could say anything to defend his new boyfriend.

Jen went across the street to talk to Yvonne, and instead of walking back across the street, she radioed to tell Ian and Riley that Yvonne had offered up her trailer for dinner. Ian elected to stay by the radio in case the Reverend called in while Riley headed across the street to help out with dinner.

They'd just gotten up on the sidewalk when faint shouts made their heart stop. Peeking behind the trailer, they saw the street was completely empty. The shouts were coming from Bravo district and falling into a staccato rhythm. Riley started to head down the alley, wondering if they would be able to see anything.

"This has been declared an unlawful assembly. Disperse immediately. This has been declared an unlawful assembly. Disperse immediately."

Even with how faint it was, the mechanical voice still grated on Riley's ears. The shouts of the crowd got louder, but Riley still couldn't tell what they were saying.

"Riley Jay! Get back here. What the hell do you think you're doing?"

Riley turned to look at Yvonne leaning out the window of the trailer. Realizing they were halfway across the empty street, they glanced around to see all of the doors were tightly shut. Tarps covered most of the windows, and those that weren't covered were dark and empty.

They opened their mouth to reply, but a faint metallic *thunk* choked off their words. Spinning around, they didn't quite know what to expect. What they didn't expect was to see nothing.

"Riley, inside, *now*!"

They were already backing toward the trailer, and once they hit the sidewalk, they turned and ran down the alley. Running up the ramp to the door, Riley threw it open.

"Riley Jay!" Jen exclaimed as Deborah screamed. The two were sitting on the couch with Deborah staring at Riley, her mouth a perfect "o" of shock. Normally Riley would've laughed, but instead they bolted through the living room and into the kitchen where Yvonne was pulling down a saucepan.

"You're not going to be able to see anything," she said as Riley grabbed the windowsill and stuck their head out. "Bravo's too far away. Well, maybe if they start throwing smoke you will, but tear gas disperses before we'd be able to see it."

Tear gas. So that was what the bandanas were for.

“We should head over there,” Riley said, stepping back from the window.

“What for?” Yvonne asked bitterly. “We’d just get gassed too. Best thing we can do is stay here, get dinner ready, be ready to patch anybody up, and brace ourselves for the smell.”

The screams had morphed into shouts as two more tear gas canisters were fired. Riley felt Yvonne flinch at each shot, and they rested their hand on her shoulder.

She shrugged it off. “Send Jen in here. Will you? She’s got more experience with this canned cheese than I do.”

Riley nodded, hurrying out of the kitchen so they wouldn’t get burned by the anger radiating off of Yvonne. Jen pushed herself off of the couch, handing Deborah one of her stuffed animals. Deborah planted her face on the top of the bunny’s head, giggling.

“I heard her,” Jen said. “Just keep giving Debbie different stuffed animals to plant her face in and she’ll be happy.”

Riley chuckled, taking Jen’s place on the couch. “Hi, Deborah!”

She looked at Riley for a few seconds and then planted her face into her rabbit again.

Riley tried to find comfort in the rhythm of giving Deborah one of her three stuffed animals, having Deborah plant her face in it, and then exchanging it for another animal. But even Deborah’s giggles couldn’t ease the tension in Riley’s chest. They kept glancing up at the cracked drywall that separated them from the window they wished they could still be staring out. Only when Deborah decided to fall into Riley’s shoulder instead of her stuffed animal was Riley able to laugh a bit and start paying more attention to her. Even then, it still felt like a coil of wire had been wrapped around their chest and was being wrenched tighter and tighter with every breath.

The door to the trailer slammed open. Deborah cried out and then immediately started to babble happily as she recognized her father. Sam was coughing, and a peppery, acidic smell swept into the room with him.

"You're okay!" Yvonne said, running toward Sam before stopping a foot away and blinking rapidly.

Riley pushed themself to their feet. "What happened?"

Sam coughed. "Stood there for a bit demandin' that the Command release everyone. They refused. We asked if they would at least release the families. They said they would tomorrow and gassed 'n' smoked us out of there. Raf's back at the Meeting House gettin' cleaned and changed. He'll be over in a minute. Speakin' of which, I need a shower too."

"Did Sergio end up going with you?"

"N-no, he said he was going to get Jen," Sam replied, biting his tongue as he glanced at Yvonne.

"He never made it," Jen said from the doorway to the kitchen. "We were hoping he'd gone with you."

Sam shook his head, pressing his lips together. "Let me get cleaned up and get my throat rinsed out. Then I can put in some calls along his route to see if anyone saw anythin'."

Sergio. Riley had managed to not think about him for over an hour. Everything came crashing back, sharp and painful, before the numbness settled in.

Riley wanted to tell Sam not to bother, that Sergio must've just gotten pulled aside to help someone like Jen said. But they knew that wasn't true. They just didn't want it confirmed. If they didn't know what happened, it was possible Sergio could walk in the door at any second.

At the same time, they desperately needed to know what happened to him so they could stop imagining horrific scenarios in their head.

"Riley, can you come watch this soup?" Jen asked as Yvonne grabbed a glass of water, scooped up Deborah, and followed Sam into the bedroom.

"Yeah, coming," Riley replied, glancing out the window at the Meeting Space. The lights were still on, but Riley couldn't see any movement. The Reverend and Ian must be in the Reverend's office.

"Riley!"

Tearing themself away from the window, Riley stepped into the cramped kitchen. Jen looked up from the stove where she was stirring tomato soup, and the two of them stared at each other. Riley figured they should say something, maybe ask if they were having tomato soup and grilled cheese for dinner, but they couldn't get their voice to work. Everything was frozen stiff, and they couldn't figure out how to move anymore.

Jen set the ladle down and held out her arms. Riley tried to get their feet to move, but they wouldn't budge. It felt like a chorus of voices was screaming in their ears, yet it was deadly silent. They couldn't decide if they wanted to cry, or scream, or vomit, or just curl themself up into a ball in the corner of the kitchen and never move again.

After a few seconds, Jen stepped forward and gently wrapped Riley up in her arms. Riley managed to get their arms to move to hug her back, resting their chin on her shoulder. All of their insides felt like they were being squeezed tighter and tighter, and they didn't know how to get them to release. They barely felt it when Jen started stroking their hair, or when she squeezed them tightly before letting them go and turning back to the stove. Riley finally managed to get their feet to move to slide past Jen and take the soup ladle.

"Just stir every few minutes so it doesn't burn on the bottom," Jen said, going through the pans hanging on the wall before pulling one down.

After two stirs Riley could hear the bedroom door open, and a few minutes later they heard Sam's low, melodic voice, presumably talking to someone on the radio. After six more stirs they heard a knock at the front door. They started stirring and stirring and stirring as three low voices drifted in from the living room. They couldn't look up when the Reverend and Ian stepped into the kitchen.

"Have you heard anything?" Jen's voice was muffled, like she was speaking underwater.

"We've called everyone we could think of," the Reverend said, just as muffled. "Nobody saw anything."

A loud *clang* made Riley jump, and they looked down to see the ladle had fallen onto the floor. The back of their hand started to sting; turning it over they realized some of the soup had splashed onto it. They recognized that Jen was hurrying to clean up the mess, but they couldn't bring themself to help her. They couldn't feel the Reverend's fingers when he grabbed their hand to see the damage, and they could only feel pressure when Ian put his arm around their shoulders to help escort them back into the living room.

This was worse than all of the scenarios Riley could imagine.

CHAPTER THIRTEEN

Ian kept his arm around Riley's shoulders as the two sat down on the couch. Riley rested their head on his shoulder, staring at the brass floor lamp on the other side of the room.

"You two going to be all right if I help Jen?" the Reverend asked, his voice scratchy from the tear gas.

"Yeah, we're fine," Ian said.

The Reverend hesitated before leaning down and kissing Ian's forehead. "Let me know if you need anything."

"Thanks, Raf," Ian said. The Reverend squeezed Riley's shoulder before heading into the kitchen.

Ian rested his head on top of Riley's. "You still with me?"

Riley forced their tongue to move, even though it felt bulky and stiff. "I don't know."

"That's okay," Ian said, pressing his forehead to the top of their head. The silence settled in again, loud and demanding, ringing in Riley's ears. It was only broken when Ian started crying.

All of the pressure and anxiety that had built up inside of Riley burst, and the numbness gave way into a piercing, aching pain. They could feel their whole-body shudder as sob after sob tore out of their throat and only increased their pain. Ian held them tightly as his sobs grew worse.

Riley's throat was burning as their tears dried up and their sobs turned into hiccupping coughs. Their sharp pain dulled into exhaustion as their eyes burned and their throat ached, yet still it felt like everything inside of them was being squeezed. When Ian tried to untangle them, Riley felt as limp as a dead fish.

"Come on, RJ, work with me," Ian said, trying to be lighthearted, but it didn't sound that way with his rough and strained voice. Riley did the best they could, and soon the two were sitting side by side on the couch again.

Jen and the Reverend came back into the room, both with puffy red eyes. Jen sat on the other side of Riley and pulled them into a hug while the Reverend sat on the armrest next to Ian. Ian looked up at him for a second, hesitating, and then slowly leaned his head down onto the Reverend's thigh. Riley's heart twinged a bit at the Reverend's soft, small smile as he began to rub Ian's shoulder.

"I'm sorry," the Reverend said, looking up at Riley, the smile gone from his face.

They didn't know how to respond, so they just stared back at him while leaning their head onto Jen's shoulder. They'd always thought it was so dumb when people apologized for something that wasn't their fault. It wasn't the Reverend's fault Sergio was g… had disappeared.

The bedroom door creaked open and Sam and Yvonne tiptoed out, Sam carrying Deborah. "I'll finish up dinner," Yvonne said, heading into the kitchen.

"How're your eyes feelin' Raf?" Sam asked, sitting down on the bench in front of the ragged upright piano while holding Deborah on his knee.

"Burning's stopped," the Reverend said, "but my throat's still on fire."

"Go get some more water then!" Sam said, nodding toward the kitchen.

"But I'm comfortable right now."

Sam glanced down at Ian. His eyes were shut, but Riley couldn't tell if he was actually sleeping. A huge grin spread across Sam's face as he looked back up at the Reverend. But when he glanced over at Riley, his smile fell a bit. He swung his legs around and tucked them under the piano, moving Deborah onto his lap. She immediately started banging on the keys, laughing.

"Gettin' late, almost time for me to broadcast," he said, running through scales and managing to avoid Deborah's fingers. "Think I should mention anythin' about goin' out tomorrow night?"

"I know you're going to even if I tell you not to," the Reverend said.

"And I know you're not goin' to tell me not to," Sam replied, breaking down chords into arpeggios. Deborah stopped playing and clapped her hands, giggling at each arpeggio.

Yvonne came back into the room with bowls of tomato soup and plates of grilled cheese that Jen helped pass around. Riley stared at the thin tomato soup and the sandwich made with canned cheese. They could already tell it was going to taste like sawdust—creamy, slippery sawdust.

"All right, Debbie. It's time for bed," Yvonne said, taking her daughter from Sam.

"Thank you, honey," Sam said, stealing a kiss from Yvonne. The ache in Riley's heart sharpened again, and they had to look away until they heard the bedroom door close. Jen's arm tightened around their shoulders, pulling them closer, and the sharp pain started to dull back down.

Sam ran up and down the keys of the piano, settling into a smooth jazz melody. "Yo, Raf, can you get the radio ready?"

"Yeah," the Reverend said, patting Ian on the shoulder. Ian yawned and sat up, his eyes still puffy as he reached for his sandwich and soup that was already growing cold. Riley glanced down at their own dinner, but they couldn't bring themself to take a bite just yet. Their entire face felt stuffed up and their mouth felt like it was full of cotton, which wouldn't help the taste.

The Reverend had pushed himself off of the couch and headed over to the radio as Sam readjusted the mic on top of the piano, continuing the melody with his other hand. It was an actual radio mic, not the handheld one at home. Riley suddenly realized they should really be home since the sun was down, but that didn't seem to matter much anymore. They'd just find another excuse to arrest them.

"You ready?" the Reverend asked, his finger hovering over the switch.

Sam nodded, "Quiet in the studio."

Riley took this as the excuse they were looking for to set down their dinner. Ian did the same, with only a single bite missing from his plate. Jen had managed two or three, from how it looked.

The Reverend flipped the switch, and Sam ran his fingers up to the top of the keys before settling back into the jazz melody again. The music was starting to melt into Riley's numbness, but along with the warmth of the music came the sharp pangs of loss. They bit the corner of their mouth to keep from tearing up as the Reverend tiptoed back over to the couch. Instead of sitting back on the arm rest, though, he plopped down on the floor in front of Ian and tugged on his hand. Ian joined him on the floor, giving Riley room to tuck their feet up on the couch and lean onto Jen's shoulder again. The Reverend put his arm around Ian's shoulders, and Ian relaxed against his chest.

Jen readjusted so she could wrap her arms around Riley, stroking their hair as she softly hummed along to the music. Riley tucked their head into Jen's neck, trying to relax, but their arms and legs felt very disconnected from their body.

"Gooood evening, Jericho! This is Shockwave, comin' to you live, and that was just a lil improvisation I've had bouncin' around in my head all day. Hope you enjoyed it. We're gonna have a shorter program tonight. I get the feelin' we're all a lil tired after today's excitement."

He'd switched over to a slow blues melody that played softly under his low, musical voice. Glancing at the Reverend, he leaned closer to the mic. "As some of you may already heard, there was a group of us that took a lil trip to Bravo to…inquire after some folks. Unfortunately we didn' end up hearin' much about them, so we're thinkin' about headin' back tomorrow afternoon to talk some more. If you're interested in joinin' us, we're gonna meet up at two p.m., no earlier, no later. Air might get a lil spicy, things might get a lil loud, but we're gonna move fast and move together. See you then. Now, lemme soothe you to sleep with some sweet sounds before I sign off."

He leaned back from the mic and began to play louder, switching to a more soulful, fiery blues. Riley could feel tears start to sting their eyes. Was Sergio in that prison? If so, why'd they taken him? For glaring at a soldier? For talking to them wrong? Or had the soldiers just…

Jen hugged them tighter, and Riley realized they'd been sniffling fairly loudly. The Reverend glanced back, reaching to rest his hand on their knee with a small, sad smile. Riley tried to force a smile back, but they couldn't get their face to contort in the right way. The Reverend squeezed their knee in understanding, glanced out the window behind them, and jumped to his feet.

"FUCK!"

Riley turned to see orange flames dancing at the feet of the Meeting Space.

The Reverend bolted out the door, quickly followed by Ian. By the time Riley made it outside, the two were booking it across the street. Riley vaulted over the railing and ran up to the Meeting Place. The Reverend leapt over the low flames that wreathed the steps and yanked the door open. Smoke wafted out. The Reverend plunged inside. Riley and Ian didn't hesitate to follow.

Smoke was filling the main area of the Meeting Space. Large orange flames blazed in the Reverend's office. Riley could hear popping and fizzling as the radio burned. Glancing inside, they saw the file cabinet that had held the Reverend's files on the ground. The doors were ripped out of their slots.

The Reverend ran into the back room where the medicine was stored. "Grab as much as you can!"

Riley spotted their medical kit by the doorway and scooped it up. The flames were licking the medication crates and boxes. Two of the boxes were up in flames. The Reverend was trying to yank another box to safety. "Grab what you can and *go*!"

Riley ducked past Ian to get to the antibiotics crate. Throwing the lid off, they shoved as much as they could in the small gap in their backpack.

"*Riley*! Fill this bag!"

Riley turned as a duffle bag flew at their face. Catching it, they zipped up their backpack and got it on their back before shoving more antibiotics into the duffle. They got through half of the box before the flames started licking their feet.

The smoke seeped into Riley's lungs. Their eyes and throat burned, but they turned to another box with vitamins and pried it open.

"Grab more ibuprofen too!" the Reverend yelled.

Riley grabbed a few more bottles of multivitamins before turning to the box the Reverend pointed at.

The flames crept closer and closer. "We're going to be trapped!" Ian yelled.

Riley spun again to see the flames from the Reverend's office spilling out into the Meeting Space, warping the metal folding chairs and scorching the floor.

"Get out. Get out. *Get out!*" the Reverend yelled.

Riley zipped up the duffle bag, slinging it over their shoulder, before following Ian out of the room. The Reverend brought up the rear, dodging the line of flames starting to cross the floor. The door had shut, so Ian grabbed the knob and screamed. He yanked back, shaking his hand in the air.

"Ian!" The Reverend grabbed Ian's shoulder and spun him around, taking his injured hand. "You're fine, darling. You got your hand away fast enough."

"There's fire on the stairs if the door's hot. We can't go that way," Riley said, looking over to the side window. "This way!"

Sliding the arms of their jacket over their hands, Riley grabbed one of the metal chairs that was farthest from the blaze and raised it in the air.

"Stand back!"

Glancing back to make sure Ian and the Reverend were far enough back, Riley smashed the chair against the dirty glass. The window cracked. Another hit and pieces flew out. One more hit and the window shattered. Throwing the chair aside, Riley pulled out the remaining shards of glass as the Reverend pushed Ian forward and helped him climb up onto the windowsill.

"*Go!*" he yelled.

Ian startled, looking back at the Reverend and Riley.

"*Ian, go!*" Riley yelled, resisting the urge to shove him to the ground.

He finally jumped down to the ground, running toward the street. Riley heard shouting, screaming, loud and fast footsteps, and two sharp *cracks.*

"Riley, *move!*"

Riley hopped up into the window, trying to counterbalance the weight of the duffle bag. The flames were licking up the sides of the wall, nearly hitting their feet. If they squinted, Riley swore the flames were springing out of an oily slick on the ground.

"*Riley!*"

Squeezing their eyes shut and nearly crying out at the burning pain, Riley kicked away from the wall and jumped out as far as they could. They rolled as they landed, nearly hitting the building next door. Opening their eyes, they saw that the duffel bag had flickers of orange at the far corner. They slammed the bag into the ground to smother the flames.

Scrambling away from the building so the Reverend could jump, Riley followed Ian's path to the road. Their feet froze as soon as they touched the pavement. Riley couldn't believe their eyes.

Soldiers were forcing people away from the building at gunpoint. The people were carrying buckets. Some had water still in them. The rest had been splashed onto the ground. Ian stood a few rows back. Catching Riley's eye, he shook his head as he glanced at the soldiers and then down the road. More soldiers must be on the way.

Riley heard a *thud* and spun around. The Reverend scrambled to get up, stomping his foot on the ground to get rid of the flickers on the edges of his pant legs. Riley helped him beat out the flames before yanking him to his feet.

"We're going around back. Soldiers in the street!"

The Reverend nodded and the two raced for the back street, skirting the fire. The flames were even, spread out perfectly along the building. Riley tripped over plastic containers, which they realized was a pile of empty gas containers

The Reverend grabbed Riley's hand and yanked them forward. Riley pulled their hand away as the two ran down the road, trying to keep from falling in the dark. Every breath was scorched, but their lungs still screamed for air with every step.

Tapping them on the shoulder, the Reverend pointed back toward the road that ran in front of the Meeting Space. Riley nodded, leading the way through an alley. Landing on the street, they looked down and expected to see one large building up in flames. Instead they saw an entire skyline of fire. Loud blasts rang out, sparks flew up in the air, and fireballs rolled up into the night sky.

"My God, my God, what have they done?" the Reverend said, staring at the flames. Riley couldn't tell if it was a prayer or a question. Maybe both.

Riley bent over and put their hands on their knees, gasping for every torturous breath. People ran toward them, screaming, reaching back for loved ones, clutching babies. Riley knew they should keep running too, but they didn't know how much more their lungs could take.

"Come on, Riley Jay. Come on. Just start walking. Just move. Please, just come with me!"

Riley registered that the Reverend was shaking them, pulling them down the road. Their tear-filled eyes cleared up enough for them to see that people weren't just running from the fires. They were running from the soldiers. A woman clutching the hand of a teenage boy was smacked in the shoulder with the butt of a gun. An older man was shoved to the ground by another pair of soldiers. Riley's feet unstuck from the asphalt and followed the Reverend down the road. The smoke thinned out, but the heat made their skin crawl with pinpricks that felt like molten iron.

Riley tried to stop coughing, tried to stop the pain that came every time their chest heaved, but their lungs were damn determined to get the soot and ash out. The Reverend tried to form words as the two staggered on, but all he could manage was raspy nonsense, lost in the screams and the coughs and crackling of the flames. People piled up at the checkpoint, trying to get through the gate as fast as possible and slowing everyone else down.

"Raf! RJ!"

Ian!

Ian appeared next to the Reverend. He slung the Reverend's arm over his shoulders and slid his arm around the Reverend's waist. Riley could feel someone manipulating them in the same way. Looking up, they were surprised to see Sam.

"Jen's okay. Yvonne noticed the kitchen was on fire soon after you ran across the street. We grabbed what we could—"

He coughed and couldn't continue. Riley pulled their shirt up over their face to try and block out some of the smoke, but it had already laced itself into their clothing. What they wouldn't give for a wet bandana!

The checkpoint gate was up. No one was manning the guardhouse. As the mass of people were shoved through, Riley could see the shadows of soldiers splashing something along the fence. They were wearing gas masks with tubes that ran from each side of their face into black metal backpacks that Riley presumed were oxygen tanks. Their matte black bucket helmets and bulky, padded armor made them look more like robots or humanoid tanks rather than soldiers.

One of the soldiers' heads slowly turned and watched Riley as they stumbled past, two black pupils in golden rings boring into them. Riley couldn't look away as their eyes watered and turned the world into up and down waves of blurred motion.

Something slammed into them and Riley could feel their feet give way. They expected to feel the scrape of the asphalt on their skin, but it never came. Instead, they felt themself hoisted into the air, onto their back, an arm tucked under their knees and one cradling their shoulders.

"Hold on, Riley Jay. We're almost to your place. Catch your breath," Sam said.

Sirens reared up and wailed as people spread into Foxtrot from the checkpoint. "Little fuckin' late for that," Sam said, coughing. "Riley, can you walk again?"

Riley didn't want to, didn't know if their knees would buckle underneath them, but they nodded. Sam set them down, keeping his arm around their waist. Riley took a few cautious steps before he let them go. Ian and the Reverend were a few feet ahead, waiting for Riley and Sam to catch up.

"Get inside! Curfew is still in effect! Get inside your homes now or you will be detained!"

Riley stared at the soldier with the bullhorn in disbelief. Inside their homes? Where? All of Echo had just *burned to the fucking ground—*

People started to run again, trying to get away from the soldiers and coalescing into a mass of humanity as if pure numbers could save them from being arrested.

The Reverend grabbed Ian's hand. "R-run!"

Whatever breath Riley had managed to catch quickly evaporated. Ducking and weaving between people, Riley tried not to trip on anyone's feet while making sure they were still getting closer to the blue-and-white "HOTEL" sign. Home.

A hand scrabbled at their sleeve. Riley reached back to grab Sam's hand. Ian and the Reverend had disappeared. The crowd started to thin out again, and Riley wasn't sure why at first. Then they saw the door to a storefront open, and a young man dart out into the streets and start ushering people inside. Next door to him, a middle-aged woman helped carry an injured person into her home. Everyone was starting to disappear into homes and buildings, but it wasn't fast enough.

A teenager ran alongside Riley, also gasping for breath. As he passed by a pair of soldiers, one of them smacked them on the back of the neck. The boy crumpled to the ground. Riley stopped to help, but Sam yanked them forward. The butt of a gun barely missed their cheek.

Riley froze. Sam yanked them up onto the sidewalk, guiding them past soldiers who cared more about the crowd than two individuals. Riley looked up, realizing they were at the hotel. Sam headed for the front door, but Riley tugged his hand, pointing at the group of people heading around the building.

"Why?" Sam asked as the two ran around the corner. Riley tried to answer, but their throat was still swollen. That was fine. They didn't have a good answer anyway. It just felt safer to go in the back door. Besides, they had a feeling they knew why people were going that way.

When Riley turned the last corner their suspicions were confirmed. Ian and the Reverend were holding the doors open, guiding people inside and up the stairs.

Ian's face lit up under the streaks of soot. "RJ! Sam! Get inside!"

"Where's Jen?" Riley asked.

"Should be right upstairs," Sam replied. "She took Yvonne up ahead. I stayed back to find y'all."

Riley hopped up next to Sam, getting out of the way so Ian and the Reverend could get inside and pull the doors shut. The darkness and silence pressed in. Riley couldn't tell if they were struggling to breathe because of the smoke or because of their growing claustrophobia.

"Let's go," the Reverend whispered, and the group fumbled their way up the stairs.

Riley was shocked to find people camping in the hallway that led to their apartment. Candles were the only source of light, their flickers much softer and calming than the ferocious blaze that had driven everyone out of Echo. Some people who lived in the hotel had opened their doors and were trying to encourage people to come inside while other doors stayed locked up tightly. Sam and the Reverend kept getting pulled aside by people. One woman was weeping so hard she couldn't get her words out, so her husband gestured for the group to continue on. An older man who was sitting with what looked like his daughter and grandson managed to ask, "What happened?"

The Reverend and Sam looked at each other. Sam's eyes snapped with fury while the Reverend's smoldered in rage.

"We're not sure, Peter," the Reverend said, clapping the man on the back. "But we'll get through this. I promise. We'll figure it out."

The Reverend's smile was too forced for him to be telling the truth. The pieces of the puzzle that had been floating around in Riley's brain snapped together, forcing them to think about the very thing they'd been trying to ignore. The empty gas containers, the neat ring around the Meeting Space, the soldiers splashing water on the fence, the fact that almost every building had gone up at once…

"Riley, you coming?"

Ian was standing in front of the apartment, key in hand, eyes wide with fear and anxiety. Riley nodded, praying that Jen, Yvonne, and Deborah were behind the door. Sam tore himself away from Peter and his family and stood slightly back from the door, his arms crossed as he shifted nervously from foot to foot. Ian swallowed, closing his eyes before unlocking the door and pushing it open. Riley's heart leapt to see candle shadows flickering on the walls.

"Ian? Riley? That you?"

"Yeah it's us, Jen!" Ian said, opening his eyes with a sigh. Relief washed through Riley as Jen hurried to the door and pulled Ian and Riley inside. The Reverend and Sam soon followed, locking the door behind them.

Yvonne poked her head out from Riley's bedroom, relief evident on her face, holding Deborah on her hip. Riley hurried out of the way so she could hug Sam. Their heart started to ache again, and it just made the pain in their chest and throat worse.

"Riley, you're bleeding," Jen said.

Really? Riley looked down at their arms and hands, which were covered in soot but not blood. Their legs were also blood-free.

"Your ribs."

Riley could see the Reverend look up from where he was examining Ian's singed hand. Frowning, Riley looked down and sure enough, a dark slash of blood and torn cloth slashed their light blue T-shirt. How the heck did that get there?

As soon as Riley looked at the wound, it started to sting.

"Here, Riley, let's get that bandaged up," Jen said, unzipping the medical kit on Riley's back. "Where do you keep the gauze again?"

"Middle pocket, alongside the tape," Riley replied. Waiting until Jen had gotten the gauze and tape out and zipped the backpack back up, they took it off and put it next to the duffel bag.

"Riley, do you have any burn cream?" the Reverend asked.

"Haven't seen that since before the Collapse."

"That's what I was afraid of," the Reverend replied, looking back down at Ian's hand.

Riley looked up at Sam, Yvonne, and Deborah. Deborah was sleeping on Sam's shoulder as her parents talked in low voices, glancing over at the group every once in a while. Riley knew they needed somewhere to stay, and there was plenty of space in the other room. Especially since Sergio wasn't here anymore.

"Sam? Yvonne? You can have the other room."

Yvonne looked over at Riley, relief on her face, but Sam looked away.

"Think there's some clothes that should fit Sam in one of the crates in there," Riley said, their voice cracking at the thought of giving up the space they'd shared with Sergio.

Sam swallowed as he looked up at Riley. "We can't ask you to do that."

"You didn't ask. I offered. Radio's in there too in case you need to call anyone. I'll pull my stuff out in a minute."

"I've got it, Riley," Ian said as the Reverend wrapped the gauze around his hand to protect it.

"Not with this hand you won't," the Reverend said. "I'll help you."

"Riley? I'm going to need you to take your shirt off so we can get this bandaged up," Jen said.

Riley glanced up at Sam and Yvonne, who scooted into the other room and closed the door. The Reverend politely turned his back, shifting Ian so he could continue bandaging his hand. Once everyone had their eyes adverted, Riley peeled off their shirt. Jen had grabbed a spare shirt of Ian's for Riley to change into, and Riley and Jen hurried to get Riley patched up and decent. Jen's hands shook as she tried to clean off the blood and soot around the wound; Riley tried to help, but it hurt too much to twist or raise their arms.

"You all right if I take over, Riley?" the Reverend asked.

"Yeah, that's fine," Riley replied.

Jen seemed both relieved and disappointed as she handed the supplies over to the Reverend. Everything went much quicker once Riley was in his expert hands.

"There you go," he said, adverting his eyes as he handed over the shirt Jen had gotten for them. Riley wondered what the purpose was since he'd basically already seen everything, but they appreciated the gesture nonetheless.

"Thanks, Doc."

The Reverend chuckled and rolled his eyes, carefully pulling Riley into a hug. "It's going to be okay, Riley Jay."

Okay? Of course it wasn't, not by any standard Riley had known. Families were missing—families they'd helped treat. The Meeting Space and Echo were gone, soaked with gasoline and burned to the ground. Glancing at the closed door that led to the other room, they could feel their heart start to ache again, and they wished more than anything that Sergio was behind that door.

CHAPTER FOURTEEN

Riley held their breath as they crawled off the loveseat and slipped past Jen's mattress, heading for the balcony door. The floor creaked, and Riley looked back, worried they'd woken everyone else. But Jen was still stretched out on her mattress, sleeping soundly, while Ian and the Reverend were curled up together in Ian's bed. The Reverend's arm was wrapped around Ian's waist, his face buried into the back of Ian's neck. Ian had his arm on top of the Reverend's, and Riley was sure their fingers were laced together.

Trying to ignore the lump in their throat, Riley slid outside and closed the door behind them.

The full moon cast enough light for Riley to find their way to one of the balcony chairs without knocking anything over. Settling into it, they let out their breath and scanned the streets. Pairs of soldiers stood on every corner, and Humvees roared down the road every few minutes. Across the street, Riley saw the corner of a window tarp raise, and the woman who lived there poked her head out. She looked up and down the road before ducking back inside.

The balcony door creaked open behind them and Riley jumped, turning their head to see the Reverend. "Just me," he whispered, sliding the door shut and heading for the other chair. "Couldn't sleep either."

He settled in, kicking his feet up to press against the balcony railing. "I was thinking about how we're going to handle tomorrow," he said. "You don't have a ton of space in your apartment, so I wouldn't be able to send a lot of patients back to you—"

"What are you talking about? I'm going with you!" Riley said.

"The hell you are. What happens if we both get arrested? The network falls apart."

"Look, you said you got surrounded today in that square. How would you have gotten patients out?"

"…I don't know."

"I'll be of more use in the square," Riley said, looking back out over the streets as another Humvee drove by. "We can try and set up an area for triage, at least somewhere to keep people out of the action if they're hurt."

The Reverend didn't reply, and Riley looked over at him. They couldn't read his expression in the moonlight, but they assumed he was trying to think his way out of this.

"I can't risk the network like that," he finally said.

"Then *you* don't go! You started the network. You've run it this whole time. I've only been around for a few months. I can't run the network if you… don't make it out."

"I can't stay away when everyone else is going to be there."

"I know. I'm not asking you to."

The Reverend sighed, leaning forward and burying his face in his hands.

"Look, leave one EMT out in each district," Riley said. "Everyone else has been here longer than I have and know systems better than I do. Any of them would be of more use if the network had to be rebuilt."

"There's not going to be any children in that square," the Reverend said, looking over at them. "Why do you need to be there?"

How could they not be there? "They took my partner from me. I'm not going anywhere else until I get him back, and I'm not going to let it happen to anyone else."

The Reverend sighed, shaking his head. "Riley, the fact that nobody saw Sergio get arrested—"

"He could've taken back roads to get around, trying to avoid soldiers," Riley said, desperately trying not to think about the implications of what the Reverend had said. "If he was around a bunch of abandoned buildings, of course no one would've seen him."

"But why would the soldiers have been back there, then?" the Reverend asked. "Unless they were trying to isolate him before arresting him, but that's not how Command works. The soldiers arrest people publicly, that way everyone sees, everyone's warned and everyone's scared. Why would they randomly arrest someone on a back street with no one else around?"

"Do they need a good reason? Maybe they were just pissed off and took it out on S-Sergio…"

Riley nearly choked on those words. They'd been vacillating between believing Sergio was in prison and Sergio was… gone, but they hadn't fully embraced the idea he'd been hurt. That just made either option so, so much worse, and they could feel their insides knot together.

"Oh, Riley."

The Reverend's sorrowful tone made it clear that he wasn't going to fight them anymore. But Riley wasn't done yet.

“Even if I can’t get him back, maybe I can help someone else not lose their partner.”

The Reverend stretched his hand out. “We’ll do everything we can to get him back. I promise.”

Riley took his hand, squeezing it in thanks. The glass door slid open again and they both jumped, turning to see a yawning Ian stumble out. “Why are you up?” he asked, directing it more at the Reverend.

“Couldn’t sleep,” the Reverend replied as he let go of Riley’s hand to take Ian’s.

Ian tugged on his arm, stepping back toward the balcony door. “Come back to bed.” He turned to Riley and mussed up their hair. “You need sleep too. Tomorrow’s going to be a long day.”

“I know. That’s why I can’t sleep!” Riley replied, shaking their head to get their hair to fall back into place.

“Well you’re definitely not going to fall asleep out here. Come on, before Jen wakes up,” Ian replied, tugging on the Reverend’s hand again.

The Reverend pushed himself out of the chair, patting Riley on the shoulder before being pulled back inside by Ian. Riley turned away as the Reverend pressed a kiss to Ian’s cheek.

They looked back out over the road as they got up. The pair of soldiers on the corner closest to Riley were looking up at them. The one on the left leaned over to the one on the right. Riley backed toward the door. The soldiers disappeared behind the railing as Riley ducked back inside, sliding the door closed as quietly as they could.

“Everything okay?” the Reverend whispered.

Riley couldn’t look at him with Ian. They didn’t want the reminder that they no longer had someone to cuddle with.

"Yeah, everything's fine."

They heard the bed rustle as the Reverend lay back down. Riley climbed in between the sheets of the bed that Jen had made up on the loveseat. Tucking the blanket up underneath their chin, they squeezed their eyes shut and tried to pretend that the back of the loveseat was Sergio's back pressed against them. Maybe if they believed it for a few minutes, they'd be able to fall asleep.

Riley had absolutely no clue if they were able to sleep. It sure didn't feel like it the next morning with how much their neck ached and how heavy all of their limbs felt. But that could be because they'd been curled up on the loveseat all night.

Deborah adored having a bunch of adults around who were willing to give her attention, so she ran from person to person, babbling about the small doll she was holding. Eventually she ended up on the Reverend's lap, trying to steal his spoon while he tried to eat the chicken casserole Jen had put together. Riley didn't want to think about how long their rations would last trying to feed eight people.

Wait, seven. Seven people. Riley winced as the knife twisted in their chest.

"Raf, do you want me to take her back?" Yvonne asked as she sat down at the table.

"No, she's fine," the Reverend replied, moving his spoon up higher to take a bite. Deborah began to fuss, stretching up higher to try and grab the spoon.

"Hey, want your own spoon?" Ian asked, holding out his own spoon.

"Ian! Eat your lunch, please!" Jen said.

“I’m not hungry,” Ian said, “and I’ll just borrow Raf’s spoon if I get hungry.”

Jen opened her mouth to protest, but Deborah grabbed Ian’s spoon and waved it around in the air. The Reverend took the opportunity to grab a few more bites while the baby was distracted.

“Here, Raf, let me take her,” Ian said, moving Deborah from the Reverend’s lap to his as Sam came in from the other room.

“Think the radio’s gonna stay quiet for now,” Sam said, glancing back at the other room.

“Here, take my spot. I’ll cover the radio so you can eat,” Yvonne said,

“Thanks, darlin’,” Sam replied, kissing Yvonne as she got up. Riley quickly looked away and back at Deborah, who was now trying to stick the spoon in Ian’s casserole.

“Hey, honey, save that for Ian,” the Reverend said, offering up his own casserole instead. He gave his spoon to Ian and looked pointedly at the casserole, raising his eyebrows. Ian sighed and took a small bite. The Reverend kept glaring until Ian gave in and took an even bigger bite.

Riley hoped nobody would notice they weren’t eating either. But they were straight out of luck when Deborah decided to attack their uneaten casserole.

“Riley Jay, you need to eat too!” Jen said, leaning on the table across from them and raising her eyebrows.

Riley really, really didn’t want to eat the casserole, but they took several small bites to appease Jen. Deborah nearly smacked her tiny fist into the Reverend’s casserole trying to reach Riley’s but then decided to actually try to grab the Reverend’s casserole.

"C'mon, I'll take her," Sam said, laughing and scraping the last few bits out of his bowl before setting it back down and pushing his chair away from the table. He kept Deborah cuddled in his arms throughout the rest of lunch, through the rest of the preparations, and up until the very moment they were about to leave out the door. Then he turned her over to Yvonne, who was staying behind to monitor the radio, giving them both kisses as he held them. At the same time, Jen gave Ian, Riley, and the Reverend hugs and kisses on the cheek.

"Keep your heads up and be smart about it," she said. "Look out for each other."

"Yes, ma'am," the Reverend replied, kissing her cheek. Ian and Riley did the same, but when Riley leaned in to kiss her cheek, Jen held them there for a minute.

"You keep an eye on Ian for me," she said. "He's not as... experienced as you. He'll need your help if things go south."

Riley tensed. How much did Jen know about their past? But they nodded, kissed Jen on the cheek, and turned to follow Ian and the Reverend out the door. The last time things had gone south for Ian, it'd been their fault. They just hoped it wouldn't be their fault this time. Or, y'know, that things wouldn't go badly. But that seemed unlikely.

Riley was sure the Reverend would've argued for Ian to stay home and cover the radio, doing news reports. But he'd just sighed while Ian packed up his survival bag. Riley wondered if they'd missed an argument, but they had no clue when the two would've argued without them hearing.

The Reverend and Ian stepped back and let Sam take the lead as the group headed out the back door. Riley stayed back, looking up and down the streets as they headed toward Bravo district. Everything was quiet, too quiet. No squadrons or

Humvees rolled down the street, and the only soldiers to be seen were the pairs on the corners. The few people on the streets weren't talking to each other, just heading in the same direction, forming into bigger and bigger groups.

As the crowd approached the checkpoint, Riley was surprised to see both soldiers were in the guardhouse. The gate went up without anyone having to show any ID. The Reverend and Sam glanced at each other, and the Reverend reached out toward Ian. Ian looked down in surprise, hesitating for a little bit before taking his hand.

They were one big mass now, around thirty people strong, marching through Bravo district toward the prison. The Reverend squeezed Sam's shoulder before tapping Riley's arm and gesturing to fall back. Sam turned his head to wave and wink at Riley before they got separated by the crowd.

"We're going to need to stay on the edges to block off a triage area," the Reverend said in a low voice, trying to hide his words in everyone's footsteps. "Hopefully we can recruit some bigger muscles to keep the area safe."

"Who's staying back?" Riley asked.

"Willow, Licorice, Turmeric, and Chamomile. I've told everyone else to pair up and disperse themselves in the crowd. Couldn't raise Cardamom or Hyssop though. Think it's safe to assume both were taken."

Four people taken, including Peppermint and possibly Sergio, who could spill secrets about the network. None of them knew the full scope of the operation, but they could still do some serious damage. Riley was sure Sergio at least wouldn't talk, if he was still alive.

Riley swallowed back their grief as the group walked into the square. Two lines of soldiers were already standing in front of the prison, a dark concrete block with no windows and the roof ringed with spirals of barbed wire. Riley wondered what it had held before the Collapse.

People were coming in from both sides of the square, and the crowd quickly grew to over a hundred strong. The side of the square across from the prison was lined by the backs of four buildings with a narrow alley between each building.

The Reverend nodded to the second-to-last building. "Think that's our best location."

"I'll grab people to help guard it," Ian said, squeezing the Reverend's hand before letting go and disappearing into the crowd.

Riley stayed close behind the Reverend as they weaved and ducked their way toward that building. People stepped out of the Reverend's way, nodding and slapping him on the back as he passed. When they reached the corner of the building, people began to press away, giving them plenty of space.

"That's probably the triage area," Riley heard one young man say to a young woman.

"Maybe we won't need the guards after all," Riley said.

"We will when the tear gas and panic starts," the Reverend replied.

Right.

Riley reached to the outside pocket of their backpack, reassuring themself with the outline of their goggles and the plastic bag with a bandana soaked in water. It wouldn't do too much for the tear gas, but hopefully it would at least keep out any smoke. Their throat still felt singed from yesterday.

"We just gonna lay people on the ground?" Riley asked.

"We'll probably want to prop people up against the wall for better safety if we can," the Reverend said. "Keep them on their feet if they can stand, otherwise… we'll just have to be careful."

A burly man with dark brown skin and a long, black beard was making his way toward them, a big grin on his face. "Rev! Good to see you!"

"Good to see you too, Baashir," the Reverend said, clapping him on the back. "You want to be in charge of security?"

"Of course!" Baashir replied, turning toward Riley. "Don't think we've met."

"Yeah, this is Elderflower," the Reverend said before Riley could reply. Riley frowned at him, and he shook his head almost imperceptibly. Guess he didn't want their real name getting out?

"Oh, Elderflower! Yeah, you helped me over the radio when my son was sick," Baashir said, holding out his hand.

"Yeah, how's he doing?" Riley asked, shaking his hand and wondering which kid he was talking about.

"Back to full health!"

Other big, burly people were heading toward them. Ian knew how to recruit. Some introduced themselves to the Reverend while others merely nodded hello before turning to face away, watching the crowd. A low murmur washed over everyone, getting louder and louder the longer they stood there.

Ian broke through the crowd in front of Riley, ducking under the arms of Baashir and the similarly sized man standing next to him. "That enough people?"

"You're a godsend, Ian," the Reverend replied, taking both of his hands. Ian grinned, glancing around a bit before leaning in for a quick kiss. The Reverend smiled, keeping ahold of Ian's hand as Ian moved to stand next to him.

"I think I'm going to make my story about this triage team," Ian said.

"I'll want to go over it first, make sure you aren't giving away any of our secrets," the Reverend replied.

"Yeah, of course."

"Can everyone hear me?"

Riley turned to see Sam standing above the crowd, holding a megaphone. Everyone cheered and called back that they could hear Sam loud and clear. Riley expected him to start yelling, start leading chants or something, but instead he started singing. Riley didn't know what the song was, but it was sweeping and grand, almost as if Sam was claiming victory before anything had happened.

Sam continued to lead the crowd in song for the next fifteen minutes, hardly pausing to take a breath. Riley didn't recognize most of the songs, but the Reverend sang along to all of them. Ian kept watching the Reverend as he sang, the look of absolute adoration on his face making Riley's insides twist with jealousy and pain.

"Hey, Shock, what're our demands?" a deep voice yelled from somewhere in front of Riley.

"What're our demands?" Sam said, and the crowd cheered. "It's simple, brother. We want our families back. We want our friends back. We want our people back. Our community has been torn apart by soldiers comin' into our homes and takin' away people for no goddamn reason! We want them back!"

Everyone roared in agreement, and the cry went up, "We want our people back! We want our people back!"

Thunk.

A metallic canister clattered in the center of the square, emitting off-white smoke. Riley scrambled for their goggles and bandana, but the tear gas was already dissipating. Their eyes stung a bit, but they couldn't tell if it was from the tear gas or if they were imagining things.

"Heard that some people were trying to come up with ways to neutralize the gas," the Reverend said, his voice slightly muffled behind his own bandana. "Guess they figured it out. Makes our jobs easier."

Riley looked around, trying to figure out where the canister had come from. They quickly forgot all about that, though, when soldiers in solid black uniforms marched up the roads and lined up on the two edges of the square not blocked by buildings. Tanks rolled up behind them, one behind each line. The bulky and stiff way the soldiers moved told Riley "body armor." They were wearing the same black bucket helmets and masks with tubes that the soldiers at the fence wore last night. But these soldiers were carrying clear plastic shields that covered most of them from below their chin to just above their feet. They shoved people back from the edges of the square, making everyone jostle around for space.

"Stay together. Watch out for each other! Make sure nobody gets trampled!" Sam called through the megaphone as two more *thunks* resulted in canisters flying into the square. People jumped back from where they landed and then rushed in to smother the gas. Those on the edges continued to press back against the soldiers, chanting, "We won't go! We won't go!"

"And this is why we're not on the edge of the square," the Reverend shouted. The people protecting the triage area pressed together and directed people to open spots. Even still, they were forced to step back, shrinking the already small square. Riley prayed they wouldn't need the space, but they had a feeling the entire square was about to turn into one big triage zone.

A shrill whistle split the air. Everything froze. Riley could feel their breath hanging in their throat, not sure whether it was okay to breathe out.

Riley jolted at a loud, discordant clacking. Peeking over the heads of the crush of people in front of them, they saw that each soldier had unfurled a black, segmented nightstick. Their heart leapt into their throat and then dropped into their stomach as the soldiers drummed the nightsticks against the shields.

"Protect your heads and faces!" Sam yelled. "Form a wall!"

Riley had a pretty good guess what that meant when they saw those with a backpack moving toward the perimeter of the square. Sometimes smaller people passed their backpacks to larger people before backing into the crowd again. The chanting had become fragmented, with some yelling, "Give us our families back!" while others yelled, "We won't go!" and even more chanting something Riley couldn't quite make out.

"Fall back. Fall back!" the Reverend told Baashir. "Give people space to spread out!"

"Fall back, guards!" Baashir bellowed. All the other guards immediately did as he said.

The Reverend threw his arm around Riley's shoulder and put his mouth up to their ear. "Your job is to not get hurt right now. The soldiers are going to charge. People are going to get hurt. Wait until they back off. Then assess and patch people up. Recruit people in to help. They'll be willing. Move fast, stay away from the soldiers."

Riley nodded as another shrill whistle split the air.

The people on the perimeter tore off their backpacks and put them up in front of their faces. Nightsticks rained down on them, thudding against the backpacks. Screams rose up along with shouts of anger.

Riley nearly fell as the Reverend and Ian were shoved into them. Baashir caught them and made sure they stayed on their feet. Turning to thank Baashir, Riley saw Sam lifting the megaphone to speak again when a sharp *crack* rang out.

The megaphone dropped from Sam's hand as he collapsed behind the crowd.

Everything froze with time floating in between breaths of pepper-gassed air. Riley knew what had happened, knew why Sam had fallen, but they couldn't believe it. It didn't feel like it'd happened.

The spell of numbness was broken by nightsticks hitting flesh and the yells of pain. Then the screams of fear.

"*Sam!*"

Riley turned to see the Reverend and Ian plunge into the crowd. They went to follow, but a man with dark brown hair a few feet away got caught across the face with a nightstick. Blood spurted out, splattering onto the people next to him.

Riley pushed their way through the crowd as the people in front of them started shouting "Medic! Medic!"

"Get him back! Get him away from the soldiers!" Riley yelled.

They realized it wasn't the smartest thing to yell when the soldiers pressed forward, trying to reach the man. Fortunately people interfered. Some helped the man get back toward Riley, others pushing back against the soldiers, and the rest jumped out of the way. Finally the man and Riley met with the man being held up by two others while Baashir stood right behind Riley.

Baashir stepped forward and carefully scooped the man up in his arms. "Can you work on him like this, Elderflower?" he asked.

"Sure can," Riley replied, swinging their backpack around to their front and unzipping it. They looked up and froze when they saw the man's battered face.

"Carter!"

His face was covered in deep red blood, his nose curved awkwardly to the left, and his right eye was starting to swell shut. Riley knew at least some of the blood had to be coming from his nose, but they couldn't tell if there were any other slashes or splits contributing to the problem. Reminding themself that head and face wounds bled a lot, they pulled out a cloth and a water bottle. They would need a second pair of hands, especially in this environment.

They looked up to see who was nearby, finding an older Japanese woman standing right in front of them. "What can I do?" the woman asked, pushing her graying black hair out of her eyes.

"We need to clean off his face," Riley said, handing the woman a bottle of water. "I'll need you to pour carefully while I clean it off and try to find where the blood is coming from besides his nose."

Someone slammed into Riley's back and they nearly pitched face-first into Baashir and Carter. The woman jumped away and nearly smacked her head against the nearby building.

"You all right?" Riley asked as the little group crowded back together.

"Yes, I'm fine. Where do you need the water?"

"Start around his injured eye. I think that's where most of this blood is coming from," Riley said. The woman nodded, carefully pouring water on Carter's forehead above his eye. Some of the blood flowed off, leaving behind only dark, dried blood. Riley wet a cloth with the water and began to sponge the wound clean.

"Medic! Medic!"

Riley looked up to see two young men holding up a middle-aged woman, whose right leg was covered in blood. "Sit her up against the wall and make sure nobody hits that leg!" Riley yelled, turning back to Carter. Clearing off more of the blood they finally found the gash and handed off the wet rag to the woman.

"Get pressure on that. I'll be right back to bandage it," Riley said, readjusting their backpack onto their shoulder to make their way over to the injured woman. They were surprised more people weren't coming to them with injuries. With the tight press of the crowd, there must be plenty of injured people who couldn't move.

Two more whistle blasts screeched out, and Riley's ears filled with the sharp cracks of gunshots. They fought the urge to fling themself to the ground. A person next to them stumbled sideways, falling into the crowd. Blood splattered onto people and dripped to the dark cobblestones.

Their stomach heaved. The chants completely disappeared into screams and cries of fear and pain. Riley tried to get to the person who'd been shot, but their feet had turned to lead.

Somebody's backpack smacked against their face. The sting shoved Riley forward. Throwing their backpack onto their back, they elbowed their way through the crowd. Finally reaching the person, they choked.

It was Kit. Her eyes were wide and glassy, blood starting to pool under her neck and ooze out of her mouth. The bullet had gone right through her carotid artery.

Swallowing back the bile that rose in their throat, Riley looked up at the nearby people. The dread of the truth was evident behind everyone's eyes. Riley shook their head and backed away, leaving them to yell out in grief. They wished they could join, but their grief was strangling them, refusing to let Riley have the sweet release of tears.

Riley fought their way back to whatever minuscule triage area was left. They noticed the soldiers had pressed in further, still beating people back with nightsticks. But the solid line had broken and people were starting to slip by, running down the streets in the cold afternoon sun. Some were chased by soldiers while others were seemingly let go.

Cold sweat dripped down Riley's back. Their chest tightened as people squeezed in on them. They wanted to scream, shove themself above the crowd to breathe and somehow climb over everyone to safety. They settled for ducking under backpacks and threading their way between bodies covered in blood, sweat, and bruises.

"Elderflower! *Elderflower!*"

Baashir's voice rang over the clamor, and Riley tried to move toward it. The crowd shifted, and instead of pushing in from the sides, they pressed Riley toward the front. They struggled to find footing, a space to break through the line, as everyone else seemed to be fighting to get away from the back of the square. When Riley managed to duck through two bulkier men, they figured out why.

Soldiers poured out from the alleyways, punching and kicking people. Riley swore they saw someone dragged down one of the alleyways by two soldiers.

They couldn't hear Baashir yelling anymore. They pushed themself up onto their tiptoes, but they couldn't see him, Carter, or the helpful woman. Nobody was propped up against the wall either. They could only hope the woman and her friends had managed to get away. The twisting in their gut told them otherwise.

"*Riley!*"

Spinning around and smacking their backpack into a few people, Riley nearly cried with relief. The Reverend pushed his way between two people dressed in all black. Riley's relief turned into horror when they saw the Reverend's shirt and face, splattered with blood. Then they realized Ian wasn't with him.

"Rev, where's Ian? Where is he?"

Tears streamed down the Reverend's face. He shook his head frantically. "I lost him! We were so c-close to the front when the soldiers r-rushed us."

"Is he dead?" The words were out of Riley's mouth before they could stop themself.

"I don't know! We got separated."

Riley's shoulders screamed in pain. They were yanked back by the handle of their backpack. The Reverend lunged forward. Riley threw their hand forward to grab his. Their fingers just brushed along the back of his hand as he was smacked in the side of the face with a nightstick.

Riley could feel his blood splatter on their face.

Their mouth tried to scream, but their throat was frozen shut. The Reverend was sprawled out on the ground, eyes closed. Two soldiers lunged past Riley and scooped him up. They tried to see if his chest was moving, but a third soldier blocked Riley's view. He grabbed their chin and forced their head back. A bright light blasted into their eyes, but they could still see the outline of the soldier's octopus-like gas mask. They could feel a piece of paper slice against their face.

“Yeah, near-perfect match. Take ’em.”

The bright light vanished as a bag was thrown over Riley’s head, and they were dragged backward by a swarm of hands.

CHAPTER FIFTEEN

Riley kicked out, trying to hold on to their backpack, but it was torn from their shoulders. Cold metal pinched their wrists as they were shoved into a vehicle. The door slammed behind them, and the vehicle rumbled off. They struggled to push themself up and steady themself as they were thrown about, scrambling for a seat. After a few minutes they were sure there wasn't one.

Riley crawled on their elbows and knees toward where they thought should be the side of the truck. If they could jam themself into a corner, they wouldn't be tossed around as much. But another sharp turn threw them backward, slamming them into the floor. Blood oozed into their mouth before they felt the pain.

Scrambling backward in the darkness, Riley's head banged against the side of the vehicle. Ignoring the ache that resulted, they felt along the wall, trying to find the corner, praying another turn wouldn't erase all of their progress. The truck screeched to a halt, throwing Riley back on to the floor.

Riley tried to take deep breaths, waiting for the truck to move again or waiting for a door to be yanked open. But everything stayed silent. They didn't even hear the driver's side door open. What was going on?

A few minutes passed before the door of the truck clacked open. Four hands grabbed their hands and arms, yanking them out. They landed on their knees, gravel pinching their skin.

"Get moving!"

Riley was yanked back to their feet, a hand on each shoulder and another grabbing their handcuffs. They were shoved forward, nearly falling on the ground again. Riley looked down, trying to see if they could see underneath the bag over their head, but the soldiers had closed it off too well. The sight made their breathing pick up, and they had to turn all of their energy to trying not to hyperventilate.

The gravel turned into a solid, hard floor under their feet. Riley couldn't hear their own footsteps over the heavy clomps of the soldier's boots that echoed around. The bootsteps became muffled by carpet, and the smell of musk and mildew grew stronger and stronger. By the time Riley was pushed into a chair and the bag was pulled off of their head, they were pretty sure they were in City Hall. The carpet confirmed it—the same ugly maroon Riley remembered.

One of the soldiers grabbed a short chain locked into the table and fastened it to the chain of Riley's handcuffs. They didn't look up until they heard the door slam shut.

They were sitting on a metal chair, chained to a long metal table in the center of the room. Besides that, the room was completely empty. Riley was thankful a soldier hadn't been left in the room. They really didn't want to have a gun pointed at them again.

It felt like hours before the door lock clacked open. Two soldiers strolled into the room. Neither of them was carrying an assault rifle, but Riley didn't trust the handguns prominently fastened on their belts.

The soldier in the back was talking to the soldier in the lead. "—not to touch the hostages. It was part of the deal."

"New orders," the other soldier replied. "Keep up the threat. It's worked well enough so far."

What? Hostages? Threat?

They didn't see the flash of silver flying toward their face. Pain seared across their cheek. Gritting their teeth so they wouldn't scream, Riley looked up to see the soldier sheathing their knife. The other soldier opened the door and walked out first, followed by the soldier who'd cut them. The door clanged as it slammed shut.

"Bastards."

A security camera light flashed red in the corner of the room. Every muscle in Riley's back and shoulders tensed. Had it been on this entire time? Can't have been. Riley would've noticed it by now.

Riley jumped at the shouts and the sounds of a scuffle out in the hallway. They tried to shuffle their chair to the other side of the room, but it was bolted to the floor. They heard a scrabbling sound at the door, and their heart pounded in their throat as their stomach sank.

The door burst open and a soldier rushed into the room. Two other soldiers were in the doorway behind him, reaching to grab his shoulders and arms. He threw them off, stepping forward and staring at Riley in abject horror. Riley nearly sobbed in terror and relief.

It was Sergio.

In a black Command uniform.

"Riley... oh, honey... *shit!*"

Sergio bolted forward and fell on his knees, wrapping Riley up in his arms and burying his face in their neck. Everything within Riley screamed, but they were so stunned they couldn't voice any of it. So much was swirling around inside them, knotting together, breaking apart, trying to sort itself out but failing. Riley grasped for any coherent thought. Two made themselves clear.

Sergio was alive.

Sergio was wearing a Command uniform.

The elation at the first one was somehow amplified and tempered by the confusion and anger at the second. They felt sick to their stomach, but also their heart was bursting with… fuck, Riley didn't know.

"What the hell happened?" Sergio said, pulling back to press his hands to their face, running his fingers under the slash on their cheek.

Riley opened their mouth to respond, but all that came out was something between a choke and a sob. Sergio's eyes watered, and he pressed his lips to their forehead. The kiss was everything Riley wanted, yet it burned like acid.

"It's okay. It's okay. I've got you now. You're safe." He looked up at the other soldiers and nodded to the closest one. "You, get those handcuffs off of them, now!"

The soldiers looked at each other. "Orders were to keep them on—"

"I'm sorry, Private. Who holds rank here?"

Riley had only heard him use this voice on raids, when he ordered around the people in the places they looted.

"Get those handcuffs off of them before I write you up for insubordination!"

The soldiers jumped, and the one on the left hurried forward, pulling keys out of his pocket. Sergio got out of the way but kept his hands on Riley's shoulders as the other soldier unlocked their handcuffs.

Other soldier. Sergio was a Command soldier. With some amount of rank.

Riley glanced up at the other two soldiers' shoulder insignias. One bar. When Sergio knelt down in front of them after the other two soldiers left, Riley saw his insignia had three bars.

"Hey, baby, talk to me," he said softly, pushing their hair out of their face before taking their hands.

Riley finally managed to get their tongue to move. Their voice sounded scratchy. "Wh-what the hell?"

Relief, despair, and fear all washed over Sergio's face. "I-I'm so sorry, Riley. I couldn't tell you. I knew I liked you the day we met, and I didn't want you to leave—"

"Th-the day we met?"

Sergio sighed, resting his forehead on their chest. Riley's hand instinctively came up to begin stroking his hair, even though they could feel their anger blazing inside of them.

How the hell had he kept all this from them?

"I was in the military. Not construction. Pre-Collapse."

Riley could feel tension leave their shoulders, as if they'd been bracing themself against something. Maybe the truth. Maybe their shoulders had known and had protected the rest of them.

It sounded ridiculous in their head, but it was the only explanation they had right now.

"So the Command found out."

He nodded, sniffling. "Soon as they ran my name, my service record came up. Officers stormed into my cell, demandin' I enlist again…"

He squeezed their hands tighter, looking back up at them. "I didn't have a choice."

"Of course you did!"

They couldn't hold back the fury that had been building up inside them. "You could've said no and asked to leave! You could've told us as soon as we left the building! We would've left!"

"I watched on a TV as a soldier pointed an assault rifle at you and switched off the safety! The general was threatenin' to kill all y'all if I didn't become a district spy!"

Riley went blank with shock. The red flashing light of the security camera mocked them with every blink.

"Sergio, I..." Any words they'd hoped to say fell away as he grabbed their face. The pain from the cut stung, but they didn't care. All of the burning anger inside of them that had flared up had been reduced to smoldering cinders. He hadn't chosen this. Of course he hadn't.

"You still should've told us. We could've left..." they started, but Sergio shook his head violently.

"Ian was hurtin'! The wound got infected. He could've died had we left! I thought maybe by joinin' them I could get help for him too, get him medical care, but then it could've reduced his rations to make up for the medicine and we were strugglin' to make ends meet as it was, then you found the Reverend and got medicine that way and I thought we were gonna be okay but Command found out we were involved and pulled me in to tell them all about the network and then I started hearin' about all of these protests in front of the prison and I was hopin' and prayin' that you weren't involved—"

"Sergio, what did you tell them about the network?"

Sergio stopped, his mouth slightly open. He glanced behind him at the security camera and lowered his voice.

"I-I translated the records, but not the codenames. Told the officers it was just a bunch of people helpin' each other out. That's all," he said. "And that Shockwave and Valerian were in charge of it."

Oh, dear God in Heaven. That was all that Command had needed.

"They shot Sam."

Sergio's eyes shot wide. "What?"

"They murdered him. In the square. Right in front of everyone. Then Ian and the Reverend went after him and then Ian disappeared and—"

"Ian's disappeared?"

Riley nodded, the tears they'd been suppressing starting to flood down their cheeks. "Rev managed to get back, but then they beat him and took him away when they got me. He had no clue where Ian was or if h-he was still alive. I have no idea if even the Rev's still alive. I couldn't tell if he was breathing—"

"Shh, shh, Riley, it's okay, it's okay," Sergio said, pulling Riley back into his arms and rubbing their back. "You're here now. I've got you. I'm not gonna let anyone hurt you."

Bit late for that.

The door swung open and an officer in a crisp black uniform strode in. At least, Riley guessed he was an officer by the black peaked cap.

"Sergeant, did you override my orders regarding the prisoner being handcuffed?"

"Prisoner?" Sergio let go of Riley to turn around and stand face to face with the officer, blocking Riley from his view. "Sir, they're my partner! They're not a hostage! We agreed that—"

"Our agreement did not extend to immunity if they were found to be assisting in the network," the officer said. "Riley Jay was found in the square with the other protestors. Several prisoners have given sworn statements saying Elderflower was a leader in the network. We have reason to believe Riley is Elderflower."

Sergio's hands were trembling, but his voice remained steady.

"There is no way Riley was a leader," he said. "I would have known. Besides, I told you, their code name was Sandstorm."

"Do not lie to a superior officer!"

Smack.

Riley screamed as Sergio crashed to the floor. They pushed themself out of their chair to help him, but the officer shoved them back into it. They didn't see his black gloved hand coming toward them until it'd already connected with their face. The force of it was so strong they were nearly thrown to the floor themself.

"I'll let Riley Jay stay with you as agreed," the officer said. "But they will have questions to answer in the morning. And, if you step out of line one more time, your *partner* will be thrown into the prison with everyone else and you will not be allowed to see them until I say so."

"Wh-what about Ian and Jen?"

Riley nearly cursed at Sergio although they'd been wondering the exact same thing. Their chin was grabbed and their head was forced back so the dim light above blinded them.

"Be thankful for what you have, Sergeant. You wouldn't want this pretty little face damaged more than it already has been. Would you?"

The officer let Riley's chin go. They dropped their head forward so they didn't have to look at him. Maybe if they didn't make eye contact, he'd back off.

The officer's boots clomped on the concrete floor, punctuated by the slamming of the door.

It was a minute before Sergio pushed himself off the floor and came back over to Riley's side. He kissed them before pressing his forehead to theirs.

"I'm so sorry," he whispered. "I'm an idiot."

"Yeah."

"When everythin' started going downhill and Command pulled me off the street and Echo burned, the officers promised to bring in you, Ian, and Jen, and we could all live together in the compound. I thought you'd be safer here. They promised to keep you all safe..."

He couldn't say it, but Riley knew what he'd finally figured out. Command hadn't promised to bring them, Ian, and Jen in as a favor to Sergio.

The officers had wanted hostages to keep Sergio in line.

The fury in Riley began to spark again. How the hell could Sergio have missed that? What happened to his mistrust of Command? When they were snatching families out of their homes...

"Why do they want you so badly?" Riley asked.

The question had been spinning around in their head. Why would Command go through all this trouble just to keep one sergeant in line?

Sergio leaned back and looked away. "Please don't make me tell you that," he said. "Please."

"Sergio..."

"Look, I know I've fucked up. I know you don't have much reason to trust me right now. I know I'm not in a position to ask you for anythin'. But please, just give me this one thing right now. Don't make me tell you."

The fury turned to fear as Sergio met their eyes again, pleading. Riley's first instinct was to punish him, demand that he tell them exactly what he'd done in thorough detail. Was he a deserter? Were they holding some war crime over his head that his unit had participated in? Or, heaven forbid, had he been part of the assault on the capitol?

They knew if they pressed, he'd eventually relent. But what would they gain for heaping on the guilt?

"Wait… did you seriously expect Ian to leave the Reverend behind?" Riley asked.

"This was before any of us cared about him! Then Ian developed his little crush, and you and Jen apparently decided he wasn't that bad after all, but Command was already suspicious of him so I knew I couldn't include him in the bargain. I didn't want to connect him to you any more than you were already connected. I didn't want Command to go after you."

"That didn't work."

"I know. I know!" Sergio said, running both his hands through his hair. "I fucked up! I didn't have any other choice! It was either join and you wouldn't get hurt, or refuse and watch you die! Even if we tried to escape, they would've hunted us down and…"

Riley's anger started to burn out again. They still thought Sergio should've told them what had happened, let the entire family decide what to do instead of taking it all on himself to keep them "safe." Maybe then the family could've figured a way out. But at the end of the day, the Command had forced him into that decision. Forced everyone into every single godforsaken decision since arriving in Jericho.

But even knowing all that, even believing it, Riley could still feel the embers of anger toward Sergio burning in their chest. But they still loved him, still never wanted him to leave their side again. The two emotions twisted together so much Riley could barely tell them apart.

"We have to get out of here," Riley said.

"I can't," Sergio said. "If I leave with you, they'll come after both of us. If I stay, they might not chase you. Plus," he glanced at the door, "if Ian's here, I need to get him out."

"And Rafael."

He looked back up at Riley, mouth opened ready to argue. Riley let go of a flame of anger to glare at him. He owed them. He owed Ian.

"I'll do my best, but if the Reverend's still alive and here, they'll have him under heavy lockdown."

"Sergio, we don't even know if Ian's alive!"

"That's a risk I'm willing to take! I don't know if I can risk it for both of them!"

"Ian would never leave without him."

Sergio let out a frustrated sigh, burying his face into Riley's chest. "Shit, Riley, I'm doing the best I can. I'll figure it out. I'm sorry. But for right now, you're my priority. I need to make sure you're safe. And that means getting you out of here."

Riley wanted to argue, wanted to say they weren't going anywhere without Ian and the Reverend. Because that meant leaving Sergio again, and that was the last thing they wanted to do. But they were scared of what might come tomorrow if they didn't get out.

They also needed to find Jen.

Sergio leaned back, taking Riley's hands again. "Soon as you're out, go home, get Jen, get the hell out of Jericho. Command knows they're in trouble. That's why they pulled me in. They will do anything to hold on to control of this city. It's gonna be ugly."

Any uglier than it already had been?

"What about you, Ian, and Rafael?"

"I'll work on that once you're out. Do you remember that abandoned town we went through with the coffee shop that still had the neon coffee cup sign in the window?"

Riley nodded, and Sergio continued. "Set up camp there so I can find you. I promise, Riley, I'm not gonna leave you forever. This is temporary. We'll be together soon again. I promise."

A part of Riley wanted to grab him and never let go, but another part of them wanted to spit in his face and never seen him again for all he'd put them through.

They settled for nodding. Sergio sat up to kiss their forehead again. "Come on, baby. I think I know how to get you out of here."

Riley kept their head down as Sergio escorted them through the hallways, his arm wrapped tightly around their shoulders. Every time boots snapped in salute as the two passed, their stomach sank a little more.

Two guards pulled open the double doors. Riley looked up as they stepped outside, shocked that night was falling. The last gasps of sunlight were still on the horizon, but the soldiers patrolling along the fence already had their flashlights out. Sergio kept them on the path that led straight to what Riley assumed was the Bravo district compound. Two soldiers were guarding the gate that led to an area encircled in a barbed-wire fence with rows of squat, cube-shaped buildings. The buildings were in concentric rings with a small square made of cobblestone in the middle that reminded Riley of the squares in the districts.

They were meant to escape from here? Sure, there was less security, but those fences looked mean.

"IDs."

Riley scrambled in their pocket, sighing in relief when the rough edge of the card scraped against their fingers. Sergio also pulled out his ID, which Riley realized had a black box around his photo—a box their photo didn't have.

"Their family ID is still being processed," Sergio said.

"You can go, then," the guard replied, handing the IDs back and saluting.

Sergio nodded in thanks, putting his arm back around Riley as the guards pushed the gate open. The ground turned from gravel into paving stones as they stepped inside. Everything was quiet with most of the homes lit by flickering light that barely illuminated the windows. It was a lot more flickering light than they'd seen in the rest of Jericho, though.

Shouts and screams pierced the night air. Riley froze as their chest constricted. Suddenly they were back in the other square with the crowd pressing in on them, covered in blood and spit and tears.

Sergio shoved Riley behind him. Riley grabbed onto his arm to keep from falling. Looking up, in the glow of the candlelight, they saw two bulky silhouettes of soldiers pulling a much thinner shadow out of one of the homes. High-pitched screaming blended with rough yells of pure fury as another shadow appeared in the doorway, grabbing for the thin shadow.

"No! No! I'm sorry, don't take her!" the rougher voice yelled.

“Left,” Sergio said, grabbing Riley’s hand. The two ducked into one of the side streets and ran around the arc of the back half of the compound. Sergio stopped in front of one of the blocks right next to the intersection, pulled out a silver key, and unlocked the door. Pushing it open he grabbed Riley’s arm and shoved them inside. As soon as the door closed behind him, Sergio pulled Riley into his arms, burying his face in their hair. Riley hugged him back, resting their forehead on his chest. He was shaking.

Riley wanted to believe they could actually have a life with Sergio where they wouldn’t have to worry about where food would come from or whether bandits or robbers would ambush them in the middle of the night. They’d theoretically get that here, but at the cost of constantly being terrified that the very soldiers who supposedly provided security would drag them away in the middle of the night.

And if they stayed, Ian and Jen would be in danger.

That was a cost Riley refused to pay.

Sergio’s trembling stilled, his breathing deepening and evening out. “Okay,” he whispered, letting them go and leading them toward the back of the house. He navigated perfectly in the pitch black, guiding them around a small table with five chairs to reach the back window.

Sergio eased it open. “All right. I know it’s dark, but can you see where the shadows are different? That’s a loose section of the fence that’s meant for an emergency exit in case the front gets blocked. Here’s some gloves.” He pulled out a pair from his back pocket and handed them to Riley. “They’re too small for me. We’re issued two pairs, but they don’t have to fit apparently. And here, my gun. You’ll need it. I’ll say you got it from me and held me at gunpoint as you escaped.”

Sliding the gloves on and tucking the handgun into their waistband, Riley squinted out the window. They thought they could see where the shadows were a little bit deeper, a little wonkier.

"It'll put you out on a side road that'll lead right into Charlie district. You can get to Foxtrot from there. Right?"

Riley nodded. At least this time they'd have gloves to protect their hands as they climbed the fence.

"This seems too easy," Riley said.

"Well, it's supposed to be. It's an emergency exit," Sergio said. "Not like there's a lot of people tryin' to get out of here."

"Guess so." Riley swallowed back the anxiety rising in their throat. "Well. Guess I'd better get moving."

"Yeah," Sergio said, so quietly Riley almost didn't hear it. He stepped closer to cradle their face in both of his hands. "I promise. I'll come find you. With Ian, and Jen… and the Reverend. I love you, darlin'."

He waited, and Riley knew what he wanted. They just didn't know if they wanted to give it to him. The last smoldering embers of fury wanted them to turn away and bolt out the window. But the ache in Riley's chest told them if they didn't kiss him now, they'd regret it. Especially if…

So they pushed themself up on their tiptoes and pressed their lips to his. He sighed, and Riley could feel the sorrow, desperation, and love rolling off of him. It was overwhelming, and Riley could feel their knees go weak beneath them. But before they could change their mind, Riley tore themself away and jumped out the window.

CHAPTER SIXTEEN

Riley crouched as they ran to the fence. The barbed wire looked pretty solid, the spiky coils all tangled up together. They held in a curse as they tiptoed along, looking for the spot Sergio had talked about. Finally, Riley saw a place where coils were misaligned, not as solid as the rest of the fence. Riley grabbed the wire and pulled on it. The fence jangled but gave way, bending toward them. Cringing and praying no soldiers were nearby, they yanked on the coils again. The barbed wire fell, leaving a sizeable gap.

Holding their breath, Riley wrangled their way through. They flinched at a sharp poke in their back. Forcing themself to remain calm, they slid their way through the rest of the fence and took off for Charlie district.

Riley fully expected to hear shouts, sirens, *something*. But the only thing they could hear were their footsteps crunching on the gravel. Sergio was right. They weren't expecting anyone to want to leave.

Don't think about Sergio. Don't think about Sergio.

Turning the corner, Riley staggered to a halt as a wave of warmth hit their face. Charlie was smoldering, reduced to piles of glowing embers, twisted metal, and scorched concrete. The air was bitter and acrid, threatening to choke them.

For some reason Riley expected people to be moving around, standing in front of burnt homes with their hands on their heads or on their knees. They expected soldiers to be scouring the remains and shoving people toward Golf. But nobody was there. The only movement came from ash that swirled around Riley's ankles and from embers slowly collapsing to the ground. If they had to guess, Charlie had been burned this afternoon while they were in Bravo.

They caught a glimpse of white within a twisted black mass under a pile of ash. Turning away, they hurried down the road. Holding up their shirt over their nose and mouth, Riley fell into a jog. As they passed gaps in between fallen buildings they could see a glow of orange light flickering brighter and brighter as they got closer to Foxtrot. With every step they could feel their stomach drop a little further into their feet. Their throat tightened, either from the smoke and heat from the outside or the anxiety rising from within.

As Riley got closer to the street, the roar of car engines got louder and louder. Gunfire split the air. Making it to the last building, Riley ducked behind it and peered out onto the road.

The city checkpoint gate was smashed. Cars barreled out of the city. Soldiers shot haphazardly at the cars. A large black SUV raced down the road. Two soldiers jumped in front of it, raising their rifles. The car ran them down. Riley's stomach lurched at the results. Another car ran over the bodies. All that was left was a mess of flesh and tire tracks. Bright red blood trickled down from the dark asphalt, coagulating in the sand.

Trying not to hurl, Riley darted across the small side road toward Foxtrot, keeping their head down. With every step they could feel the heat rising until it felt like their face was starting to sunburn. They finally allowed themself to look up, acknowledging what they'd already known but refused to believe.

Foxtrot was up in flames. Cars were screaming toward the checkpoint. People on foot were being pulled up into the cars and trucks. Some were yanked down by much bulkier shadows, who then put pistols to their heads.

There was no way Riley would be able to get in.

Every step back felt like moving through hot soup. Their insides felt like dark static, buzzing and overwhelming at the thought of what might have happened to Jen. And Yvonne. And Deborah.

They hadn't even thought about Yvonne and Deborah. Had they heard? Were they even still alive?

Riley tried to push the image of Sam falling down out of their head. It wouldn't budge. It was as seared into their mind as the images of Foxtrot burning right in front of them. They didn't want to turn away, didn't want to admit defeat, but with how heavy the fire was Riley was positive the hotel had already burned to the ground.

But they really, really wanted to check.

Resisting that self-destructive impulse, Riley finally turned away from the firestorm. Heading back down the road, their mind spun with options.

They could head out into the desert alone and try their luck out there, but that seemed like surefire death by dehydration.

They could try and get in with one of the cars speeding by, but they didn't want to attract the attention of the soldiers or get hit by a speeding vehicle.

They could return to live with Sergio.

Riley's stomach churned. They were terrified of the idea of living in a Command compound, where they could be taken away at any second. But their heart fluttered at the idea that they could be with Sergio, maybe help him get Ian and the Reverend out...

"Riley! *Riley!*"

Spinning around, Riley saw a shadow leaning out the side of a black pickup truck.

"Come on! We have got to go!"

Riley recognized the voice, but wasn't entirely sure he actually existed. He seemed like a mirage, some sort of angel offering them a way out of a situation that they shouldn't be able to get out of. He couldn't be real.

"Riley, come on!"

Well, it wouldn't hurt to check.

Pushing themself forward, Riley felt their lungs struggle for air as they tried to run. As they got closer, they confirmed it was Rami, Aisha and Kamal's brother. He was in the back of the truck, holding his hand out. Riley jumped off the ground to grab it, relieved when it was solid and warm and real. Rami yanked them into the truck bed before pounding on the back window.

"Go! Go! *Go!*"

He pushed Riley to stay down, dropping to his stomach himself as the truck took off. Bracing themself against the wall, Riley squeezed their eyes shut as the rapid sputter of gunfire pierced their ears. They felt something hot drop against their neck. Swatting it away they realized it was a bullet. They felt their blood run cold as the truck sped up.

"You all right, Riley? Where is the rest of your family? Where is the Reverend?"

Riley couldn't answer. Not because their throat was scorched, not because they couldn't get their tongue to move, but because they didn't want to face the answers to those questions. So they just shook their head. Rami mercifully nodded, settling back against the other side of the truck.

When the road evened out, and the roar of other car engines grew quiet, Riley crawled to the back of the truck and pulled themself up on the tailgate. The city of Jericho was all aglow. Everything shone with a warm orange light that seemed to flicker and wave with all the fury of a candle, with Jericho as the wick. Their heart squeezed, full of anxiety over every material thing they'd lost, and an aching, bone-piercing sorrow over the things and people that were much less replaceable.

From this distance, Jericho looked so much smaller than the void it left in Riley's heart.

The sun peeked over the horizon as the truck rolled to a halt, and they heard a door of the truck bang open. Riley pushed themself up to see Aisha pelting out of the cab, jumping up to try and climb into the bed.

"Riley! You're okay! You're okay!"

Riley certainly didn't feel okay. They felt empty. But they tried to ignore that as they jumped over the side of the truck. Aisha threw her arms around their neck and hugged them tightly, nearly knocking Riley over. The emptiness inside them didn't feel as sharp as they hugged Aisha back.

Two other doors opened, and an older couple climbed out, the woman holding Kamal in her arms. "You must be Riley Jay," she said, readjusting Kamal to sit on her hip. "I'm Nabila, and this is my husband Hasan."

"I-I'm honestly surprised we haven't met before," Riley said, wincing at how raspy their voice was.

"So am I!" Nabila said, laughing a bit. "With everything you've done for our family, I feel like we have."

Hasan's eyes were darting up and down the road. "Rami, hand me a gas container. I want to get back on the road as soon as possible."

"Yes, Dad."

Hasan nodded to Riley. "I'll ride in the truck bed. You need to get cleaned up. We have supplies in the cab."

"Thank you," Riley replied, wishing they could say something more.

"Are you armed?" Hasan asked.

"Yes."

"Good."

Riley was surprised he didn't ask how. Then again, they had no idea where he'd gotten the handgun that was visible on his back through his T-shirt, but the outline looked identical to the gun they now carried.

Nabila handed Kamal to Aisha. Kamal protested and reached back out for his mother. Nabila kissed the top of his head and motioned for all of them to get back in the cab.

"You look like you had a long night," Nabila said, putting her arm around Riley's shoulders and escorting them to the driver's side of the car. "Let's get that cut on your back patched up, and did you get the chance to clean out the cut on your face?"

"No, I didn't," Riley replied, cautiously running their finger over their cheek. The cut was scabbed over. Well, it had been a while since they'd gotten sliced up by the soldier.

"We'll still get the soot off of you," Nabila said, opening the door and sitting Riley down on the driver's seat. "That will at least make you feel better."

Aisha awkwardly pulled up a backpack from the cab floor and pushed it toward them. Riley grabbed it and passed it to Nabila, who unzipped it and pulled out a towel and water bottle.

"Here, use this to clean your face while I fix your back."

"Thank you." Riley turned away from Nabila with the towel and water. They adjusted the rearview mirror so they could see their face, which was streaked with soot. Their lips were cracked open, the bright red blood stark against the soot. The slash across their cheek was ugly and precise as it started to turn brown. But Riley was surprised at how dull their eyes looked. They had no idea what they were expecting, maybe fear, maybe relief, but instead they just looked... empty.

"Careful, this is going to sting."

Riley winced as Nabila began to rub alcohol along the edges of the wound. "How'd you manage to get alcohol wipes?"

"The Reverend made them for us."

Riley's chest tightened, and they could feel tears threatening their eyes. But they didn't have the energy to cry. They barely had the energy to take off their gloves and scrub at the soot on their face as Nabila started to tape gauze over the scratch on their back.

"What happened to the Reverend?" she asked in a low voice so Aisha couldn't hear.

Riley wiped the soot off of their forehead. "He was knocked out by a nightstick and taken by Command. I..."

They couldn't go on. Nabila patted their shoulder and set back to work.

"Nabila! We are ready to go. Are you finished?" Hasan yelled from the other side of the truck.

"Yes!" she replied, taping one last piece of gauze on Riley's back. "Do you want me to drive?"

"Yes please!" Hasan replied.

Aisha reached out the passenger-side door, taking the keys from her dad and passing them to her mom. Riley folded the wet towel and wiped off the last of the soot as Hasan poked his head into the car.

"Dust is getting kicked up on the road behind us," he said. "We must move now."

"Scoot over, Riley," Nabila said.

Riley did as she said, putting the rest of the medical tape and gauze away as Nabila hopped in and closed the door. Hasan shut the other door. Riley heard him and Rami jump into the back of the truck. Aisha held Kamal tightly on her lap. He squirmed and tried to climb down into the floor.

"Stay *still,* Kamal!" Nabila snapped as she turned on the engine. Riley pushed the backpack onto the floor of the cab as Nabila hit the gas.

Bracing themself against the dashboard, Riley turned around to see two separate but identical dust plumes flying up in the air. Their best guess was Humvees. They wondered why Command would be coming after them now, when nobody had even tried to chase them down last night. But they didn't feel scared. Didn't feel anything, really.

Rami banged on the back window of the cab. Riley slid it open. He had to yell over the wind. "Can I have your gun?"

Riley nodded but hesitated as their fingers wrapped around their handgun. It was the last thing Sergio had given them, his last means of protecting them. They didn't really want to hand it over. Besides, what would it do against a Humvee? But their rational brain took over, knowing it was better than nothing. So they passed it to Rami. He nodded his thanks, crawling back to the other end of the truck.

Sliding the window closed, Riley turned back to look out the windshield. Row after row of rubble and barely standing buildings passed, slightly familiar blurs from when Riley had driven down the road in the other direction. With different people. In a different truck.

They crested over a hill. A long line of mostly standing concrete buildings stretched out in front of them. Riley recognized it as the area where the coffee shop was.

Shit.

Looking out the back again, Riley really hoped the dust plumes would be gone, but they were still sputtering in the distance. Adrenaline kicked up inside them, flooding away the numbness. A plan coalesced in their head.

"Let's lose them," Riley said, yelling to be heard over the roar of the road and engine. "There's a good hiding spot 'bout fifty feet ahead. Look for the neon sign in the shape of a coffee cup and pull behind that building!"

"The soldiers'll see us!" Nabila replied.

"No they won't. They're behind the hill!"

Nabila glanced back and nodded. She pressed down harder on the gas. Riley braced themself against the console. Aisha screamed as she and Kamal were nearly thrown into the dashboard. Kamal started crying. Aisha tried to shush him, but he just cried harder.

"Is that it?" Nabila asked, pointing at the familiar coffee cup sign.

"Yeah!"

Nabila spun the wheel. The truck careened off the main road onto a cragged side road. Riley threw out their arm to keep Aisha and Kamal from falling into them. It didn't work. Sharp pain shot through their shoulder as Kamal's head banged into it. Gritting their teeth to keep from screaming and freaking Kamal out even further, Riley grabbed onto the dashboard.

Nabila turned the car off the road and forced it fully behind the store. "Shut down the engine," Riley said, but Nabila was already one step ahead of them.

The back window slid open. "What are you doing?" Rami asked furiously.

"Shh!" Riley hissed. "We can't outrun them, so we hid while they were still behind the hill. Get down and stay quiet!"

Rami's face lit up, and he scrambled away to whisper into Hasan's ear. Hasan nodded toward Riley, and they both lay flat on the bed of the truck.

"Get in the floor!" Riley said, kicking their feet up on the seat. Aisha stuffed Kamal and herself onto the floor on the passenger's side while Nabila slid under the steering wheel and folded herself to fit.

"What about you?" she whispered.

"I'll hide behind the truck!" Riley replied, sliding toward the driver's side door and pushing it open with their foot. Hopping out, they ran for the other side of the truck. They ducked down between the tire and the wall of the coffee shop.

The purrs of the Humvees' engines quickly grew into deafening roars. The engines stopped after a minute. Riley thought they could hear multiple car doors slamming. They reached back for their waistband and realized Rami still had their gun. Fear washed over them. They racked their brain for their options. Try to get the gun back from Rami? Hide under the truck and hope they could roll out of the way of any bullets?

Everything in their head became muddled as nearby footsteps crunched in the sand. Holding their breath, Riley scooted as far as they could along the wall, trying to slide under the truck. Their feet slid out from under them and they caught themself against the side of the truck, wincing at the dull, metallic *thunk*. They could hear the soft crunch of the sand stop and then speed up as they got closer and closer and closer and they squeezed their eyes shut.

BANG! BANG! CRACK! CRACK!

Riley's ears rang. They'd always thought it would hurt when they got shot. But they just felt the rough press of the concrete against their back and their feet shoved up against the toes of their sneakers. They peeled open their eyes and looked up into the bed of the truck. If they hadn't been shot, Rami and Hasan had to have been doing the shooting.

But the two men were just standing up, peeking over the sides of the pickup truck. The adrenaline started to fade away as Riley climbed out from behind the truck.

"What..." Rami started, but Hasan hushed him with a hand on his shoulder. Riley was about to round the truck to see where the bodies were, but more footsteps made them duck back down behind the front of the truck. Rami and Hasan hit the floorboards of the truck bed again as the footsteps got louder and then stopped. They were replaced by scuffling sounds and the low murmur of voices before a high, raspy voice spoke up.

"Y'all are okay to come on out now!"

Riley didn't move, didn't know if they trusted the voice. They were shocked when Rami and Hasan popped right up.

"Keith, is that you?" Hasan called.

"Wait—Hasan? Rami!"

A loud whoop went up, and the truck rocked as a thin, pale man leapt up into the truck bed and pulled Hasan into a bear hug. Nabila, Aisha, and Kamal scrambled up from the floorboards and leapt out of the truck. Riley ran around the corner to see what was going on.

Five people were standing over four bodies, looking up as Riley and Nabila rounded the corner. "Nabila!" one of the women shouted, running forward to pull Nabila into a hug.

Riley stepped back to get out of the way, ending up by the side of one of the men. "How many survivors are here?" they asked.

He looked up and his deep, suntanned face broke into a grin. "Your voice sounds familiar. You Elderflower?"

Riley squinted, trying to place him. "Yeah, my real name's Riley Jay. I'm sorry, but who're you?"

He held out his hand. "I'm Jeremy, but you'd know me as Birch. Helped us out with—"

"—your daughter who had knocked out one of her teeth. Yes, how is she?"

He was about to reply when a bang made Riley jump. "That'd be the front door of the coffee shop," Jeremy said, turning around. "Wonder what—"

"Riley! *Riley!*"

It felt like the wind had been knocked out of them although nobody had touched them. They knew what they were seeing, knew that it was real, but they couldn't believe it. It was everything they hadn't dared to hope for.

"Jen!"

Riley refused to let go of Jen as the two walked into the coffee shop. They expected the room to be empty, but there were actually a dozen people crawling out from behind crates and boxes, helping each other up.

"Riley?" a familiar voice asked, devoid of all emotion.

"Yvonne."

Yvonne was holding Deborah in her arms, sitting on one of the wooden crates. Her eyes looked even more lifeless than Riley felt. It was clear she'd already been told.

Jen sat Riley down on another crate next to Yvonne and lowered herself to her knees as she put both her hands on their shoulders. "Tell me about Ian and Rafael."

Riley took a deep breath, trying to quell the squeezing in their chest. "Ian got lost in the crowd. Rafael got taken by the Command. Got hit in the head. Couldn't tell if he was breathing."

They wanted to tell Jen that Sergio was alive, that he was okay, but then they'd have to explain how and why and they didn't have the strength to tell the truth yet. So they asked instead, "How'd you all get out?"

"Nozomi," Jen replied. "She saw the flames go up in Charlie and ran to get us, told us to pack. We threw together what we could and got it into the truck. Then we waited for you all to get back. But then soldiers started running through the streets grabbing people and fires were going up everywhere. We tried get out but the truck wouldn't start. Nozomi ordered us into her car and got us out of the city…"

A small gasp cut off her words, and she threw her arms around Riley.

"I thought I'd lost you too," she said through quiet sobs.

Riley hugged her back, burying their face into her shoulder. They thought they were going to cry too. They could feel the knot in their stomach welling up into their throat, but it kept dying down before it could spill over into tears.

As they held Jen, they saw her navy-blue backpack sitting at the feet of one of the nearby crates. “What did you manage to grab?” Riley asked.

Jen sat back and turned to also look at the backpack. “Not much of your stuff, I’m afraid,” she said. “I-I didn’t want the Command soldiers knowing more about the network than they already did, so I grabbed all the medical records out of the truck. That way if somebody talked and the code was broken—”

Pure, sweet relief rushed through Riley, and tears finally came to their eyes. The network was safe. Any of the families that hadn’t been compromised by the initial breach wouldn’t be at risk now, even if they’d been captured. The network would seem smaller. Maybe the Reverend wouldn’t be in so much trouble if he was still alive.

“We need to move out.”

Riley looked up to see a familiar man standing in the middle of the room. They couldn’t miss the horn-rimmed glasses or black blazer that was now covered in dust and rips in the cloth. It was the same man from the alley where they’d hidden with Ian from the tank. They were shocked to see that he had a shotgun, which he had lazily tucked under his arm.

“Eh, sit down Mark, we can talk this out,” a slurred voice said from the corner of the room.

“No! We need to go immediately.”

“Why?” Riley asked before they could stop themself. Jen let go and stepped back, looking worried. A surge of confidence from who-knows-where made Riley nod reassuringly and get to their feet.

“Why?” Mark said, snorting incredulously. “We’ve been found! When those four bastards don’t return, more soldiers’ll flood out here!”

"Not gonna happen. This area's known for bandits—ones that aren't afraid of taking on soldiers. Command will assume there's bandit activity this way and leave another direction. We'd do better to hunker down here for a while until we're sure the city's empty—"

"We? Where's the we in this situation? Every man for himself, I say!"

Murmurs sprang up among the group of twenty or so, and Riley could see people glancing at the doors.

"Why do you think they're leaving anyway?" Mark asked.

"What is there left to stay for? *Who* is left to stay for?"

They could hear choking, sobs, and muttering from the others, but they pressed on. "Command's got no reason to stay with nobody and nothing to rule over. As I was saying, we'd do better to stay here and collect more supplies until we're sure Command has left the area. Then we can go back to Jericho and see if anything can be salvaged."

Mark laughed, looking around at the crowd. "Do you hear this? Who even are you?"

"Somebody who's right, Mark," Yvonne said, pushing herself to her feet, adjusting Deborah on her hip. He immediately fell silent, looking down at the ground.

"We don't have a chance out here with how little supplies we have, and we don't know where the nearest settlement is," Yvonne said. "This area has housing for all of us, a chance for salvaging more supplies, and some protection from bandits, which is more than the open desert has. I'm staying. You can leave if you want."

The murmuring had stopped, and Riley could see most people listening with rapt attention to Yvonne. Those who weren't were glaring at Mark.

Mark scoffed again, looking around for support. When nobody would meet his eye, he shook his head.

"Well, then. Guess I'll be off on my own."

He stepped toward one of the crates, but Hasan and Rami stepped forward to stand in between him and the crate. He huffed, turning back to Yvonne who was shaking her head with her lips pursed.

"We said you could leave, Mark. We didn't say that crate could leave."

Riley wanted to protest, wanted to say that it wasn't fair since presumably it was his stuff he'd brought from Jericho. But if it meant keeping those materials to keep everyone else alive, even for just one more day…

"This is outrageous!" Mark said.

"You can stay with that crate, or you can leave without it. Those're your options."

Mark growled something Riley couldn't make out. He pointed the shotgun at Yvonne. Everyone gasped, some stepping back and others stepping forward to stand in the way. Riley stepped back to Yvonne's side, taking her arm. Jen took Deborah from Yvonne and backed far away, next to Aisha and Nabila, stroking the baby's hair and bouncing her to stop her fussing. Hasan jumped forward and put Mark in a headlock while Rami wrestled the gun out of his hands.

"Now that wasn't very nice of you, Mark," Yvonne said soothingly, throwing off Riley's hand and stepping forward. "Why would you do that?"

He sputtered and struggled, his eyes darting wildly from one person to another before landing back on Yvonne.

"I think we'll keep your shotgun as well if you're so damned determined to shoot someone," Yvonne said. "Now, you have two options. You can stay with us, with someone keeping an eye on you at all times, or you can get in your truck with all the shit you still have in it and head out. It's up to you."

Mark huffed, his face going red. Throwing off Hasan, he straightened out his shirt and headed for the door. Riley shifted so they remained between Yvonne and Mark as he shoved open the door and stormed out. Riley sighed as the car engine faded away, some tension leaving their shoulders. They turned to see Yvonne rubbing the temples of her head.

People slowly started moved around and started talking again. Jen and the Kader family walked over, Jen handing Deborah back to Yvonne. "What's in the crate, again?" Jen asked.

"Medicine," Yvonne replied. "Whole shitload of it. No clue how he got it, but Raf always said he was pinching stuff. Couldn't prove it, though. That's why he always tried to stay out of Delta. He knew Mark had that district locked tight."

Even more tension left Riley's shoulders. An entire crate of medicine? It was heaven.

"It's not enough, though," Yvonne said, pressing her hands to her cheeks. "We've got some medicine, food, soap... but not nearly enough for everyone."

"How many people you got here?" Riley asked.

"Twenty or thirty," Yvonne replied. "Most managed to bring something, but there were a few that just got plucked of the streets and run out here with nothing."

"Yeah, I was one of them," Riley replied. "Look, we're not that far out from a gas station that's closer to Jericho. A couple lives there. They were getting supplies from Jericho I'm pretty sure. They'll have enough to keep us going for quite a while."

Yvonne's eyes widened. "You sure?"

"Yeah, I'm sure."

"Well, it's the best option we have right now. You up to leading it? Maybe in a few hours?"

Riley looked at Jen. They weren't so sure. Go back up to the same group they'd robbed previously and shot one of their members? That wouldn't be a warm welcome. But they were the only person who knew where it was, meaning they had to be the one to lead the expedition. Plus, this time they had stuff to barter with.

"I'll go with you, Riley," Hasan said.

"Me too," Rami chimed in. "And I have a few friends I can ask to go with us as well."

"Wonderful," Yvonne said, clapping her hands. "Well, we need to get this place a little cleaner and a little more settled in. Paul said his crew was looking at moving out with the Youngs to a nearby building, which means we can fit you all in here with us. Now, let's see if we can find some bedding..."

Yvonne headed off toward the back of the coffee shop, followed by Nabila, Aisha, and Kamal. Hasan was called over by a group of men to help open a tightly closed crate while Rami stayed by Riley's side.

"Here," he said, handing back over their handgun. "I am sorry I could not get it back to you sooner."

"Didn't really have much time," Riley replied, nodding in thanks. Rami nodded back, keeping the shotgun in both hands as he went to join his father.

Tucking the handgun into the back of their jeans, Riley turned to Jen. Jen smiled sadly as she ran a delicate finger down the cut on Riley's cheek.

"You don't have to tell me everything that's happened to you yet if you don't want to," she said. "But I need you to tell me if you're up for this little trip."

Riley looked out at the blazing sun. The rays stretched down toward the earth, piercing worn-out buildings and flowing down from piles of rubble. It was so similar to other abandoned towns they'd lived in with Sergio, places where the two had cuddled and fought and fallen in love. The numbness was barely pierced by a sudden ache in their heart as they thought of those days. The ache only grew when they thought of their days in Philippi too, with Ian and Jen. Then their mind turned to Jericho and Rafael and Sam, and the ache just kept growing and growing until it threatened to tear them apart.

"Riley?"

The ache dulled as they turned back to Jen, who was tapping her bitten fingernails on her arm. "I don't know if this is a good idea," she said.

Riley shook their head, reaching out for a hug. Jen accepted it, rubbing Riley's back as they stood there, swaying a little. The ache lessened even more, and soon Riley could feel themself breathe a little easier.

"I'll be safe, Jen."

ACKNOWLEDGMENTS

Thank you to everyone who has helped me bring *Jericho* to life, whether you helped me write it or just finished reading it. This book has been one of the most rewarding projects I've ever done, and I hope you enjoyed it.

Thank you, Mom, for giving me a laptop without internet connection when I was twelve, forcing me to entertain myself by writing stories. You've always encouraged me to get my stories published, so I hope you're proud of this one. Also, thank you, Dad, for reading an early version of *Jericho* and offering up a lot of ways to tie up plot holes that I didn't even see. Thank you, Grandma and Grandpa, for being excited about this book since I first let on I was writing it. Finally, thank you, Dan, for all of the memes and links to watch SpaceX launches, forcing me to take a break from writing once in a while!

Noah, thank you for being my emotional rock. From the constant questions of "will anyone actually read this book?" to the days where I didn't feel like I could finish, you were always there with a hug and reassurance.

I couldn't have gotten through this book without Collin Yarborough, my author friend. Thank you for telling me about this publishing opportunity and for mutually freaking out with me about the insanity that is writing your first book.

You can check out his book, *Paved a Way: Exploring How Infrastructure Impacts Our Cities*, on Amazon.

Mrs. Pizzuto, I don't know why you made us write a story about a clam in first grade, but I'm pretty sure that's what started me on my journey to become a writer, so thank you. Professor Rubin, thank you for giving me my technical story crafting abilities. Finally, Mr. Olson, I'm sorry you had to read all of my horrible high school writing for years. Thank you for your feedback on those pieces, and on *Jericho* as well.

Besides my dad and Mr. Olson, I owe a huge debt of gratitude to Nic Wells and Keegan for also reading early drafts of *Jericho* and giving me invaluable feedback. Nic, I've loved reading every script you've written, and your storytelling abilities were so helpful in fleshing out the world of *Jericho*. Keegan, you were the first person I told about Jericho, back when it was just a soup of ideas. Thank you for being a constant sounding board over the past few years, for all of the sarcastically loving comments, and for being one of my best friends. More than anyone else, I hope *Jericho* makes you proud.

Without a doubt the two people who have had the most impact on *Jericho* are my editors, Clayton Bohle and Stephanie McKibben. Clayton, you were so invaluable in creating the stories, characters, and world of *Jericho*. I couldn't have asked for a better developmental editor. And Stephanie, my dragon editor, who swooped in and tore up my first draft and helped me stitch it back together better than ever. You two are the only reason *Jericho* has any level of coherence. So thank you so, so much.

Writing *Jericho* has been the journey of a lifetime, and it wouldn't have been possible without the support of the Book Creator's Institute and New Degree Press. Huge thank-you to Eric Koester and Hayley Newlin at the BCI, and Brian Bies, Amanda Brown, Kyra Ann Dawkins, Gjorgji Pejkovski, Mackenzie Joyce, Sdrjan Filipovic, and everyone else at NDP. Y'all are amazing.

Finally, a special thank-you to the people who preordered Jericho and supported the book early on:

Adam L.
Aisha A.
Albert L.
Alex M.
Alison W.
Ally S.
Alexis J.
Ariana D.
Aron D.
Austin R.
Becky S.
Betty M.
Candice C.
Caroline C.
Carolyn K.
Cathy D.
Cecily C.
Charlotte and Jonathan B.
Cheyenne M.
Cindy & Dan B.
Cindy H.
Courtney M.
Curtis F.
Dan & Amber S.
David K.
David M.
David & Sheri M.
Dean S.
DeAnna C.
Elizabeth B.
Elmer D.
Emily R.
Emma W.
Eric K.
Erin R.
Evan H.
Evan H.
Evan S.
Gabriella G.
Gideon L.
Gordon V.
Hannah H.
J.J. S.
JaeJun Daniel C.
Jay H.
Jill D.
Joan M.
Joshua R.
Julianne R.
Justin K.
Kaleigh C.
Kimberly H.

Lamisa M.
Laura P.
Lauren Anne C.
Lee T.
Lil S.
Lindsay B.
Lydia H.
Lynda F.
Mandi H.
Marge G.
Peg M.
Maria G.
Matthew L.
Matt N.
Melissa N.
Mollie M.
Nathaniel M.
Neha H.
Nic W.
Nicole L.
Noah S.
Patricia D.
Rachael P.
Racheal K.
Rachel D.
Raisch T.
Ray J.
Rhonda C.
Rosedanny O.
Sally R.
Sara E.
Sarah B.
Sarah M.
Sarah S.
Sidra I.
Steven L.
Sungman (Tyler) K.
Tae Ho J.
Teri & Mike M.
Thomas R.
Tim & Katie C.
Travis Z.
Trent J.
TJ D.
Willene C.
William A.
Zack P.

Thank you, from the bottom of my heart.

APPENDIX

A NOTE FROM THE AUTHOR

ACLU. "Surveillance under the Patriot Act." Multimedia. Updated 2021. https://www.aclu.org/issues/national-security/privacy-and-surveillance/surveillance-under-patriot-act.

Ali, Safia Samee. "Tamir Rice Shooting: Newly Released Interview Reveals Cop's Shifting Story." *NBC News,* April 26, 2017. https://www.nbcnews.com/news/us-news/newly-released-interview-footage-reveal-shifting-stories-officers-who-shot-n751401.

Hansford, Justin, Robert F. Kennedy Human Rights Global Justice Clinic, New York University School of Law International Human Rights Law Clinic, University of Virginia School of Law. *Excessive Use of Force by the Police against Black Americans in the United States.* Inter-American Commission on Human Rights, 2016. https://rfkhumanrights.org/assets/documents/iachr_thematic_hearing_submission_-_excessive_use_of_force_by_police_against_black_americans.pdf.

Hill, Evan, Ainara Tiefenthäler, Christiaan Triebert, Drew Jordan, Haley Willis, and Robin Stein. "How George Floyd Was Killed in Police Custody." *New York Times,* May 31, 2020. https://www.nytimes.com/2020/05/31/us/george-floyd-investigation.html.

Johnson, Marty and Lauren Vella. "Federal Agents Deployed to Portland Did Not Have Training in Riot Control: NYT." *The Hill,* July 18, 2020. https://thehill.com/homenews/administration/507976-federal-agents-deployed-to-portland-did-not-have-training-in-riot.

Kirby, Jen. "Concentration Camps and Forced Labor: China's Repression of the Uighurs, Explained." *Vox Media,* September 25, 2020. https://www.vox.com/2020/7/28/21333345/uighurs-china-internment-camps-forced-labor-xinjiang.

Leatherby, Lauren, Arielle Ray, Anjali Singhvi, Christian Triebert, Derek Watkins, and Haley Willis. "How a Presidential Rally Turned into a Capitol Rampage," *New York Times,* January 12, 2021. https://www.nytimes.com/interactive/2021/01/12/us/capitol-mob-timeline.html.

Lee, Jessica. "Were Portland Protesters 'Kidnapped' by Federal Officers in Unmarked Vans?" *Snopes,* July 22, 2020. https://www.snopes.com/fact-check/feds-unmarked-vans-portland/.

Lee, Kurtis. "Officer Convicted in Killing of Fifteen-Year-Old Jordan Edwards—A Rare Outcome in Police Shootings." *Los Angeles Times,* August 28, 2018. https://www.latimes.com/nation/la-na-jordan-edwards-verdict-20180828-story.html.

Levenson, Eric, "A Timeline of Breonna Taylor's Case Since Police Broke Down Her Door and Shot Her." *CNN,* September 24, 2020. https://www.cnn.com/2020/09/23/us/breonna-taylor-timeline/index.html.

Parks, Brad. "George Floyd's Death Was 'Murder' and the Accused Officer 'Knew What He Was Doing' Minneapolis Police Chief Says." *CNN*, June 24, 2020. https://www.cnn.com/2020/06/24/us/minneapolis-police-chief-comment-george-floyd-trnd/index.html.

Razek, Raja. "Missouri Police Officer Who Killed Michael Brown Faces No Charges." *CNN*, July 30, 2020. https://www.cnn.com/2020/07/30/us/ferguson-missouri-michael-brown-darren-wilson-no-charges/index.html.

Southern Poverty Law Center, "Flags and Other Symbols Used by Far-Right Groups in Charlottesville," Hatewatch, updated August 12, 2017. https://www.splcenter.org/hatewatch/2017/08/12/flags-and-other-symbols-used-far-right-groups-charlottesville.

Thebault, Reis. "Police Laughed and Joked As He Lost Consciousness in Handcuffs. Minutes Later, He Died." *The Washington Post*, July 31, 2019. https://www.washingtonpost.com/nation/2019/08/01/police-laughed-joked-he-lost-consciousness-handcuffs-minutes-later-he-died/.

The Trevor Project. "Research Brief: Pronouns Usage Among LGBTQ Youth." Blog & Events. Updated July 29, 2020. https://www.thetrevorproject.org/2020/07/29/research-brief-pronouns-usage-among-lgbtq-youth/.

Wagner, Peter and Bertram, Wanda. "'What Percent of the US Is Incarcerated?' (And Other Ways to Measure Mass Incarceration)." *Prison Policy Initiative*, January 16, 2020. https://www.prisonpolicy.org/blog/2020/01/16/percent-incarcerated/.

Wamsley, Laurel. "In Portland, A 'Wall of Moms' and Leaf Blowers against Tear Gas." *NPR,* July 22, 2020. https://www.npr.org/sections/live-updates-protests-for-racial-justice/2020/07/22/894197681/in-portland-a-wall-of-moms-and-leaf-blowers-against-tear-gas.

Worland, Justin. "What to Know about the Dakota Access Pipeline Protests." *Time,* October 28, 2016. https://time.com/4548566/dakota-access-pipeline-standing-rock-sioux/.

Yabroff, K. Robin, Jingxuan Zhao, Xuesong Han, and Zhiyuan Zheng. "Prevalence and Correlates of Medical Financial Hardship in the USA." *Journal of General Internal Medicine* 34 (2019): 1494-1502. https://link.springer.com/article/10.1007/s11606-019-05002-w.

Made in the USA
Columbia, SC
11 May 2021

37738898R00183